Children and FAMILY Ministry Handbook

Practical • Tested • Backed by Research

SARAH FLANNERY

Abingdon Press

Nashville

CHILDREN AND FAMILY MINISTRY HANDBOOK

Editor: Brittany Sky
Production Editor: Rhonda Delph
Designer: Kent Sneed

All Web addresses were correct and operational at the time of publication.

ISBN: 9781501896231
PACP10579538-01

20 21 22 23 24 25 26 27 28 29—10 9 8 7 6 5 4 3 2 1

MANUFACTURED IN THE UNITED STATES OF AMERICA

CONTENTS

CHAPTER 1

FAMILY AND INTERGENERATIONAL MINISTRY

The Gossip in Jesus' Neighborhood

Have you ever stopped to imagine what the folks in the hometown of Mary and Joseph must have said when Mary became pregnant? Or how the neighbors might have told the story of Jesus' birth? I picture a scene in which baby Jesus toddles out into a yard where two neighbors are working. In my imagination their conversation sounds like this:

Neighbor 1: Have you heard the story about that kid? Oh, my gosh! I've got to fill you in! You won't believe it. Scandalous is the only word for it.

Neighbor 2: I believe I know their situation. Didn't his sweet little mother, barely more than a child herself, claim that there was no father?

Neighbor 1: No, she said that God was the father, of all things. The moment she became pregnant, she ran away to live with her cousin, which makes sense. Nobody wants damaged goods.

Neighbor 2: It sounds like she was overwhelmed. She probably needed some time away to gather her thoughts and feel safe.

Neighbor 1: Well, unwed mothers have no place in a society where we're trying to raise up good men of God.

Neighbor 2: Even though I can't understand how she got herself into this mess, I am glad for her sake that she has some extended family to provide support. I can't imagine how alone she'd feel otherwise.

Neighbor 1: Her father had already arranged a marriage for her. Nobody expected that to last once her baby bump started to show. But incredibly, the fiancé decided to go through with the ceremony! There is no prize for raising another guy's kid, that's for sure; but he said that he was following God's orders, if you can fathom that.

Neighbor 2: It's not the way I would want to start my own family, but to each his own. This kid is the son of a single mom with an adopted dad. Or is he a stepdad? I'm not sure about the right terminology in this situation.

Neighbor 1: By all accounts, he was there when the baby was born, although I'm sure he had mixed feelings about the whole thing. The word is that the kid's mom gave birth to him in an animal keep, and no sooner had she wrapped him up than filthy shepherds barged in and gathered close to bow down and worship him. They've had more kids the normal way too, you know. But I can tell there's just something strange about that kid right there and his patched-together family.

Introduction to Family and Intergenerational Ministry

Looking at Jesus' family through the eyes of two neighbors reminds us that what constitutes a "normal" family is defined by culture. Family and intergenerational ministry can mean many different things, depending on your cultural ideas of family. This chapter will spend a bit more time exploring Jesus' family as a case study for families we encounter in churches today. This biblical case study will help us broaden our definition of family, which is necessary for effective family ministry. Next, the chapter will briefly review the history of the family unit, from ancient to modern times. Finally, the chapter will link those scriptural and historical concepts of family to family and intergenerational ministry in the church.

Jesus' Life: A Case Study

Many families resemble Jesus' family in one way or another. It's alarming to admit that if a family that looked like Jesus'— a working-class, blended, brown-skinned, Jewish family—walked into the average American church, the church may not be prepared to receive them. Much has changed since Jesus' time, and much has not.

Unexpected Pregnancy

Even with the angel's assurance that there was nothing to fear ringing in her ears, Mary must have felt all the feelings in the days following her Holy Spirit conception. We don't know Mary's personality type, but her anticipation of judgment and misunderstanding from her parents and neighbors likely caused her great anxiety. She faced some of the same worries and decisions that women in her situation face today.

In 2006, nearly half of pregnancies in the U.S. were unintended, with young women (ages 18-24) comprising a substantial percentage of these unplanned conceptions.[1] Surprise pregnancies are more stressful than anticipated ones and can lead to increased health risks for mother and child. A crisis can ensue when the mother, the father, and other family members face difficult decisions about acceptance or rejection of the child, partnership or separation of the parents, costs of medical care, and many other stressors.

According to the Guttmacher Institute, teen pregnancy in the United States peaked in the 1990s at 12 percent, but due to increased use of birth control, by 2013 the pregnancy rate for teenagers fell to the lowest level in 80 years: 7.6 percent for black women, 6 percent for Hispanic women, and 3 percent for non-Hispanic white women.[2] This does not mean that teenagers are having less sex, but simply that their sexual encounters produce fewer pregnancies.

While we are less likely now more than ever before to encounter pregnant teenagers in our ministries, we must remember that a significant number of the mothers and grandmothers in our churches experienced this stressful situation years ago during its peak.

1   Lawrence B. Finer and Mia R. Zolna, "Unintended Pregnancy in the United States: Incidence and Disparities, 2006," *Contraception* 84, no. 5 (November 2011): 478–85, https://doi.org/10.1016/j.contraception.2011.07.013.
2   Kathryn Kost, Isaac Maddow-Zimet, and Alex Arpaia, "Pregnancies, Births and Abortions Among Adolescents and Young Women in the United States, 2013: National and State Trends by Age, Race and Ethnicity," Guttmacher Institute, August 16, 2017, https://www.guttmacher.org/report/us-adolescent-pregnancy-trends-2013.

A Blended Family

Many of the kids in our ministries can relate to Jesus' position as a stepchild. All parenting is complicated, and stepparent relationships add an extra layer of complexity to the family. We hope that Joseph raised and taught Jesus with as much love and attention as any good father would, but we don't actually know much about their relationship. We do believe that Jesus learned Joseph's trade as a carpenter, which indicates Joseph at least remained present in Jesus' life and accepted him as a member of the family. We also know that when God spoke to Joseph through angelic visits, Joseph obeyed. All parents, whether biological, foster, or adoptive, would benefit from following Joseph's example of listening to God's voice.

Almost half of modern stepfathers report that it can be more difficult to love a stepchild than a biological child, although research shows that stepfathers often achieve loving, authoritative, healthy relationships with their stepchildren.[3] The strength of the relationship between a stepparent and the children often depends on the marital relationship in the home. Marriage health and satisfaction lead to better relationships between the stepparent and children.

A Family Living in Poverty

While we do not know if Jesus' family was destitute or simply working class, we do know that they did not operate in the upper crust of society. Joseph's trade as a carpenter was decidedly blue collar, and the birds they purchased to sacrifice at Jesus' dedication in the temple were known as the poor person's option. We can assume that this family lived in a modest dwelling in a poorer part of town, and that they worried over their expenses as much as any family with a low income. There is no doubt that Jesus' background affected his ministry. His consistent efforts to humble the well-to-do religious leaders, as well as his deep appreciation for the underdog, were most likely cultivated in a childhood of lack.

Research demonstrates that childhood poverty is correlated with

---

3   William Marsiglio, "Stepfathers With Minor Children Living at Home: Parenting Perceptions and Relationship Quality," *Journal of Family Issues* 13, no. 2 (June 1, 1992): 195–214, https://doi.org/10.1177/019251392013002005.

adverse experiences, such as incidences of abuse, divorce, incarceration, and substance abuse in the home.[4] While this correlation is troubling, it is important to remember that low socioeconomic status is nothing to be embarrassed about or ignored. It is tempting for the affected family and ministry leaders to avoid discussing financial struggles. Silence only adds to the sense of shame. Jesus was poor; there is nothing shameful about that.

What Is Family?

Jesus' family structure defies many of our typical expectations—which means we may need to reconfigure those expectations. The goal of this chapter is to outline resources for designing a church ministry that Mary, Joseph, and Jesus could smoothly assimilate into. Gather together your spirit of adventure as we tackle some slippery and complicated definitions of family and intergenerational ministry.

First, the word *family* is seriously tricky. The word connotes different meanings for various people because of their unique experiences of family relationships—or the lack of them. When asked to define this word on the spot, most people will talk about relationships based on love, the people who take care of us and make us feel safe, and the place where we learn to trust others. And that's beautiful! At the same time, it's not reality for everyone. Ministry leaders will run into problems if they don't consider how exclusive this sanguine perspective can be for people who experienced abuse, rejection, or neglect in their families.

Just as people's experiences of family relationships are vastly different, so, too, are their definitions of "family." It is important for ministry leaders to define "family" in a way that allows for multiple family configurations. Here's one attempt to define "family," from *The Book of Disciple of the United Methodist Church*:

> We believe the family to be the basic human community through
> which persons are nurtured and sustained in mutual love, responsibility,

---

4   Michelle Hughes and Whitney Tucker, "Poverty as an Adverse Childhood Experience," *North Carolina Medical Journal* 79, no. 2 (March 1, 2018): 124–26, https://doi.org/10.18043/ncm.79.2.124.

respect, and fidelity. . . . We also understand the family as encompassing
a wider range of options than that of the two-generational unit of parents
and children (the nuclear family).[5]

As this definition implies, there is more than one way to think about
the family. First is the *structural* or *nuclear* definition. Families who fit this
definition correspond to the picture of family in many Americans' heads—
mom, dad, and kids. As we'll discuss in the next section, this understanding of family is brand new in historical context. Not only do a minority of
today's families comply with this structural definition, this kind of family
has always been a rarity.

Somehow, this structure of married, heterosexual parents with two
children has become the normative and socially ideal model of family.
Many American Christians accept that not every family looks like this but
believe this is the way that families *ought* to be in a perfect world. I would
posit that when it comes to families, there is no such thing as a perfect
world. There is also no perfect kind of family. This is an important starting
place when creating a family ministry plan.

In contrast to the *nuclear* or *structural* definition of families, I would
draw your attention to a *functional* perspective. Rather than declaring
family to consist of only legal, biological, aspirational relationships, the
functional view describes what families actually are and how families
relate. A functional view of family allows for a wide array of organized
relationships to constitute family. According to Diana Garland in her text-
book *Family Ministry*, family can be "a group of people characterized by
roles, rules, and distribution of power" through which people seek to meet
their needs for belonging and to share life purposes and resources.[6]

Under this broader definition there is room for a single person with
adopted children, roommates who take in a pregnant teenager, grandparents raising their grandchildren, or a same-sex couple with biological
children. I have no interest in convincing you of the morality of each family
type; that is a discussion for a different book. But I hope we can agree that

5   The United Methodist Church, *The Book of Discipline of the United Methodist Church*
(Nashville, TN: The United Methodist Publishing House, 2016), 111.
6   Diana R. Garland, *Family Ministry: A Comprehensive Guide*, 2nd edition (Downers
Grove, IL: IVP Academic, 2012), 56.

the church isn't the place for perfect people. Rather, the church is where imperfect humans hold other imperfect humans accountable for discipleship, being formed more and more into the image of God.

The way we define family is crucial during the planning and design phase of family ministry. I think most of us can honestly say that we would want to welcome any kind of family into our ministries, and we can take comfort in that desire. The real question is, would non-traditional families feel welcome at our event offerings? Would they make it past a review of our website? Is it obvious that our design took them into account? When we chose verbiage for the event flyer, set up the meeting room, and picked a stock image for the banner, how many kinds of families did we picture in attendance? Our invitations contain important subtext (or sometimes even overt text) that tell the real story. We can bet that families outside the nuclear mold will look for key words to clue them in as to whether they'll be safe in our spaces.

The collective fear that grips many of us at the thought of accepting such an expansive definition of family makes sense to me. Let's name that discomfort right now. The slippery slope argument is out there. It goes like this: *If we broaden the term "family" to include any group of people who care for one another and meet one another's needs, does the term become useless? Is there anyone in our churches who wouldn't qualify as a family member at this point?* I do hear this and have wrestled with these questions myself. Here are the two reasons why I have landed firmly on the side of affirming a functional view of the family.

Family as Metaphor

Family was God's original invention. The Bible consistently speaks to family relationships as a metaphor for all of God's people. At times God is positioned as the parent, ever-ready to protect us (Psalm 91) or to discipline us when we need to learn (Hebrews 12:6). At other times, God's people are encouraged to treat one another as family (1 Timothy 5:1-2).

With unflinching consistency, God's injunctions to God's people require them to become more inclusive over time. Prophets and apostles urged the church (and thereby families) to incorporate orphans and widows into their care. (Isaiah 1:17; Zechariah 7:9-10; James 1:27) The apostle Paul and his comrades made it their life's mission to open the doors of the church to Gentiles, a diversity initiative that must have felt bewildering to God's chosen people at the time (Ephesians 3:6).

Perhaps God places us into families so that our first, most basic human experience provides a blueprint for the church. Every scriptural instruction to obey our parents and care for our children can be mirrored in church relationships as well. Just as God fulfilled God's will through dysfunctional families all throughout the Bible, God continues to work in and through a divided, imperfect church. Scripture makes it clear that both the family and the church are meant to include God's people in a variety of roles and circumstances, all working together to bring in God's kingdom.

Adoption

Adoption is a significant scriptural metaphor for our relationship with God (Romans 8:14-17). In a trinitarian relationship too wonderful for us to comprehend, God our Parent invites us through the Holy Spirit to be adopted into the family along with the Son, Jesus. Our very identity as children of God happens through adoption. This idea is integral to our faith.

Just as we have been adopted into God's family, God asks us to adopt others into our families. The college student far from home, the widower who doesn't know how to live alone, and the guy who hangs around the church every day because he has no other place to go—all these folks and more can be members of our church family. Through adoption, the church has received an imperative to leave no one in isolation. But a definition of family implying any one household is better than another is too exclusive to fit into a theology of adoption.

Families Throughout Time

All of this talk of God's design for the family leads into a discussion of how the family has evolved since the earliest times. While some things have remained constant, such as the family's inexorable ties to one another and the instinctive love of parents for their children, the structure, roles, and purposes of family members have changed many times over.

There is not a word in Greek or Latin that corresponds to our modern English word for *family*.[7] In ancient times, *family* existed in the context of the *household*. Every person in a household, whether a blood relative, a guest, or a slave, was considered a part of the family unit.[8] The larger the household, the stronger and more powerful the family was considered to be.[9] Households could comprise 50-100 people, generating the sum of all production for the economy.[10] Individualism was a curse back then, and anyone with solid standing in a household would not have given individual interest a second thought.[11] A person's identity rested without question in that person's inclusion in a household. This is the reason that anyone not attached to a household—an unmarried woman, an orphan, a leper—had so little power in society. There was literally no socially accepted category for them, and their very lives were in constant jeopardy.[12] Once again, adoption arises as the key to understanding the inclusiveness of God's family. When Scripture enjoins us to adopt outcasts into our families, it is the voice of God speaking a new identity into lives that were never meant to be lived alone. Abraham, Lot, Mary and Martha, and others in Scripture welcome travelers into their homes, exemplifying not just a culture of hospitality but a belief that they are called to protect and provide for those who cannot do so for themselves.

All areas of life in these households were intertwined. Babies were cared for by a myriad of aunts, grandparents, siblings, and, in upper-class

---

7   Halvor Moxnes, ed., *Constructing Early Christian Families: Family as Social Reality and Metaphor*, 1st ed. (London: Routledge, 1997), 2–3, 20.

8   J. H. Elliott, "Temple versus Household in Luke-Acts: A Contrast in Social Institutions," *HTS Teologiese Studies / Theological Studies* 47, no. 1 (January 9, 1991): 88-120, https://doi.org/10.4102/hts.v47i1.2356; Mauro Pesce and Adriana Destro, "Fathers and Householders in the Jesus Movement: The Perspective of the Gospel of Luke," *Biblical Interpretation* 11, no. 2 (January 1, 2003): 211–38, https://doi.org/10.1163/156851503765661285; Moxnes, *Constructing Early Christian Families: Family as Social Reality and Metaphor*, 22.

9   Roland Boer, "By Clans and Households: On the Malleability of the Kinship-Household in the Ancient Near East," *Memoria Ethnologica* 13, no. 48/49 (2013): 6–21.

10   Garland, 26.

11   Boer, 6–21.

12   Garland, 26.

households, servants.[13] Children worked in the household business along-side cousins, interns, slaves, and elders.[14] Meals were shared among the whole group.[15] Households were places of unquestioned belonging.

Between 500-800 BCE, exchanges of power due to wars and conquests transformed the major economies of Europe and the Middle East to a feudal system, creating social castes of lords on estates and peasants who paid tribute to those lords in exchange for protection.[16] One major result was that the rich continued to keep large households, but the poor survived in small ones. Peasants' households were restricted because they were not powerful or resourced enough to sustain larger numbers.[17] This transition marked the first instance of what we would call the *nuclear* family.

Skipping ahead several centuries, we find that the colonization of North America radically altered previous experiences of family for both the colonists and the First Peoples whom they invaded. Exposure to the sicknesses that the settlers brought with them wiped out a large percentage of the native people, while exposure to the elements and poor preparation for frontier life decreased life expectancy for colonial people. Those settlers who survived combined their forces into new, blended families.[18]

In the early years of America, families existed more as households than as individuals. The survival rate of children was low,[19] but those who survived past the age of 5 quickly began to contribute to the production of the group. An entire household joined together in the same pursuit, whether that was farming, hunting, or some other trade.[20] Existence was a matter of scraping by for most, and life was hard. Only property owners could

---

13   Leo G. Perdue et al., *Families in Ancient Israel.* (Vol. 1st ed). Louisville, Ky: Westminster John Knox Press.
14   Ibid., 27.
15   Carolyn Osiek and David L. Balch, *Families in the New Testament World: Households and House Churches* (Louisville, KY: Westminster John Knox Press, 1997), 210–14.
16   Garland, 29.
17   John R. Gillis, *A World of Their Own Making: Myth, Ritual, and the Quest for Family Values* (Cambridge, MA: Harvard University Press, 1997), 10.
18   Donald M. Scott and Bernard W. Wishy, eds., *America's Families: A Documentary History* (New York: Harper & Row Publishers, 1982), 2–8.
19   Alex Liazos, *Families: Joys, Conflicts, and Changes* (New York: Routledge, 2015), 15.
20   Ibid., 14.

marry legally,[21] a rule that greatly affected the growth and formation of new households. As people were kidnapped in Africa and brought to America as slaves, the wealthy treated them as property and expanded their fortunes by refusing to recognize their family relationships. Under oppression, people of color became the most accepting of all family types, allowing any combination of family members within a household that contributed to their survival. Another trait of African and African American households during this time was gender equity, with both men and women assuming equal responsibility and leadership within the family.[22]

With the Industrial Revolution in America and Britain, families changed drastically once again. At first, all members of the family continued to work, only in mills and factories rather than fields. During this time, charitable people capitalized on children's one day off each week by initiating the first Sunday schools, using the Bible to teach children to read.[23] But with the merciful passage of child labor laws, for the first time children became an economic liability rather than a benefit. Work became individualized, with adults and older children taking various jobs. Families became consumers of the products from these factories rather than producers of their own and others' needed products.

The American Civil War disrupted this system by sending fathers and sons to fight and leaving the elderly, women, and young children at home to carry on the work of farms and factories. The loss of hundreds of thousands of men meant that life after the war could never return to normal. Two-generation households became common for the first time. Roughly 150 years ago, the concept of a breadwinning father and homemaker mother emerged as men took back the workplace.[24] As hard as it is to believe, the nuclear family consisting of a father, mother, and two children living in a household has existed as an ideal for only a small fraction of history.

---

21   Allan Kulikoff, *From British Peasants to Colonial American Farmers* (Chapel Hill, NC: The University of North Carolina Press, 2000), 227-29.

22   Liazos, 31.

23   Anne M. Boylan, *Sunday School: The Formation of an American Institution, 1790-1880*, Revised (New Haven: Yale University Press, 1990), 6–7; Pamela Mitchell Legg, "The Work of Christian Education in the Seminary and the Church: Then (1812) and Now (2012)," *Interpretation* 66, no. 4 (October 1, 2012): 425, *https://doi. org/10.1177/0020964312451420.*

24   Liazos, 17–20.

Families Today

Today, families result more from choice than biology. The majority of our children are growing up in single-parent households.[25] Unwed mothers and fathers are no longer forced to marry to satisfy cultural expectations, divorced parents are less and less likely to remarry, and single adults have more options for bearing or adopting children than ever before. Couples have the option to cohabitate or remain engaged long-term without legally marrying. Single adults find it harder and harder to afford housing on their own, and therefore, have begun establishing non-sexual roommate relationships that sometimes last for years. There is really no end to the ways we can choose the people who are in our family.

Economic forces exerted upon modern families cause them to make choices not just about who is included in the family but about how the family functions. The cost of childcare and the availability of reliable of birth control determine the number of children families choose to bear. Longer life expectancy means that adults in their prime can no longer count on receiving an inheritance of money or business to help them succeed financially in their prime production years.

With significant financial burdens and a persistent cultural emphasis on individualism, the task of parenting has become a monumental responsibility that parents feel they must do in isolation. Parents believe they should be capable of handling all the questions and challenges of raising children, not even realizing that until very recently this idea would have been completely out of place. Both the parents and the children suffer from this arrangement.

Church staff who are parents tend to be particularly prone to raising their children in isolation. During the first few years of my kids' lives, I worked full-time at a church that was at least a 30-minute drive from our home. My husband's job was an even longer commute. Church work requires nights and weekends, and between sleep training our younger child and caring for the constant needs of our preschooler, we hung on only by a thread. I remember a particularly painful night when I brought the boys home from daycare, quickly pulled together dinner, then headed back out

---

25   Garland, 42.

the door for the work commute again to attend an administrative council meeting. My preschooler sobbed and screamed as I removed him from my person in order to get in my car. Exhausted already, I felt like I had to physically fight off my child when all I wanted to do was wrap myself around him and stay home. It was a horrible experience that I know many other ministry parents share.

Later, I relayed this story to my supervisor. He looked at me appalled and said, "Why didn't you call me? Why didn't you tell me you needed the night off? There are times in ministry when the church has to come first, but those should be much less frequent than the times your family comes first." I appreciated his wisdom enough not to forget it these years later. But would I ever follow it? Doubtful. American individualism feeds me the lie that I should be enough all on my own. If I admit to any weakness or let people see what my family life is really like, there is the legitimate fear that they could use that against me. Vulnerability can sometimes feel like a privilege not available to "paid Christians" representing family values on a church staff.

Paradoxically, today's families enjoy increased volition, while they simultaneously suffer immeasurable shame, financial burdens, and isolation due to perceived or actual cultural expectations.

What Is Family Ministry?

There are two basic tenets to insist upon when defining family ministry. While the nuances of the definition may differ from church to church, these two non-negotiables give us a starting point. Before presenting these criteria, a couple of definitions would be helpful. Throughout this book, words such as *child* or *kid* apply to anyone under the age of 22 who is dependent on a caregiver for financial resources or shelter. An *adult* is anyone age 18 or older who is financially independent. That said, here are the major principles of family ministry:

1. The target audience is a child and that child's primary caregiver(s).
2. All programs within the ministry are intended to strengthen family relationships with God and one another.

A true family ministry intentionally includes those family types that are underrepresented in many of our churches, such as single parents, kids being raised by someone other than their biological parent, and families of divorce. At the same time, this definition is intentionally exclusive of any household that is not somehow connected to a child or young person. Households composed of retired adults with adult children, a single person in their 30s without children, or the group of older adults who meet monthly in the fellowship hall do not generally have a place in family ministry. That is not to say that these other kinds of households would never participate in a family ministry offering. Rather, those who design family ministry do not do so with these households in mind. They may be an occasional audience, but they are never the target audience. (Don't worry, we still care about these folks, even though they're not directly connected to a child. Check out the next section on Intergenerational Ministry!)

Moral Definitions of Family Ministry

Christians of good conscience have come to differing conclusions about moral and ethical issues affecting family ministry, such as divorce, same-sex marriage, and non-married couples raising children. Very smart people disagree with one another when interpreting Scriptures on these topics. It is important that your church staff has a conversation about how you will respond to different types of families in your ministry, and that everyone in leadership be prepared to implement your church's policy with kindness and love. Every church is different, and there is no one approach that works for everyone. However, if your church is looking for concrete ways to be supportive and inclusive of all family types, you can find concrete ideas in Chapter 2.

Intergenerational Ministry

Ministries to households with or without direct connections to children fit into the category of **intergenerational ministry.** This broad designation includes everyone; if you have an age, you are a member. The goal of intergenerational ministry is to create and strengthen adoptive relationships between all the generations of the church. There should be one of those equal opportunity disclaimers here to make it abundantly clear that intergenerational ministry does not discriminate based on age or any other status. All are welcome, and everyone in a church that values intergenerational ministry will find themselves frequently exposed to members of other age groups.

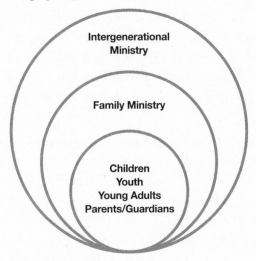

Intergenerational ministry is not synonymous with *church* or *congregation*. Intergenerational ministry is church *plus* intentional mixing of generations in the areas of worship, discipleship, and service. While an intergenerational church will offer some events exclusively for families and some exclusively for non-families, its primary worship services will include everyone. A church intent on intergenerational ministry will provide childcare for parenting classes and welcome single adults into the annual Jesus' Birthday Party event.

Intergenerational ministry is an old idea that is making a comeback. It fell out of popularity in the past one hundred years as other cultural experiences began segregating by age as well—such as schools dividing children by grades, childcare, and work taking place outside the home, sports and extracurricular experiences separating family members from one another until bedtime, and older adults receiving care in nursing facilities. These age-based divisions aren't necessarily bad, but there is no reason they must extend to our church experience.

I champion intergenerational ministry for all churches. I also realize that some churches may have well-established, age-segregated ministries, and challenging long-standing traditions can be extremely difficult. Wholesale change will never happen in a day. There are no cookie cutters, so find out what makes sense for your own congregation. Every church can seek to empower parents and include all ages in churchwide events and worship. However, the most successful intergenerational ministries are those with the support of the senior pastor and collaboration of multiple staff or volunteer leaders. Check out Chapter 13 for ways to initiate change without losing your mind—or your job. For now, here are a few things to keep in mind as you ponder where and how to get started.

Biblical Basis for Intergenerational Ministry

There is strong support for faith sharing among generations in Scripture. The passage I consider to be the best starting point is Deuteronomy 6. This passage appears in every family ministry manual, on the walls of many churches, and in a plethora of Christian parenting books.

> Israel, listen! Our God is the Lord! Only the Lord! Love the Lord your God with all your heart, all your being, and all your strength. These words that I am commanding you today must always be on your minds. Recite them to your children. Talk about them when you are sitting around your house and when you are out and about, when you are lying down and when you are getting up. Tie them on your hand as a sign. They should be on your forehead as a symbol. Write them on your house's doorframes and on your city's gates. (Deuteronomy 6:4-9)

We call this foundational passage the *Shema*, which is the Hebrew word for "listen," because that is the first word of the passage in Hebrew. God was saying, "Listen up!" In my head, God's audience for these instructions has always been parents. After all, God says to share these instructions with children at home and on the road, at bedtime, and in the morning. In my experience, those are times with immediate family.

But upon a closer look, the audience for God's words was much broader. God addresses Israel, the entire community of people. This is not parenting advice; this was "people of God" advice. And as we've already discussed earlier in this chapter, on the day these words were first spoken, children were raised within much larger households than the ones I've experienced. It would make sense for a grandfather to speak God's commands to a child at bedtime and for a neighbor to share them with that same child along the road. Life happened together, which meant the whole community of adults received the responsibility of raising everyone's children in the love of God.

A Shoutout to Singles

Notice that the way to incorporate single adults into households is not simply to marry them all off! We have done a poor job of celebrating the worth of unmarried adults in our churches, to the point that single folks often feel as if there is no place for them in the church at all. Young adult ministries easily devolve into an in-person version of Christian dating apps, communicating the lie that married adults are better than single ones. In fact, one could easily put together a biblical argument for the beauty of and calling to a single, celibate lifestyle. There are even a few scriptural examples of people (namely, Jesus) who fulfilled God's mission for their lives without ever marrying. A recently divorced friend attended her long-time Sunday school class a few years ago and felt caught off-guard when the icebreaker question of the day was, "Tell the story of how you met your spouse." The language, curriculum, leadership rosters, and even bylaws that we operate upon convey our assumptions clearly. Be sure marriage is not an expectation or status symbol in your church.

Final Thoughts

Would Mary, Joseph, Jesus, and siblings be welcomed in our churches if they were to walk into the worship space one week? Have you stopped to consider, both as an individual professional and as a member of a corporate worshiping community, what *family* means to you, or how you are pursuing intergenerational ministry already? Knowing the boundaries of family ministry and setting up an inclusive environment for people of all ages to belong in the church is a critical calling for each of us. The start of every great family ministry lies in understanding what it is and setting goals for including everyone in it that we can.

Ministry to families is a wonderful, scary, overwhelming, godly calling. Churches who celebrate the diversity of today's families and design realistic, meaningful ministry experiences to meet their spiritual needs will be the difference between the life or death of the church. Without family ministry, we risk further individualization of a faith that only can be truly lived in community with others. In the following chapters, we'll plunge into the specific categories that await under the heading of family ministry.

CHAPTER 2

PARENTS, GUARDIANS, AND CAREGIVERS

If you do not bear in your heart a particular love for parents, guardians, and other caregivers of children, you will want to excuse yourself from family ministry now. These wonderful, anxious, earnest creatures are what our ministry is all about. Their responsibility is overwhelming, but their love for their children is often rewarded with pride and delight as those children grow.

This chapter will discuss the role of parents and caregivers, including some key differences between the role of the church and the role of caregivers in the holy work of raising children in the faith. Perhaps most importantly, this chapter will provide tools for equipping adult caregivers in their own faith journeys. Finally, we will conclude with a section on caregivers with particular needs and suggestions for supporting them.

Raising Children as a Calling

Do you have any friends who just exemplify #lifegoals? For me, that would be my friends from college, Adam and Allison. They're smart, they eat healthy food, they have meaningful and challenging careers, and their cat named Bluegrass maintains an active profile on Instagram. I'm hoping to be like them when I grow up. I asked them several years ago if they planned to have kids, and Allison's response took my breath away. "You know," she said, "We have just never felt called to have children." Honestly, that was the first time someone ever posited to me that raising kids was not the default role of married people. If it's not the default role, then what is it?

To raise a child is to accept a call of God on your life.[1] Whether someone raises a child they hoped for or a child who showed up in their lives unexpectedly, parenting is a calling. The job of parents and guardians is to love, teach, and discipline their children, all in preparation for the day those children will accept God's call for themselves. For many caregivers, this will mean spending 18 or so years pouring into these young lives before setting them free. Children start out utterly dependent on others; good parenting is the daily, slow, conversation-by-conversation process of getting them to independence and letting them go.

In 1 Samuel, Hannah provides us with an extreme example of letting go. She is introduced to us as a woman in utter misery because she had been struggling to become pregnant. At one point, she went to the temple and swore in prayer that if she had a child, she would dedicate that child to God's service. And she meant it! She soon gave birth to a boy and named him Samuel. When Samuel was weaned, Hannah took him to the priest in the temple and literally gave him up to serve God as a priest. While I really don't want to encourage any parents or guardians to drop off their kids at my church for a lifetime of service, I do wish that more caregivers raised their children with an appreciation for God's unique call on their children's lives.

The Calling Takes a Community

When my first child was born, there was a lot of crying in my house, and it wasn't just his. One night I stood in his pitch-dark room, bouncing him on my shoulder and trying desperately to get him to sleep, and it hit me. I am a well-educated, financially secure, very connected and supported

---

1   A word here to anyone who feels called to parenthood but has faced the barrier of infertility, miscarriage, or loss of life: We see you, and our hearts mourn along with your heart. You are not forgotten.

parent—and I felt absolutely overwhelmed by the sleep deprivation and stress of his crying. How much more overwhelmed might a caregiver with less support feel?

And that was just in the first month! Raising a child is a marathon, and the task is monumental. It constitutes a task that is way too great for two adults, much less one. To give our kids all the instruction, encouragement, experience, and nurturing they need takes a whole network of loving adults who all commit to raising up these children together. That is where the church comes in. While no one else can substitute for a child's primary caregivers, every adult in the church should understand their responsibility to model their faith and mentor the children of the church. We cannot expect caregivers to prepare their children to receive God's calling without support. That task belongs first to them, but secondly to all of us.

Feelings of Inadequacy

In addition to the practical responsibilities of raising a child—food, homework help, carpool, bathing, nose-wiping, and so forth—there is the mental and emotional weight of this work to consider. Most caregivers I know feel unworthy or unable to disciple their children adequately, admitting to having more questions than answers. Don't be surprised to hear parents express anxiety to you over the high stakes involved in parenting—many parents are incredibly anxious about screwing up their kids. Approach adults who are raising children with grace, knowing that no matter how competent and confident they appear, it is likely that doubts lurk beneath the surface.

I call these feelings of inadequacy Imposter Parenting Syndrome. It seems that for many parents, the very thought of discipling their children feels terribly hypocritical. Anyone who works with kids knows that they are constantly watching the adults around them, absorbing knowledge like sponges. For some caregivers, it can feel disingenuous to teach their children about Christian values when they don't always live up to them. Parents and guardians have asked me many times some version of *"How can I teach my child why breaking rules is wrong when he saw me run that red light last week?"* Another question I hear often is *"How can I teach my child about God's Word when I myself know nothing about it?"* The reason many caregivers rely so heavily on the church or Christian schools to disciple their kids is that they are afraid to try it themselves. While church leaders often bemoan the failure of parents to immerse their kids in faithful practices at home, we must realize that this is not due to laziness or indifference. It's a self-esteem problem.

Guiding the Faith of Adults Raising Children

Because parents and guardians are the primary faith guides for their children, I would argue that for family ministers, nurturing the faith of the *parents and other caregivers* supersedes the importance of nurturing the faith of children. If the caregivers are living faithfully, they naturally will be equipped to raise their children faithfully. Yet, by and large, the discipleship of primary caregivers in our congregations needs some work.

Spiritual Practices for Caregivers

The faith of parents and guardians, like that of everyone else, is strengthened best through practice. The number-one, most basic way for caregivers to combat their feelings of helplessness and inadequacy in raising children is to spew those feelings out to God in prayer. Ministry professionals can offer a variety of parenting curricula, adult Sunday school classes, or retreats with speakers who are parenting experts, and all these offerings will likely do some good. But we should ask ourselves whether we have been clear enough in our ministries that daily prayer is the first answer to the feelings of inadequacy and uncertainty we have just discussed. Parents need to hear from us that, over time, their prayer practices will bloom into sources of spiritual nourishment in the work of parenting, so that they aren't just sending up white flag prayers in the midst of crisis, but conversing with God in an intimate back and forth. Encourage caregivers to start small and let their prayer lives grow like a friendship—the best friendship of one's life.

And while extensive Bible scholarship is not a requirement of good parenting, personal reading of Scripture in some form is needed. A few years ago, my supervisor asked me in a weekly meeting if I was making time to read the Bible devotionally. I told him no, that I had fallen out of the habit when I got married. He looked me squarely in the eye and told me that I had absolutely no right to be working on a church staff and creating discipleship opportunities for families if I wasn't practicing devotional habits myself. I told him I'd work on it. When we met the next week, he had the audacity to follow up and ask if I was reading my Bible yet. Of course, I wasn't, and he called me out on it again. He clearly wasn't going to let this go. After that, I got a new Bible as a gift and started on one of those read-the-Bible-in-a-year plans. Even though this method was basically just skimming through Scripture, within two months I felt like it had changed my life.

The secret to empowering caregivers to fulfill the heavy responsibility of discipling their children is to increase their own faith first. If this is new territory for parents, encourage them to start small. Introductory faith practices can include:

- listening to a chapter of the Bible a day through an app or podcast
- setting a phone reminder to pray each morning or evening
- writing a sentence of gratitude in a journal once a day
- checking out a Bible study book from the library

Our goal should be to develop a church full of adults who are faithfully walking the path of discipleship themselves, even if they are simply taking baby steps. Those who seek with all their hearts will find God.

Ministry to All Caregivers

At the end of this chapter we'll identify several types of caregivers who might require extra or specific care. But for now, let's go over the approaches we should take when guiding the faith of any caregiver.

One-on-One Conversations

In my experience, almost all discipleship opportunities take place through personal, face-to-face conversations. When I run into parents while grabbing coffee at the hospitality table, that's when I learn that their child is on a new medication, their grandparent is dying, or they're burnt out from overscheduling. When a caregiver asks me to coffee, we talk about the benefits of counseling, the best children's Bibles on the market, and FAQs about bedtime prayers. I'm not sure I've ever sent an e-mail that has truly helped someone to become a better person, but I know that when I look into a caregiver's eyes and talk about raising kids faithfully, we both grow. If we want revival of the Holy Spirit in the lives of families, we've got to get ourselves across a table from parents and guardians, coffee or tea in hand, and listen. Ministry only happens through relationships, and when it comes to relationship-building, there is no substitute for physical presence.

Calendaring for Discipleship

Pick up your church calendar and ask this question: *"Are these events empowering opportunities for parents, guardians, and caregivers?"* Church events require ridiculous portions of your time and budget, but do they have a lasting impact? Most events offered by churches are wonderful experiences and, with a shift in perspective, can be transformed into whole-family discipleship opportunities. For instance, perhaps you have planned a youth lock-in for a Saturday night. It's going to be a blast, and you'll have no trouble getting youth to come and even bring their friends. What extra step could you take to create space for parents and guardians to grow through this event? A few ideas:

- Reserve a room or recruit a host home where caregivers can gather after drop-off for coffee and conversation (i.e., seek the commiseration and support that caregivers of youth so often need).
- The week of the event, e-mail the parents an article about the benefits of spiritual friendships for young people or the importance of spending time away from home.
- During the event, take youth through an exercise of naming the one important conversation they wish they could have with their parents or guardians but don't feel comfortable having. Then, with permission, publish an anonymous list of their answers to their parents and encourage parents to invite their teens to ask questions while they listen with an open mind.

If empowering and discipling caregivers is your main goal, your events will start to look different. You will not spend hours and hours on a program that only considers the faith lives of kids and teens. Find a way to speak life into caregivers' faith experiences through the events you plan for their kids.

Counseling

Everyone needs therapy at some point. Any family minister worth his or her own salt needs to assemble a list of qualified, trusted local therapists and make this list available on a regular basis. Sometimes I feel like I should earn a commission for the number of parents I have urged into counseling over the years.

The truth is, although I have placed great emphasis on the power of face-to-face conversations with parents, there is a hard limit to the depth a lay person can reach in a parent's life. It is our job to invite vulnerability and help uncover the brokenness that exists in every one of our souls. But there are points at which we must refer the caregivers in our care to mental and spiritual health professionals for the rest.

Do not be shy about suggesting counseling and following up with parents to ask if they've taken that step. Better yet, if you have not already experienced professional counseling yourself, schedule an appointment. Allow a therapist to walk with you all the way into your inner child. Confront the dysfunction and pain you've been holding onto with the safety of a guide. Model the way to healing and wholeness for your church families, and in so doing, help to remove the stigma around asking for help.

Now that we have established the roles of the church—of parents, guardians, and caregivers; and of ministry leaders—let's tackle the nitty gritty details of working with and for caregivers in the church.

Working with Caregivers

For the purposes of this book, a *parent* is anyone who is a primary caregiver for a child. Primary caregivers may be the biological parents, stepparents, grandparents who live in the household with the child, foster parents, adoptive parents, other relatives who live with the child, or responsible adults who love and are very present in the child's life. These are the adults who experience many or all of the progressive stages of a child's life, from pregnancy to empty nest. Parents of infants will often define their lives by a set of rules and structures such as rigid nap times and exact millimeters of breast milk in the bottle. Parents of preschoolers will not shut up about the adorable mispronunciations their child makes out of common words. My preschooler used to refer to the bathroom as "brafroom" and called our family his "flamly," and I prefer to use those pronunciations 50 percent of the time myself. During the school years, parents have stress about grade reports, interactions with peers, teacher conferences and snow-day childcare. Extracurricular activities slowly take over the family's schedule until parents are equally thrilled and terrified to take their teen to the DMV to obtain their driver's license. With that license in hand, the teen now has their own schedule, resulting in a painful loss of control that parents grapple with until one day their child is an adult.

Every one of these new stages brings with it a multitude of emotions and stressors. One thing most caregivers will tell you is that raising kids is a moving target. As soon as you grow accustomed to one stage and feel you have a handle on it, they change again. The problem a parent worries about in May will be different by July. Every time you interact with caregivers, remember that they are treading water in a raging river, constantly approaching a new turn or obstacle, always trying to keep their heads up amid the changing stream. Approach parents and guardians with empathy. Keep a lifeline handy to throw to parents when they start to go under.

God, the Good Parent

God is the only truly good parent.[2] Jesus presented God this way in the parable of the prodigal son in Luke 15:11-32. The father in this story played the role of a loving and forgiving God. But if the story happened today, we easily could find ourselves judging the father as harshly as his son. If he had just been a little stricter, maybe his son wouldn't have left. If he had spent more time with his son, maybe he would have been happy to stay in the family business. But when the son came crawling back home in submission, it is as if the father cared nothing for our admonitions! He not

---

2. I try to be careful about referring to God as a parent when praying before large groups, knowing that for some listeners that reference could be a huge turn-off.

only allowed the son to return, he raced down the driveway to wrap him in a bear hug, then threw a huge "welcome home" party. Thank goodness, God doesn't pay attention to our judgmental attitudes toward parents. God is full of grace for each of us—the ones who keep up good appearances as well as the ones who wear their scars on the outside—and this is how we must strive to be with our own children. And with one another, for that matter.

Caregivers Seeking the Best for Their Children

Most parents want the best for their children. Unfortunately, wanting the best for children can easily devolve into anxiety and feverish control issues. I myself constantly assume (incorrectly) that my children's well-being rests on me and me alone, and this belief escalates to blame, shame, and complaining whenever something happens to threaten my kids' health or happiness. This means that when parents approach a church leader with questions or concerns, what seems like a grown-up temper tantrum is actually just that same old fear and feeling of inadequacy. A guardian's questions about the overnight retreat, small-group curriculum, or cliques in the peer group reveal their deepest fears and must be met with a combination of understanding and accountability. Be wise to worried caregivers. Ask questions to help them uncover what they're truly feeling, and only then work to solve the problem.

On the first evening of a faith and sexuality retreat for preteens a few years ago, a dear friend of mine, whose son was participating in the program, pulled me aside, and laid into me hard! Her son had brought two friends from outside the church, and our leadership team had intentionally placed them in different small groups for the duration of the weekend. We reasoned that they might be better able to open up and interact with kids outside their friend group if they were separated. However, my friend saw this very differently! She expressed how furious she was that we had separated the three kids. Even though they would only spend a small fraction of the retreat in small-group format, she was ready to pull all three of them out of the event. While I remember thinking that she was clearly overreacting, to this day I kick myself about my response. Instead of taking the time to get to the root cause of her loud emotions, I said I would talk to the team and get back to her. We agreed to acquiesce and put the boys in a group together, then moved on.

Later, my friend apologized to me for getting so angry. But I still do not know why. Did she fear the reaction of the other boys' parents if they had a bad experience? Was it a struggle to get her son to come at all, and she feared a clash in their relationship if he was separated? Did she have a bad experience in her own childhood that this situation had called up? If I had asked the right questions and listened, it is possible we could have both grown closer to each other and to God by dealing with heart issues. Instead, we moved on, same as ever.

Jesus, on the other hand, was a total genius when it came to working with parents. Once, a father brought his son to Jesus for healing. The son was mute and experienced seizures, and his condition brought danger and destruction to their home on a regular basis. The disciples had tried to heal him, but failed, and the father must have thought of Jesus as a last, faint hope. Jesus was not flustered by this situation. He asked the father several questions about the boy's condition, almost like a medical technician would do. Then Jesus brought the conversation to its spiritual core by telling the man that anything is possible as long as there is faith. The father then verbalized the battle cry of all fearful, barely hopeful parents: "I have faith; help my lack of faith!" (Mark 9:24b). So say we all.

Recruit the Complainers

Here's one of my favorite subversive ministry tips of all time. A complaining caregiver is simply a volunteer waiting to be recruited. Many of us ministry leaders complain about two major problems: volunteer shortages and dissatisfied parents. The solution to these two problems is the same! Realize that a parent or guardian who complains about a situation in your ministry either truly cares about improving the situation or is cluing you in to a real hurt or need within themselves. There is a simple, easy way to find out which is the case—ask that person to become the solution to the issue they're complaining about. If the caregiver's goal is to fix a problem, that caregiver will agree to be a part of the solution. If the parent does not want to become part of the solution, that's our signal to come alongside them to discover what the real problem is.

For example, a parent once approached me with a concern that the children in her kids' age groups weren't really developing solid friendships. In our large church, we could have 20 children in an age-based Sunday school class, representing 15 different schools. These kids weren't spending any time together other than Sunday mornings, and therefore, she didn't feel like her kids had any real church friends. The more we talked, the more invested this mom became in being a part of the solution. By the end of the conversation, she had developed an idea for a friendship-building initiative within each of our children's Sunday school groups. She recruited parent coordinators for every age group, and those parents designed simple, fun get-togethers outside of the church for the kids to play together. Other parents were thrilled to gather at a casual restaurant after church with other 3rd-grade families or spend a school holiday at the bowling alley. The best part of this situation was that I, the staff person responsible for children's ministry, didn't send a single e-mail or set up a solitary event for this purpose. It took place from start to finish at the behest of a parent who came to me with a problem, who then agreed to solve it.

Once we begin to view complaints as recruiting opportunities (or, when that doesn't work, a cry for help that we can be honored to respond to), we actually can look forward a little bit to hearing feedback from parents. With a little humility, turn those caregiver concerns into a stronger, better ministry.

Caregivers Needing Extra Care

As family ministers we care for all parents and guardians, of course. But there are a few circumstances that require us to give extra thought and intentionality in order to include families in our care. Every family struggles; no particular kind of family has a monopoly on or exemption from suffering. However, some family types are either at a cultural disadvantage or simply tend to boggle us church types, and if we want to change that trend, we should actively seek strategies to support folks we may not entirely understand.

Single Parents

Parenting alone can result from divorce, death of a spouse, becoming pregnant while single, or single-parent adoption. Regardless of the cause, raising a child or multiple children alone is a difficult task. We cannot allow single parents to walk this path alone. It is typical for parents to saddle themselves solely with the job of raising well-adjusted kids, and this is especially true of single parents. When this plan falls apart because it is impractical, their sense of competence can unravel.

Everything is more complicated for a single parent. If a spouse died, the surviving parent and children usually experience lifelong grief. If there is an ex-spouse, then life may be affected by lawyers, visitation, dating, stepparenting, and co-parenting. Divorce can be a much more difficult tragedy to overcome than death, because it is an adverse experience that sometimes unfolds over many years.

Following are strategies to consider when caring for single parents:

- Remember that single parents and their children may not be able to attend church regularly. If the children visit another parent on the weekends, or the parent struggles to get the children out of the house on weekend mornings, that family may miss worship and family ministry events. Avoid any focus on perfect attendance in Sunday school, and provide take-home sheets or e-mail updates for missed lessons if the family is interested.

- Offer childcare for anything and everything. If you do not have a childcare staff person, either hire one or recruit a team of volunteers with a heart for young ones. Make childcare available either as a default or upon request for any Bible study, worship service, small group, or special event. Providing quality childcare is the best way to include a single parent in discipleship opportunities.

- No matchmaking! Single people are complete, whole persons of God outside of marriage. If a single parent wants to talk to you about dating or marriage, fine; otherwise, leave their love lives alone.

- Accompany to court parents going through a divorce, if their proceedings require that procedure. Pray with them and their attorneys.

- Be careful about celebrating Mother's Day and Father's Day. If you want to do a craft or activity to mark that day, be intentional to suggest a wider range of people to celebrate than simply moms and dads. Let kids write notes to any woman or man who loves them.

- Do not pressure single parents to volunteer in the church. If they are in a life stage that will allow them to serve and they desire to serve, plug them into roles that will give them freedom to stay home with a sick child, if needed.

- Welcome single parents into small groups. These groups do not have to include only single people.

- Provide mentors for the children of single parents. Give single parents another person or family who will be there for them day in and day out. If their children are old enough, partner them with another adult in the church who can spend time with them and help to disciple them. Help single parents know they are not alone in this.

Don't hesitate to ask the single parents in your church what they need and listen closely to their answers. So many kids in our congregations live with only one parent. We cannot afford to neglect these families.

LGBTQIA Caregivers

The abbreviation LGBTQIA stands for Lesbian, Gay, Bisexual, Transgender, Queer or Questioning, Intersex, and Asexual. According to the Gallup Daily Tracking Survey, about 4.5 percent of adults in the U.S. identify as LGBT,[3] and other estimates say that 37 percent of LGBT adults have been parents.[4] Unlike most portrayals in TV and media, families headed by LGBTQIA adults are more likely to live in or near poverty than families of different sex parents, and same-sex couple parents and their children are more likely to be racial and ethnic minorities.[5] Consider also that some

---

3   Frank Newport, "In U.S., Estimate of LGBT Population Rises to 4.5%," Gallup.com, May 22, 2018, https://news.gallup.com/poll/234863/estimate-lgbt-population-rises.aspx.

4   Gary Gates, "LGBT Parenting in the United States" (The Williams Institute, February 26, 2013), https://williamsinstitute.law.ucla.edu/research/census-lgbt-demographics-studies/lgbt-parenting-in-the-united-states/.Gates.

5   Ibid.

children with LGBTQ parents were born from heterosexual relationships,[6] meaning that they may have experienced their parents' divorce and may maintain a relationship with a biological parent outside the household.

While some of those demographics concerning LGBTQIA families are cause for extra support from the church, it's important to remember that there is also much to be celebrated. For example, we know that children with LGBTQIA parents are often more accepting of diversity.[7] After accumulating a substantial body of research on children raised by same-sex couples, one researcher concluded, "Regardless of whether children had one mother and one father, two mothers, two fathers, or caregivers (e.g., older siblings, grandparents, extended family members), they thrived in homes that provided stability and love."[8] There is broad, undeniable consensus in the literature that children raised by same-sex parents fare just as well as children raised by different-sex parents across all major categories, such as academic performance, emotional health, substance use, social and psychological development, and so forth.[9] In this way, LGBTQIA families are exactly like every other—in need of the same supports and the same kind of discipleship as heterosexual families.

The need for extra support emerges when LGBTQIA families encounter discriminating or excluding behavior from their communities, and this happens too regularly in the church.[10] When church becomes an unsafe place for any family based on their identity, we have a problem. Consider the effect on LGBTQIA parents and their children of the stigma they

6   American Academy of Child & Adolescent Psychiatry, "Children with Lesbian, Gay, Bisexual and Transgender Parents," *Facts for Families*, August 2013.

7   L. Saffron, "Raising Children in an Age of Diversity-Advantages of Having a Lesbian Mother," *Journal of Lesbian Studies* 2, no. 4 (1998): 35–47, https://doi.org/10.1300/J155v02n04_04.

8   Sherri Sasnett, "Are the Kids All Right? A Qualitative Study of Adults with Gay and Lesbian Parents," *Journal of Contemporary Ethnography* 44, no. 2 (April 1, 2015): 196–222, https://doi.org/10.1177/0891241614540212.

9   Wendy D. Manning, Marshal Neal Fettro, and Esther Lamidi, "Child Well-Being in Same-Sex Parent Families: Review of Research Prepared for American Sociological Association Amicus Brief," *Population Research and Policy Review* 33, no. 4 (August 1, 2014): 485-502, https://doi.org/10.1007/s11113-014-9329-6.

10   Valerie Q. Glass and April L. Few-Demo, "Complexities of Informal Social Support Arrangements for Black Lesbian Couples," *Family Relations* 62, no. 5 (2013): 714–26, https://doi.org/10.1111/fare.12036.

are constantly reminded of. The church is not the only culprit, not by a long shot. Relatives, friends, and professionals, such as doctors and school pesonnel, can have a difficult time understanding and giving credit to families headed by LGBTQIA adults. If we follow the example of Jesus in Scripture, then our ministries will be places of inclusion and empowerment for everyone, especially those who are often misunderstood or excluded. Let's make our churches places where people are confident that they'll be treated with as much grace and love as Jesus showed.

Following are some ideas for supporting and including LGBTQIA caregivers and their families in practical ways:

- Ask for their opinions. LGBTQIA adults are the best resources you can have for identifying discriminatory language, policies, or practices in your ministry, so ask them what is working and what is not, and act upon their suggestions.
- Use their preferred pronouns.
- Do not make sexual identity into their one, predominant characteristic. Avoid talking to LGBTQIA parents about sexuality more than you would to a cisgender, heterosexual parent, and do not feel compelled to prove your open-mindedness to them. Treat, introduce, and talk to them as you would to any caregiver.
- Respect LGBTQIA adults' need for privacy or self-disclosure.
- Involve LGBTQIA caregivers in your ministry teams, teaching roles, and parenting groups.
- LGBTQIA parents may be more likely than other parents to need our support through an adoption or foster-care process, or a legal custody process. Attend court proceedings with them, if invited, write letters of recommendation for them, and pray with them through these potentially contentious experiences.
- For heterosexual, cisgender ministry leaders, it is essential that we educate ourselves about the truth, the data, and the beauty of LGBTQIA caregivers and their families. We will have opportunity to correct misinformation and prejudice, if only we are prepared to do so. Straight for Equality (*http://www.straightforequality.org/*) is one resource for becoming a better LGBTQIA ally.

- If the LGBTQIA adults in your family ministry are not connected to other LGBTQIA spaces, help them find friendly communities either inside or outside your church. Organizations such as PFLAG (*https://pflag.org/*) offer connections to local chapters as well as resources for LGBTQIA caregivers.

Adoptive and Fostering Parents

To prepare for this section I reached out to adoptive or foster parents to ask for input.[11] The gratitude and excitement of their responses overwhelmed me a little. I found that families who have experienced the expense, time, isolation, stress, and learning process of adoption or fostering don't often feel that their church understands or cares for their needs.

Many families adopt because their church champions the theology of adoption, but then once their children come home and the real work of becoming a family begins, church is no longer a safe or helpful space. It is our responsibility to support adoptive and foster parents throughout their journey. Following are a few important considerations:

Do:

- Ask each individual family what terms they are using in their household to refer to parents and kids.
- Use "adoptive" or "fostering" to refer to families.
- Refer to the parents who conceived and gave birth to the child as "biological" or "birth" parents.
- Ask families to clarify who is allowed to pick up their child and who is not.
- Educate yourself and your leaders on issues that might affect an adopted or foster child. Provide a mentor or buddy to build relationships with adopted or foster children, allowing parents to worship with peace.
- Support an adoption organization that helps families overcome the financial hurdles of adoption.

---

11   Special thanks to Amy Kinnell, an adoptive mom of three and adoption specialist at Adoption Assistance, Inc., and Kristina White, foster mom, children's pastor, and friend to me, for the experience and advice I'm about to share.

- Provide respite care, educational events, and training to help your church support and care for adoptive families.
- Remember other siblings in the family! Don't focus so exclusively on an adopted child that the biological children in the family feel neglected.
- Provide meals to a family receiving a child.
- Offer gift cards to shop for clothes or even gently used clothes from your family.
- Remember the foster and adoptive families in your church in prayer and on prayer lists that are distributed to prayerful people in the community.

Don't:

- Use terms such as "real parents"—both biological and adoptive adults are real parents.
- Use terms such as "gave up for adoption"—this phrase implies indifference or heartlessness that is almost never at work in a biological parent's situation.
- Ask children to explain their family situation. Accept them as they are, whether or not their skin color, last name, or behavior matches that of their family members.

Fostering and adoption involve a great deal of uncertainty. Foster care parents often coordinate with biological parents, which means being available for supervised or unsupervised visits, and dealing with the fallout if anything goes wrong. Children not living with their biological parents often have experienced trauma or abuse of some kind. In the process of transitioning into a new family unit, all members confront the spiritual, psychological, emotional, and physical consequences of trauma.

The first few months of a child's life in a new home require huge adjustments from every family member. Give the family all the prayer and resources the church can muster, but also give them space. They need concentrated time with one another to form bonds and learn new routines. Once these families are ready to ease back into church, be flexible with them. If an adoptive child wants to stay with a sibling of a different age, make room for them both. If a parent needs help getting kids unloaded from the car and dropped off in appropriate rooms, recruit a volunteer to meet them in the parking lot.

Last, if an adoption or foster relationship must be dissolved for any reason, accept and support each family member without inserting your own emotions. This turn of events plunges the family into deeply complicated territory, and it takes a long time to recover. Believe families when they tell you what they need.

Financially or Food Insecure Caregivers

Lack of food or funds for basic necessities can place incredible stress on a family's mental, physical, emotional, and spiritual health.[12] Poverty is also an uncomfortable topic for many, and people living with it will often choose to suffer silently or only go to a couple of trusted friends about their needs.

One major caution is to avoid becoming a part of a family's chronic financial problems. In the church, we feel honored to bless someone out of our benevolence funds when the opportunity arises. Keeping funds on hand to help those in need is a priority. However, my church is careful not to reach into this fund repeatedly for the same family, believing that giving money for repeated emergencies can lead to more and more emergencies, without ever dealing with the root cause of the financial problem. If a family seems to face persistent financial difficulties, following are some other ways to help:

- Offer job counseling. Help caregivers craft resumes and job-seeker profiles, and suggest business owners in the community who may be hiring.
- Provide financial counseling. Ask an accountant, business professional or financial advisor in your congregation to meet with the family to discuss strategies for long-term financial peace.
- Include scholarships in every event budget. If a church event has

---

12   Lynette M. Henry, Julia Bryan, and Carlos P. Zalaquett, "The Effects of a Counselor-Led, Faith-Based, School–Family–Community Partnership on Student Achievement in a High-Poverty Urban Elementary School," *Journal of Multicultural Counseling and Development* 45, no. 3 (2017): 162–82, https://doi.org/10.1002/jmcd.12072.

a cost, make it clear in all publications that scholarships are available. Whenever humanly possible, require every family to pay something, even if only a couple of dollars. It's important for families to invest what they can.

- Gather a list of food pantries and shelters. Provide the list to those who may walk into the church to ask for assistance as well as to families within the congregation. Agencies whose purpose is to serve those who are homeless, jobless, or in financial need will do a better job of caring for these families than even a wholehearted church staff person can do.
- Communicate clear boundaries. If a family receives financial help from the church, let them know if and when they can expect to receive it again. If the assistance is a one-time gift, explain why and discuss next steps to help ensure it won't be needed in the future.

Above all, listen and provide pastoral care. At some point or another, many of us know what it's like to budget so we can make it to payday. And some of us know the feeling of uncertainty that we will be able to eat until then. Encouragement, acceptance, and offers of non-financial assistance are always appropriate.

Caregivers Affected by Mental Illness

Mental illness is an invisible disability. According to the National Alliance on Mental Illness, 1 in 5 adults experiences a mental illness every year.[13] But do you know all the adults with a mental-health diagnosis in your congregation? It's likely you don't. The persistent stigma surrounding mental illness, leading to discomfort in relationships and even punitive treatment in social or employment spaces, tends to keep people quiet about their mental-health diagnoses.[14] The risks outweigh the rewards of sharing, because sharing often leads to expressions of blame or other harmful assumptions.

13 https://www.nami.org/Learn-More/Mental-Health-By-the-Numbers
14 Stephen P. Hinshaw, "The Stigmatization of Mental Illness in Children and Parents: Developmental Issues, Family Concerns, and Research Needs," *Journal of Child Psychology and Psychiatry* 46, no. 7 (2005): 714–34, https://doi.org/10.1111/j.1469-7610.2005.01456.x

Detecting signs of mental illness in members of your church is tricky. In my experience, folks with mental-health diagnoses are experts at putting on a strong front in social situations, only manifesting symptoms in the safety of their own homes. A few signs to watch for could show up at church: excessive worry, fear, or confusion about what's happening; avoidance behaviors or abstaining from church activities or conversations; talk of multiple physical ailments (upset stomach, headaches, and so forth) without an obvious cause; talk of drugs, excessive alcohol, or suicide.[15] Or a person's mental illness can be completely undetectable to an outsider.

Just as with other kinds of families, families that include a person with a mental illness benefit in unique ways. Mental illness in a family often fosters greater resiliency when dealing with other kinds of challenges. It also leads to greater levels of sensitivity, courage, and optimism about life and what life can afford.[16] For families that are able to overcome the fear of stigmatization and seek therapy, medication, and support for the illness, there is a deep appreciation to be found for the minds and bodies God has given us and the way God knits us into community with others.

If a parent shares a mental-health diagnosis with you, consider it an honor and sign of trust. Be worthy of that trust! If you are not the pastor, ask permission before sharing the diagnosis with the pastor. Most of all, do not shy away from conversations about mental illness or sweep it under the figurative rug. People with mental illness desperately need safe spaces to talk about their experiences, but those are incredibly hard to find. Ask questions and check in on these folks from time to time. Prove to them that you're not scared of their experiences or condition. And finally, help them (and their children) get connected with a good therapist if they don't already have one.

Final Thoughts

Short of writing an encyclopedia, there is no way to include every situation and word of advice for working with parents, guardians, and caregivers in this chapter. The hope is that the information here will be

---

15   National Alliance on Mental Illness, "Know the Warning Signs," accessed September 30, 2019, https://www.nami.org/Learn-More/Know-the-Warning-Signs.

16   Hinshaw, "The Stigmatization of Mental Illness in Children and Parents."

a starting point for developing more confidence and grace when leading primary caregivers, the most important members of our ministry. If we provide for the spiritual needs of caregivers, all other members of the family will follow. The call of raising a child is not meant to be answered alone. In fact, parents cannot fulfill their duties alone—that's not the way God set it up. And that's our in! Find out the greatest needs of the caregivers in your church and meet them there.

CHAPTER 3

CHILDREN'S MINISTRY

This is where I cut my ministry teeth. I started as a nursery volunteer, moved on to teach children's Sunday school, and eventually made a career out of leading the children, parents, and volunteers who make up a children's ministry. Ministry with children presents particular blessings and challenges. Leaders in children's ministry receive the blessing of seeing God through the eyes of children, where I believe God often shows up more clearly than anywhere else. But in a church culture that often prizes the members who can give the most or serve the best, children's gifts are often underestimated. Likewise, the leaders who work with kids are sometimes overlooked or worse, perceived as immature or unambitious. I'd like to propose a different estimation of the children in our churches and the folks who lead them. Our children are not the future of the church; they are the most valuable, most faithful present.

This chapter will begin with an overview of child and family development. Next, the chapter will review the importance of safety measures for children, one of our most vulnerable church populations. Then the chapter will address specific strategies for leading each age group in children's ministry: nursery (birth to 2 years), preschool (ages 3 to 5), and elementary (kindergarten through 3rd grade). The chapter will wrap up with a discussion of best practices for ministry with children.

Child and Family Development

Understanding how the brains, bodies, and souls of children develop, and how those developments interact with family systems, will change the way you design ministries for children and families. As leaders of children, we have a responsibility to advocate for them wisely, and that cannot be done if we do not understand how they age and grow.[1] A full treatise on child development is beyond the scope of this book. Instead, I will share some key discoveries about child development and family systems that have shaped my ministry.

Sleep

For the first five years of a child's life, the family is held hostage to sleep issues. Naptime and bedtime determine a family's availability—those times are not to be trifled with! I dare you to plan a preschool event for 2:00 p.m. and see who comes. A new dad commented to me just a couple of days ago, "You know, if you only get one and a half hours of sleep at night, there's just really not much you can do." Sleep is the time when children's bodies produce growth hormone, and they have a whole lot of physical growing to do during this stage.[2] When my husband and I switched shifts with our newborn son in the middle of the night, he would sometimes comment that the sleep deprivation we were experiencing constituted "cruel, inhuman or degrading treatment" under Article 5 of the United Nations' Universal Declaration of Human Rights.[3] Caregivers of young children are glorified zombies, and this condition can last longer than any of us would like to think. Ministry events and volunteer recruiting should respect parents' death grip on nap schedules and early bedtimes.

---

1   Catherine Stonehouse, *Joining Children on the Spiritual Journey: Nurturing a Life of Faith* (Grand Rapids, MI: Baker Academic, 1998), 11–12.
2   Rachel Leproult and Eve Van Cauter, "Role of Sleep and Sleep Loss in Hormonal Release and Metabolism," *Endocrine Development* 17 (2010): 11–21, https://doi.org/10.1159/000262524.
3   UN General Assembly, "Universal Declaration of Human Rights," 1948, https://www.un.org/en/universal-declaration-human-rights/index.html.

Childcare

Access to quality, affordable childcare is such a problem that it is some-times considered to be a bipartisan issue. Without live-in grandparents or nearby extended family relationships, parents have difficult decisions to make about childcare. If there are two parents, they must weigh the costs and benefits of who will work and who will care for the children, or how both will work and afford childcare. One of my friends has three kids, and both she and her husband work full-time. One child is in school, one is enrolled in two different partial-day preschools, and the baby attends a separate day care but also spends one or two days a week at a friend's house. Setting aside the costs of each childcare program, the shuffling back and forth is enough to put stress on any family system. Another dear friend desires to work outside the home, but as a trained social worker she cannot make enough money to justify the childcare expense. She stays home and works just one day a week when her husband can stay home with their kids.

The Economic Policy Institute published a study in 2015 finding that childcare costs exceed rent costs for most American families and that childcare simply is not an affordable option for low-income families.[4] Raising kids is already expensive and sometimes stressful. The added com-plication of finding and keeping good childcare in place has a monumental impact on family life.

Change

Young children change every single day. To adjust to this constant change, these youngsters make constant requests to learn. Parents and caregivers can truly grow weary of all the teachable moments that present themselves, especially since kids' questions and needs can arise at the least opportune times. A family that walks through the door of the church on Sunday morning has likely already had a shoe-tying lesson, a conversation about the size of Jupiter in relation to the size of the child's school, and an explanation of why they can eat pancakes for breakfast but not leftover birthday cake. (Would still like someone to explain this to me, please and thank you.)

---

4   Elise Gould and Cooke Tanyell, "High Quality Child Care Is out of Reach for Work-ing Families," *Economic Policy Institute* (blog), October 6, 2015, https://www.epi.org/publication/child-care-affordability/.

If caregivers seem to be playing catch-up at all times, it is because they are. As soon as they figure out their child's current stage, it changes. I can't tell you how many times I have bragged that we identified a new vegetable my son would eat or that we succeeded in sleep training, only to have all his tastes and habits change the following week.

Childlike Faith

When it comes to faith development, James Fowler describes the interplay of cognitive development and spiritual awakening of young children. Children ages 3-7 typically exhibit what Fowler calls the Intuitive-Projective Stage, which is characterized by imagination unhampered by logic.[5] He explains that young kids have the ability to be imaginative, but they only can use concrete objects and their limited lived experience to do so. Therefore, they are extremely open to symbolism, story, and mystery, because they are constantly searching for new language for the wonderings and anxieties of life that they haven't yet been able to put into words.[6]

In this stage, kids are constantly experiencing new thoughts and events and that no previous experience or teaching can make sense of. The line between reality and fantasy is very thin or sometimes not there at all, which means that fairy tales and exciting Bible stories are particularly real and appealing to them. This means that the story of Daniel in the lion's den might feel quite real and scary to a child in this stage. Adults leading kids in this stage need to share powerful, meaningful stories in the context of a loving relationship. Tell the story of Noah, and include both the good and the evil there, but then do not fail to provide the space for kids to process the story. Ask questions and invite their questions as well. And when they venture into imaginative territory that makes no sense or seems to make light of the story, listen and accept their wonderings. They are simply making meaning out of Scripture under the guidance of an adult who makes them feel safe. This process is healthy and beautiful.[7]

---

5   James W. Fowler, *Faithful Change: The Personal and Public Challenges of Postmodern Life* (Nashville: Abingdon Press, 2000), 58.
6   James W. Fowler, *Stages of Faith: The Psychology of Human Development and the Quest for Meaning* (San Francisco: Harper & Row, 1981), 129–30.
7   Ibid., 133-34.

If you can listen to children communicate their spiritual understanding to you, consider it an honor. Sofia Cavalletti and Gianna Gobbi, two early childhood faith educators, speak of the unique joy children express when confronted with God. They write that the image of God is "reflected with a special transparency in children."[8] Children have some mysteriously special purchase on sacred truth, an inexplicable bond between themselves and God that they probably can't describe without using story or symbol.[9] David Hay and Rebecca Nye have referred to this spiritual ability as a "relational consciousness," meaning that children reflect everything they learn onto their relationships with self, God, and the created world.[10] There is a reason that Jesus admonished the know-it-all adults to become more like a child. Children do not accept God simply or without question. They seem to have insight, an imaginative aspect of faith that many adults lose. As ministers we are to nurture rather than squash children's innate spirituality. The way children are taught about faith—whether in a didactic, legalistic manner or an explorative, wondering, welcoming environment—influences the way they internalize faith in adolescence and adulthood.[11]

When it comes to prayer, faith, and acceptance of God's nature, never underestimate children's ability to understand and engage. In these imaginative years of natural spirituality, it is our job to recognize the deep level of formation that is happening in their minds and hearts. It's our job to find ways to cultivate that openness to God, to give it room to grow, and to lay the foundations for a life of faith.[12]

Safety Concerns for Children

We can do little to nurture children's spirituality if we don't meet their basic need for safety, and every age group presents different challenges to this goal. As I share with children's ministry volunteers, this is not the most

---

8   Sofia Cavalletti et al., *The Good Shepherd and the Child: A Joyful Journey*, 1st edition (Chicago: Liturgy Training Publications, 1994), 14.

9   Sofia Cavalletti, *The Religious Potential of the Child: Experiencing Scripture and Liturgy With Young Children*, trans. Patricia M. Coulter and Julie M. Coulter, 2nd edition (Chicago: Liturgy Training Publications, 1992), 22.

10   David Hay and Rebecca Nye, *The Spirit of the Child*, Revised (London: Jessica Kingsley Publishers, 2006), 113–14.

11   Stonehouse, *Joining Children on the Spiritual Journey*, 21.

12   Ibid.

fun conversation you and I will ever have about children, but knowing the dangers our kids face is an essential first step. Before you begin designing ministry environments for children, consider these threats to their safety.

Abuse and Safe Sanctuaries

According to the American Academy of Pediatrics, as many as 1 in 4 girls and 1 in 8 boys will be sexually abused before they are 18 years old.[13] That source suggests that 1 in 20 children experience physical abuse. In 2017 the Department of Health and Human Services claims that more than 9 in every 1,000 children experience physical abuse, sexual abuse, or neglect annually,[14] and over 90 percent of abusers are the victim's parents.[15]

In our ministries we likely will encounter children who have suffered unspeakable harm, whether we recognize that or not. Equally frightening, there is also a good chance that we will encounter adults who seek to harm children through the guise of serving in our ministry area, usually in the role of pastor, youth minister, or other staff or volunteer leadership role.[16] News reports regularly tell of children who suffered abuse from a religious authority figure, even though churches are often considered safe places where parents can let their children participate without worry.

Trained church leaders and children's ministry volunteers can observe children and identify signs of abuse. It is our duty to keep our eyes open and to be willing to ask difficult questions if our suspicions are ever aroused. Read over this list of symptoms of child abuse published by the U.S. Department of Health and Human Services,[17] and ask yourself if any of the children in your ministry meet multiple criteria:

13   American Academy of Pediatrics, "Child Abuse and Neglect," HealthyChildren.org, 2018, http://www.healthychildren.org/English/safety-prevention/at-home/Pages/What-to-Know-about-Child-Abuse.aspx.
14   US Department of Health and Human Services, "Child Maltreatment 2017," 2019, 20.
15   Ibid., 25–26.
16   Andrew S. Denney, Kent R. Kerley, and Nickolas G. Gross, "Child Sexual Abuse in Protestant Christian Congregations: A Descriptive Analysis of Offense and Offender Characteristics," *Religions* 9, no. 1 (January 2018): 7, https://doi.org/10.3390/rel9010027.
17   Child Welfare Information Gateway, "What Is Child Abuse and Neglect? Recognizing the Signs and Symptoms" (U.S. Department of Health & Human Services, Administration for Children and Families, Administration on Children, Youth, and Families, Children's Bureau, 2019), 5–6, https://www.childwelfare.gov/pubs/factsheets/whatiscan/.

Physical Abuse

Physical abuse is defined as "a nonaccidental physical injury to a child caused by a parent, caregiver, or other person responsible for a child and can include punching, beating, kicking, biting, shaking, throwing, stabbing, choking, hitting (with a hand, stick, strap, or other object), burning, or otherwise causing physical harm."[18] Children who have experienced physical abuse may have the following signs.

- Unexplained injuries, such as bruises, bites, burns, broken bones, or black eyes
- Fading bruises or noticeable marks after an absence from school or church activities
- Seems scared, anxious, depressed, withdrawn, or aggressive
- Seems fearful of parents, caregivers, or specific adults
- Changes in eating or sleeping habits
- Reports injury by a parent or another adult

Sexual Abuse

Sexual abuse is defined as "activities by a parent or other caregiver such as fondling a child's genitals, penetration, incest, rape, sodomy, indecent exposure, and exploitation through prostitution or the production of pornographic materials."[19] Children who have experienced sexual abuse may demonstrate the following signs.

- Attaches quickly to strangers or new adults
- Demonstrates bizarre, sophisticated, or unusual sexual knowledge or behavior
- Has difficult walking or sitting
- Suddenly refuses to go to school or participate in certain activities
- Reports nightmares or bed-wetting
- Experiences a sudden change in appetite
- Runs away from home
- Reports sexual abuse by parent or another adult

---

18   Ibid., 3.
19   Ibid..

Neglect

Neglect is defined as "the failure of a parent or other caregiver to provide for a child's basic needs."[20] Children who are being neglected may exhibit the following signs.

- Frequent absence from school
- Steals or begs for food or money
- Lacks needed medical care, such as dental care or glasses
- Lacks clothing that is sufficient for the weather
- Consistently dirty and has severe body odor

Each state has different mandatory reporter laws, and it is essential for church workers to be familiar with their state's requirements and ensure that their church's safety policy is in accordance with those laws.[21] Regardless of your state's laws, as leaders who shepherd children and their families, we are mandated by love and by Scripture (Matthew 18:6,10; Proverbs 24:11-12; Psalm 82:3-4) to safeguard our children. That means taking swift and appropriate action to seek care and protection for any child we suspect could be in danger of abuse or neglect of any kind.

Safety Policies and Volunteer Training

The United Methodist Church requires every congregation to adopt a set of safety policies and procedures that we refer to as Safe Sanctuaries™. Regardless of what your church calls it, every church absolutely must put a plan in place to protect children and the adults who care for them. Some churches, like mine, adopt highly specific policies that outline sleeping arrangements for overnight retreats, a detailed process for reporting abuse, and step-by-step procedures for supervising bathroom breaks during ministry time. While this level of detail is not absolutely necessary, providing your volunteers with a plan to deal with dangerous contingencies is an ethical obligation.

Policies like this must be approved and revisited regularly by your

---

20   Ibid.

21   Child Welfare Information Gateway, "Clergy as Mandatory Reporters of Child Abuse and Neglect" (U.S. Department of Health & Human Services, Administration for Children and Families, Administration on Children, Youth, and Families, Children's Bureau, 2019), https://www.childwelfare.gov/topics/systemwide/laws-policies/statutes/clergymandated/.

church's governing board. Putting a safety plan for children into place only works if everyone in the church believes in it. Volunteers may complain about having to follow rules that are inconvenient. But rest assured, if and when the worst-case scenario occurs on their watch, they will stop complaining. I speak from experience when I say that it is truly reassuring to fall back upon a detailed, written set of instructions during a crisis.

Safety policies do not just protect children, but also protect adults who care for them. Our church requires that two unrelated adults be present and responsible for every group of children during ministry time. If a child requires bathroom assistance during that time, both adults communicate and observe one another to provide accountability in that sensitive situation. If the child happens to go home that day and comment to a parent that "Ms. Sarah saw my underwear today," that second, observing, impartial adult's report of what really happened is a safeguard for Ms. Sarah.

Children's ministry is one of the most exclusive areas of service in the church. Not just anyone can get in! Children are an extremely vulnerable group, and only the most trusted and mature leaders should be allowed to care for them. When we recruit leaders for children, we do not announce it. We handpick those volunteers and issue personal invitations to serve. Once someone agrees to serve with children, that adult undergoes a nationwide background check and a safety training with me, either in person or over the phone. We never, ever allow anyone to have direct contact with children until that person has participated and been known in the ministry of the church for at least six months. This delay in access to children could deter a predator looking for easy access to minors, while also giving church staff and families a period of time to get to know a new church attendee and build trust. Keep in mind, however, that pastors and church staff are the most likely culprits for abuse in the church, using positions of authority to take advantage of the most vulnerable.[22] Accountability for volunteers is important, and a watchful eye on anyone in a paid or unpaid position of church authority even more so. One of the extra resources you can access for free on *cokesburykids.com* is a volunteer safety training outline. Please take it, fill in the blanks, and make it work for your context!

---

22   Denney, Kerley, and Gross, "Child Sexual Abuse in Protestant Christian Congregations."

Adverse Childhood Experiences

Abuse is not the only danger facing children. If you live in the world of social work, adoption, foster care, or children's health, you are familiar with ACEs. These are traumatic events in a child's life that can have negative effects on the child's future.[23] This category includes abuse and neglect, along with other traumas, such as witnessing someone else's abuse, substance abuse in the home, a parent's divorce or separation, or mental illness in the household.[24] Experiencing these kinds of trauma in childhood makes it harder for people to live healthy lifestyles or contribute to healthy relationships as they grow older.[25] While children are resilient and childhood trauma does not determine anyone's future, there are lifelong effects that can only be resolved or accommodated through therapy and the care of others. Train your volunteers to be aware of ACEs, and do your best to provide stable, supportive relationships to children and families affected by them. Connect families with trauma-informed therapists and other healthcare providers as appropriate.

Mental Health Needs of Children

The National Alliance for Mental Illness (NAMI) tells us that half of all mental illnesses begin before a person turns age 14.[26] The most common private conversations I have with caregivers regard the diagnoses or medications they have received from pediatricians or children's mental health specialists. I have participated in NAMI events myself where parents of

23   Marilyn Metzler et al., "Adverse Childhood Experiences and Life Opportunities: Shifting the Narrative," *Children and Youth Services Review*, Economic Causes and Consequences of Child Maltreatment, 72 (January 1, 2017): 141–49, https://doi.org/10.1016/j.childyouth.2016.10.021.

24   Robert F. Anda et al., "Building a Framework for Global Surveillance of the Public Health Implications of Adverse Childhood Experiences," *American Journal of Preventive Medicine* 39, no. 1 (July 2010): 93–98, https://doi.org/10.1016/j.amepre.2010.03.015.

25   V. J. Felitti et al., "Relationship of Childhood Abuse and Household Dysfunction to Many of the Leading Causes of Death in Adults. The Adverse Childhood Experiences (ACE) Study," *American Journal of Preventive Medicine* 14, no. 4 (May 1998): 245–58.

26   National Alliance on Mental Illness, "Closing the Gap for Children's Mental Health," May 8, 2012, https://www.nami.org/Blogs/NAMI-Blog/May-2012/Closing-the-Gap-for-Children-s-Mental-Health.

children with mental illness express feelings of exhausted surrender at one moment and outrage toward mental health practitioners who won't listen to them the next. Many caregivers find the mental healthcare system for children to be outdated at best and callous at worst.

Children diagnosed with a mental illness or emotional/behavioral disorder encounter significant problems at school, with lower graduation rates and deficits in academic performance across the board.[27] Those are the kids receiving medical care and support. For others, mental illness is overlooked or misinterpreted.[28] Ministry leaders sometimes write off anti-social behavior as shyness, hormones, or a temporary phase. We have come to accept kids' fascination with apps and websites, such as YouTube, not re-alizing that a world of suicide tutorials, violence, and hateful self-talk is at their fingertips. Or we do notice mental-health symptoms, but we moralize them—that kid is a bad egg; the parents must have done something wrong.

The best support church staff can offer to families whose children have a mental-health diagnosis is to ask loving questions and listen empathet-ically to the answers. Many families desire space to open up about their family life without scaring people away. At the very least, do not ignore families who are taking their child to therapy or trying new medications. Approach them with love, then stick with them. See Chapter 12 for more resources on supporting families with mental-health needs.

Advertising to Children

How many of us have watched an unboxing video before? These are the genius invention of today's toy makers. Unboxing videos feature a child or adult who literally opens a brand-new toy and takes it out of the box. That's it. Children could watch these videos for hours, and they do.[29]

27   J. Ron Nelson et al., "Academic Achievement of K-12 Students With Emotional and Behavioral Disorders," *Exceptional Children* 71, no. 1 (2004): 59–73.

28   Berit Hjelde Hansen et al., "Non-Obsessive-Compulsive Anxiety Disorders in Child and Adolescent Mental Health Services--Are They Underdiagnosed, and How Accurate Is Referral Information?," *Nordic Journal of Psychiatry* 70, no. 2 (2016): 133–39, https://doi.or g/10.3109/08039488.2015.1061053

29   Mireille Silcoff, "A Mother's Journey Through the Unnerving Universe of 'Unboxing' Videos," *The New York Times*, January 19, 2018, https://www.nytimes.com/2014/08/17/ magazine/a-mothers-journey-through-the-unnerving-universe-of-unboxing-videos.html.

The Internet and phone apps are cluttered with videos and messages aimed at children. They have learned that parents have a hard time saying no to a child, so if they can get the child to want their product, it sells. And children, who have close to zero impulse control and very little executive function cannot see the harm of click after click after click. A majority of kids in the United States have televisions in their bedrooms and exercise unsupervised enjoyment of the Internet at home,[30] which means their exposure to effective advertising is immeasurable.

One way we can help families navigate the advertising landscape is simply to talk about the problem. As kids reach the age of 10, they develop the ability to see through advertisers' intentions for the first time.[31] It is therefore appropriate to start talking to kids approaching that age about how to evaluate the underlying messages of the ads they see. It is also a good idea to talk to parents about the need for supervision of screen time to mitigate some of the harmful effects.

Bullying

Researchers tell us that 21 percent of children in the U.S. experience bullying at school,[32] but I cannot imagine that to be true. Surely, the real number is much higher! Can any of us look back on our childhoods and honestly claim we never experienced bullying in some form? Our kids have access to bullying not just in the school cafeteria or church fellowship hall, but on their phones and computers as well. It pains me to have to include this problem with all the rest of the dangers facing our children; we would be willfully blind to ignore it.

Watch out for bullying in your ministry areas, especially if you see kids poring over their phones or other kids being left out. Make it clear to the

30   Brian L. Wilcox et al., "Report of the APA Task Force on Advertising and Children" (American Psychological Association, 2004), https://www.apa.org/pi/families/resources/advertising-children.pdf.

31   Rozendaal, Esther, Buijzen, Moniek, and Valkenburg, Patti. Children's understanding of advertiser's persuasive tactics. *International Journal of Advertising*, 2011, 30(2): 329–350.

32   L. Musu-Gillette et al., "Indicators of School Crime and Safety: 2017" (National Center for Education Statistics, March 2018), https://nces.ed.gov/pubs2018/2018036.pdf.

children in your ministry that cliques and exclusive clubs are not tolerated. And talk to the kids in your small groups about bullying, how to recognize it, and whom to seek out for help.

Creating Safe Spaces Through Holy Listening

I wish you could meet my friend Leanne Hadley (You really can at *www. leanne-hadley.com.*). Leanne has spent her career as an elder in the United Methodist Church conceptualizing Jesus' life, death, and resurrection as a model for children's spiritual transformation. She started this work several years ago when she began listening to children who were hurting.

Leanne does not shy away from the evils and awfulness of the world. She recognizes that children suffer from abuse, illness, death, and divorce, and they need safe places to share what they're feeling. However, children may have more difficulty putting their suffering into words than adults do.[33] So Leanne spends her time teaching church leaders how to employ the power of symbolic language in order to take children out of their normal orbit, into a safe space where they can share their hurt, then back to a place of wholeness and normalcy.

The tools that can help bring about this nonverbal communication are simple. If you know of a child in your church family who is hurting, ask the parents' permission, then introduce that child to what Leanne calls *Holy Listening.*[34] Assure the child that they do not have to share anything they don't want to—this is their time with God, not yours. Give the child several objects to choose from, such as a variety of colorful candles, a small sandbox with a stylus, blank paper with markers, a box of beads, or listening stones, which are simply rocks with simple shapes or symbols painted on them. Ask the child to choose an item they can use to express where they are in that moment.

After that sharing, the child will feel exposed, so there needs to be a ritual to help them cover up and exit gracefully. It is at this point that you

---

33   Meredith Edgar-Bailey and Victoria E. Kress, "Resolving Child and Adolescent Traumatic Grief: Creative Techniques and Interventions," *Journal of Creativity in Mental Health* 5, no. 2 (2010): 158–76.
34   Visit https://www.leanne-hadley.com/holy-listening for Holy Listening resources.

would lead them through a simple breath prayer, give the child a spoken blessing, or allow the child to light a candle. Choose any ritual (or let the child choose one) that gives closure and communicates your acceptance.

These Holy Listening sessions are not therapy, and there is nothing mystical about them. The idea is simply to learn to speak the language of children when acknowledging that our hurtful world sometimes hurts them too. It could take many repeated listening sessions for a child to open up, or they may get hooked on them and want to return and relive the session over and over. Either way, this is one powerful method for offering hope to children when they can't find it other places.

Best Practices for Each Age Group

This section outlines best practices for children's ministry areas from youngest nursery-goers to the elementary age group. Note that while many children's ministries include preteens, I have devoted the following chapter to that specific age group. In my experience, there is a real developmental shift somewhere around 4th grade; at that point, kids begin to desire and gain the ability to worship, serve, pray, and fellowship with peers in new ways. While there certainly isn't a clear-cut line demarcating children from youth in most churches, I believe a unique, targeted ministry plan for 4th-through 6th-graders is needed, which is why I have excluded them in this chapter in favor of focusing a whole chapter on them.

Nursery (Birth-2 years)

The older children get, the less of a burden their safety becomes. This means that in the nursery, safety needs are at their height. Outlet covers, rolling cribs, straps for the cradles—the nursery is basically an emergency preparedness zone. This is the one area of the church where I insist on having a dedicated, paid staff person. Making the nursery a paid position is the only way to reasonably expect someone to work there consistently. Nursery volunteers are wonderful and sometimes even reliable, but they cannot and should not be expected to be there more than 45 weeks out of the year.

The benefits of a consistent presence in the nursery are manifold. Seeing the same face in the nursery is hugely reassuring both to babies and to their parents. Many nursery kids cannot yet speak for themselves, but a the staff person who sees them every week learns quickly which bag goes with whom, and who is/who is not allowed to eat crackers. Regular nursery workers also maintain consistent drop-off and pick-up procedures. These little people who cannot speak or make wise decisions for themselves are some of our most vulnerable members. Ensure that there is a secure check-in procedure and that all children are returned to their rightful caregivers!

While it is easy to leave this age group to play and snack time, we are missing out on a beautiful opportunity if we do not involve them in a time of worship when they are in our care. Of course, their attention span lasts for only about 30-90 seconds at best, so I do not advise breaking into a homily. Simply setting down some round placemats and inviting the children to sit on them so that you can sing a simple worship song and pray over them is a great start. There is nothing quite like listening to a circle of babies singing "This Little Light of Mine," with little finger lights dancing in front of them. I also encourage you to pull out a toddler Bible and read a story, incorporating hand motions or repeat-after-me activities, if possible.

Preschool

The attention span with preschoolers is slightly longer. This age group can now experience a longer Bible story with corresponding activities! However, with greater verbal ability and hand-eye coordination come some other considerations as well.

This is the age when biting, aggression, escapes, and difficult drop-offs can cause problems. While many babies get their biting stage out of the way in the nursery, it can be a problem for our 3- to 5-year-olds too. For most children, aggressive behaviors such as biting are used to communicate a need or desire only until they are socialized to more appropriate methods of communication.[35] We should do everything we can to avoid alarming or persecuting parents when a preschooler bites. That said, biting and other forms of aggression are the one cause I find to invite a child to worship separately from a peer group. Following are some strategies to ensure the safety of a child who is aggressive (as well as peers).

---

35   Bridget Murray Law, "Biting Questions," *Monitor on Psychology*, February 2011.

- Inform the caregivers of both the biter/aggressor and any victims. Best practice is not to disclose the identity of the child who caused harm.
- Require preschool leaders to complete a written report every time a child is aggressive. Having details in writing will help you to communicate with caregivers and possibly identify triggers to be avoided in the future. Reports should be kept on file permanently.
- Ask the caregivers of an aggressive child to share with you any advice or strategies that work at home or have been suggested by teachers or pediatricians. Ask about triggers and customize your ministry time to avoid those.
- Clearly communicate boundaries and expectations. In my church, we take some sort of direct preventative action beyond simple communication after two infractions. Let caregivers know what to expect if the biting or aggression happens a second time.
- Train your preschool leaders in sensory-friendly classroom management[36] and inform them of any strategies the caregivers have shared that may help the child feel comfortable.
- If biting or aggression takes place more than twice, take one of these actions:
  - Invite the caregiver to attend preschool time along with the child. (This strategy may cause as many problems as it solves.)
  - Recruit a staff member or volunteer adult to accompany the child during ministry time to try to watch for and prevent incidents. (This is a caregiver-friendly option, but unfortunately often fails because kids are so incredibly speedy and therefore hard to stop in time!)
  - Provide two staff members or volunteers to temporarily care for the child outside the peer group. After a few weeks, reintroduce the child to the group to see if things go better. If not, repeat.

---

36   Robin H. Lock and Kelly Prestia, "Incorporate Sensory Activities and Choices Into the Classroom," *Intervention in School and Clinic* 39, no. 3 (January 1, 2004): 172–75, https://doi.org/10.1177/10534512040390030701; Barbara Wilmes et al., "Coming to Our Senses: Incorporating Brain Research Findings into Classroom Instruction," *Education* 128, no. 4 (2008): 659–66.

º   Ask the parents to take the child with them for a week or two, providing activities or materials to keep the child occupied.

Regardless of which strategies you employ, assure the child's caregivers that there is always a place for them and their child in your ministry.

Other safety hazards when working with preschoolers include assisting with toileting, integrating kids with separation anxiety, and preventing escapes. Some preschoolers may be in diapers, while others use the bathroom independently. The most important priority is being sure that you uphold your church's safety policies when helping children in the bathroom. If you must enter a bathroom or stall to wipe a child's bottom or help with those impossibly cute leggings, always inform another responsible adult beforehand, and if possible, have that other adult accompany you.

Helping a preschooler who has separation anxiety from a caregiver can be difficult. All preschool rooms should be equipped with a variety of play options—puzzles, blocks, books, crafts—so that children who experience a difficult drop-off can choose an activity that suits their personality. Offer parents and kids lots of grace, which may mean offering to hold their child for them or giving them space to work it out on their own.

This is the most common age group for flight risks. You cannot count heads too many times with this age group! Maintain a complete list of kids present, and count heads before and after every transition to ensure you still have everyone. Childproof door handles are not a bad idea either.

Finally, there is no prayer like the prayer of a preschooler.[37] These kids are just learning how to express themselves verbally. What better way to encourage this developmental milestone than by teaching them to pray? They are not yet embarrassed to pray out loud, and their sweet, simple hearts are fully attuned to God. Pick up a toy microphone, a candle, or a beanbag, and let them pray while holding it, then pass it along. Teach them how to pray for one another, pairing them up and letting them hold hands as they say their prayers. Pray blessings over them by name. Invite them to repeat prayers after you. As a group, learn a prayer by heart and pray it together in a circle at the end of your worship time. Find as many ways as you can to pray along with preschoolers.

---

37   Cavalletti, *The Religious Potential of the Child*, 23.

Elementary

The most insidious temptation with this age group is to mirror children's church after the school experience. Remember, the purpose of church is not education! We are not here to teach kids, but to share our faith journey and hold them accountable for theirs through relationship. Let's ditch the idea of Sunday school and find ways to meet the actual spiritual needs that kindergarteners and 1st-, 2nd-, and 3rd-graders have today.

Attention spans lengthen substantially once children learn to abide by the structures and expectations of elementary school. I usually count on a solid 3 to 6 minutes per activity with this age group, although sometimes a single activity can be stretched up to 10 minutes if it is interactive and engaging enough.

Safety concerns with this age group include rowdy behavior, lack of body awareness, and impulse control issues. The combination of fast physical growth and increased physical strength means that these kids often do not realize how strong they are or how much their actions can affect others. It is common for elementary worship times to be interrupted by claims that someone stepped on someone else's foot or Matilda's swinging arms accidentally slapped Oliver in the face. The best strategy I have found to keep bodies still is to stagger quiet activities with movement-based activities. That means that before we ask the kids to sit quietly and listen to a reading, we dance to a worship song. Or between each activity we practice a breath prayer or yoga pose. Following are some ideas for both active and quiet activities to intersperse throughout your worship time with kids:

Still or Quiet Activities

- **Music and meditation**—My church kids love when I allow them to assume a comfortable position and meditate on the words of a hymn or worship song.
- **Journaling**—Stock your worship room with loose paper or notebooks and pencils. Encourage kids to access these journals anytime and either draw or write their thoughts to God in prayer.
- **Breath prayer**—Breathe God's love in, pause, breathe God's love out. Repeat.

- **Blessing balm**—While the kids sit, leaders walk from child to child with a tube of unscented lip balm. The child will hold out a hand, and the leader will make the sign of the cross on it while speaking words of blessing, such as, "Kylie, you are a blessing from God. Now go and bless others."
- **Prayer**—It's never a bad time to circle up to say a prayer together!
- **Sandbox**—Obtain a plastic tub and fill it with dry materials, such as sand or terrarium stones. Allow the kids to draw in it with a stylus or their fingers.
- **Candle lighting**—If you want to see kids quiet down, give them the honor of lighting a candle as a visible symbol of their prayer for the day. You decide if this means lighting a candle with real fire or a battery!

Movement or Noisy Activities

- **Stretches**—Lead the group in reaching their hands as high as they'll go, then as low as they'll go. Direct them to wrap themselves in a hug, then stretch their arms out wide. Channel your inner coach and help them work each muscle group in turn.
- **Vocal warm-ups**—Talk to a music or voice teacher to learn some warm-up activities. They have some of the best ones!
- **Simon Says**—Encourage the kids to copy you as you jump, lunge, spin, or otherwise work out the energy.
- **Dance party**—Turn up the worship tunes and encourage kids to show you their best dance moves. Try not to pull a muscle yourself.
- **Nature walk**—If you need a change of scenery, line up and take a quick walk. If going outdoors is not safe, simply walk up and down a hallway, being careful not to disturb other worshipers.
- **Interactive Bible story**—Choose a keyword from your Bible story that day, and assign a motion to it so that every time the kids hear that word, they perform that motion.
- **Dramatic Bible story**—Assign parts from the Bible story to kids and let them act it out as you tell it.
- **Reading aloud**—While no child should ever be put on the spot

or forced to read out loud, some kids will love it. Open the floor for Bible readers sometimes and let them explain what they've read afterward.

Responding to the needs of your group for movement or quiet will help open everyone's eyes and ears to receive God's Word during worship. Be attentive, and if even one child cannot sit still and focus, be willing to change your plan a little in order to engage everyone in a time of quiet or structured movement.

Finally, many churches invite children in this age group to participate in part of sanctuary worship. If this is the case for you, keep in mind that transitions are some of the most difficult times for kids to manage. Explain the plan and expectations to everyone from the very start, and plan to begin each new phase of worship with an intentional movement or quiet activity to help kids transition mentally and emotionally to a new space.

Best Practices for All Children

One principle that guides my ministry to children, whether in a large-group worship or small-group format, is that there is nothing wrong with repetition. Repetition. Repetition. Because children can be so energized by flashy colors and new things, we often fall prey to the false belief that we must keep things new and exciting for them all the time. We take upon ourselves the responsibility to engage them, when children are way better at engaging themselves than we could ever be. They do not need us to produce thrills—they generate thrills just by being present! There is no shame in choosing one format that works for your context and sticking to it.

It is freeing to understand that our role is to build relationships and guide children through discipleship *practices* rather than lessons. Following are some ideas for practices you may want to experiment with:

- *Liturgy*—Whether your church uses a liturgical worship format or not, giving children a set of words that they can hide in their hearts and possibly relate to in a variety of church contexts is a wonderful gift. When my family visits an unfamiliar church, my kids can still join in worship whenever they hear the Lord's Prayer or sing the Doxology, because these are words they've grown accustomed to repeating every Sunday. Singing the "Gloria Patri" together or reciting the Apostles' Creed are wonderful ways to impart lasting and foundational truths to our kids. Circling up at the end of ministry time and leading kids in reciting "May the Lord bless you and keep you…" (Numbers 6:24-26) not only gives them closure to your time together but teaches them Scripture. Liturgy is one of the most child-friendly worship elements in our churches.

- *Bible storybooks*—Choose a solid Bible storybook and read a story from it each week. After a year of reading through the stories, start over, reading the same stories to the same group of children the next year. The stories of the Bible grow with us! Our understanding changes from reading to reading; there are always new questions to ask about these stories. Bible stories can be interpreted through journaling, drawing, dramatization, games, and retelling. Choose the application that best fits with your group and allow the kids to express their reaction to it with their own creativity. And when they complain, "Hey, we've heard this one before!" at the beginning of the story, remind them that God's Word always has something new to tell us. Challenge them to figure out what God wants them to hear in the story this time.

- *Routine*—Many children's ministry workers fear that routine will be boring to kids and that parents will complain that we're not working hard enough if we just do the same thing over and over. I hope I have put those fears to rest here. Routine should not be a dirty word in children's ministry! In fact, setting an expectation that kids can rely on fuels their sense of belonging in your ministry space. Ministry to children generally happens through a set of activities, such as:
  - Snacks
  - Prayer requests
  - Prayer time
  - Bible story/passage
  - Scripture memorization

- ° Application (crafts and games)
- ° Meditation/quiet time
- ° Journaling
- ° Service project

Choose the elements you need to include in your ministry event and the order in which you will do them. This order becomes your routine. Cycle through this routine every week; be sure the kids in your ministry know what the routine is and take responsibility for leading it. If you begin by lighting a candle, assign a child or two to perform that task each week. If you need to set up chairs or cushions, let the kids do that at the beginning of your time together until it becomes the ritual. And if you are worried that this will become boring, remember that simply including time for prayer requests will deliver all the entertainment and excitement you would ever need.

Final Thoughts

Children's ministry is a time of building foundations and setting expectations for both parents and their kids. Create open lines of communication now so that parents know they can come to you down the road as well. Caregivers tend to be open to volunteering at this stage, which is wonderful! But do not burn them out. The parent volunteer you have come to rely on this year will need a break next year. Keep prep time and number of volunteer commitments as low as possible, giving your children's ministry volunteers freedom to build relationships without getting completely exhausted. Perhaps these parents will be confirmation mentors or high school small group leaders for these same kids down the road, especially if they develop a special place in their hearts for them now.

Last, we have ignored and underfunded our children's ministries for far too long. Declining church attendance and giving should prove to us that what we are doing is not working. It is time to start paying closer attention to what our children say and need, and see where that takes us. Children are not just our future—they are our present and our past, too.

CHAPTER 4

PRETEEN MINISTRY

"Tell me one of your most memorable experiences from your preteen years." I threw that question out to friends from all walks of life, and these are just a few of their responses:

"Getting caught in our fort in the woods with beer and cigarettes we had stolen from my parents. [It was the] summer before 4th grade, so [we were] around 10."

"The day in 6th grade when my friends decided not to talk to me. It really only lasted a day, but it hurt badly. I'll never forget it."

"I was in 6th grade and received every single academic award for the highest GPA in each subject, and all around. I was beaming with pride, then I was laughed at and felt humiliated. It was the first time I realized it was no longer 'cool' to be smart. My self-confidence was instantly shattered because I had never been laughed at that way before."

"[My] first kiss was in the 6th grade at the roller-skating rink—my friend told me to make sure I kept my eyes open, then I closed them and thought I had done it wrong forever."

These stories should remind all of us that the preteen years make an indelible impact on our development. No longer little kids and not yet teenagers, 10- to 12-year-olds experience wild changes in their bodies, minds, and social worlds. They are by far my favorite kids to lead and serve.

This chapter begins with an overview of developmental changes at work during the preteen years, such as brain development and adherence to cultural scripts. Then we discuss the roles of parents and caregivers as they shepherd preteens, followed by ministries the church can offer preteens through mentoring, apprenticeship, and peer-based discipleship. The final section covers the unique protections we must offer to our preteens, from safety measures we put in place to sexuality education and more.

Middle Childhood

There is a significant shift in development during the preteen years, and understanding this stage is critical to designing ministry spaces for these kids. For many years, churches divided children's ministry from youth ministry with a hard line at 6th or 7th grade. More and more, however, we are learning that this short span truly deserves its own distinct plan, separate from young children and youth. The years from age 9 to 12 are the pre-adolescent or "onset of adolescence" phase, when kids begin to encounter some of the challenges and privileges of full adolescence.[1] What follows is an overview of brain development, cultural scripts, and the lasting memories made during this developmental stage.

Preteen Brain Development

Preteen and teenage years are notorious for being times of adventure, risk-taking, and deviance. It is common for parents and professionals alike to approach these years with some anxiety. The most popular explanation for the increased risk-taking behaviors that occur throughout adolescence is the growth imbalance between the brain's logical, rational area (the frontal cortex) and its more affective, emotional, adventurous area (the amygdala).[2] It seems that the brain's capacity for emotions and stress expands dramatically with the onset of adolescence, but its ability to foresee consequences and plan ahead remains childlike for a while longer.

---

1   Eveline A. Crone and Ronald E. Dahl, "Understanding Adolescence as a Period of Social-Affective Engagement and Goal Flexibility," *Nature Reviews. Neuroscience* 13, no. 9 (2012): 636, https://doi.org/10.1038/nrn3313.
2   Ibid., 637.

It is important to realize that while this explanation is helpful, it also represents an oversimplification of the pre-adolescent brain. This stage is much too complex to be explained entirely by a delay in the development of the frontal cortex, as brain researchers have begun to discover.[3] They are finding that close relationships in a preteen's life, as well as intentional education, can mitigate the effects of this maturity gap in the brain. Healthy communication with primary caregivers paired with education that helps preteens understand their big feelings and respond appropriately can lead to a much smoother, more harmonious preteen experience. But brain development is not the only factor at play; the social environment also has a role to play, and that acto Invite the children to mimic you. r is even further outside the control of parents and practitioners.

Cultural Scripts for Preteens

Most adults are intimately familiar with the process of following a cultural script, whether or not they realize it. A *cultural script* is the socially idealized succession of events in a person's life—in other words, a set of "culturally important transitional events" that are expected to take place over the typical course of life.[4] Studies have found that young people's expectations for their future and older persons' reminiscences of important life events in their past align with a high degree of overlap. It seems that while cultural scripts can differ from one geographic place to another, they remain largely the same from generation to generation. Cultural scripts that are pertinent to the lives of preteens may include puberty, birth of a sibling, going to school, and beginning to date.[5]

These scripts go largely unnoticed by children until they enter the preteen years. Children aged 9, 10, and 11 begin to think a lot about what is expected of them—dressing a certain way, knowing the words to the right songs, watching the right shows, owning the right devices. They learn by watching others suffer the social consequences of not fulfilling the script.

---

3   Ibid., 640.
4   Annette Bohn, "Generational Differences in Cultural Life Scripts and Life Story Memories of Younger and Older Adults," *Applied Cognitive Psychology* 24, no. 9 (2010): 1325, https://doi.org/10.1002/acp.1641.
5   Ibid.

We socialize preteen boys to be tough, and to earn sexual desirability by being big and strong, while our culture teaches preteen girls to be small, prizing sexual inexperience and seeing them as solely relational and able to be manipulated. In other words, the ideal boy is strong and unemotional, and the ideal girl is small and emotional. Both of these scripts are, obviously, harmful.

Learning the cultural script and following it can take a toll on young people's physical and emotional well-being. They have never before had so much to learn in such a short period of time with such high stakes for failure. Preteens' seemingly sudden adherence to perceived social cues can flummox their parents and caregivers. I have lost count of the number of times the parent of a 4th-grade girl or a 5th-grade boy has approached me to bemoan the loss of their sweet, good-natured kid who has been replaced by a stranger with a smart mouth and a new penchant for throwing tantrums with seemingly little cause. The truth is, the cause of all this tumult is not just hormone development or inadequate sleep or overdependence on screen time, although all those things certainly play a role. The main issue is one most preteens cannot consciously identify, but which has become of utmost importance: that of fitting into the script set by their social environment.

Imaginary Audience

The necessity of following a cultural script is coupled with an internal monologue that begins to speak into preteens' subconscious called the "imaginary audience," the idea that "other people are as concerned with their behaviors and appearance" as they are themselves.[6] In short, preteens begin to make predictions and assumptions about how others will react to them, and their behavior is guided by this phenomenon. When the concept of this imaginary audience was first raised in the 1960s, it was thought to be a product of egocentric beliefs, with no basis in reality. Today we understand that the feedback from this imaginary audience emerges from real social experiences and events. As noted in the Journal of Research on Adolescence, "with 'likes' and 'followers' and Instagram stories, the

---

6   Julie Y. Takishima-Lacasa et al., "Self-Consciousness and Social Anxiety in Youth: The Revised Self-Consciousness Scales for Children," *Psychological Assessment* 26, no. 4 (December 2014): 1292–1306, https://doi.org/10.1037/a0037386.

imaginary audience is real for many adolescents."[7] There is a strong tie between preteens' fears and the real opinions and consequences they face in life.[8]

When a parent tells a preteen to put away their phone and their child throws a fit, a natural reaction might be to respond with anger and/or punishment. While the preteen's disrespectful behavior might be legitimately unacceptable, responding with anger only furthers the preteen's belief that they are misunderstood and deepens their fears of not belonging. They see the phone as the primary tool of social engagement, and putting it away threatens their image among peers. Preteens are too young to see the big picture and understand where their parents are coming from; the pressure to perform for their imagined audience is too high.

The imaginary audience is seen to be as critical or as admiring of the individual as they are of themselves.[9] As a result, preteens' own self-criticism is magnified by their imaginary audience. This is the stage when concepts of beauty, especially for girls, become self-destructive and oppressive. A study in 2010 found that girls as young as 8 or 9 years old frequently report body-image dissatisfaction.[10] While body-image struggles are especially common in girls, boys experience body-image dissatisfaction as well, and in increasing numbers.[11] Research suggests that more and more men and boys experience eating disorders.[12] Children's negative feelings about their bodies—not strong enough, not small enough, not fill-in-the-blank enough—result in plummeting self-esteem and self-confidence. Trends toward disordered eating or self-inflicted isolation begin during preadolescence. These coping mechanisms are attempts at numbing the pain of listening to an angry crowd of internal critics.

7   Amanda Sheffield Morris et al., "Adolescent Brain Development: Implications for Understanding Risk and Resilience Processes Through Neuroimaging Research," *Journal of Research on Adolescence* 28, no. 1 (2018): 4–9, https://doi.org/10.1111/jora.12379.
8   Joanna H. Bell and Rachel D. Bromnick, "The Social Reality of the Imaginary Audience: A Grounded Theory Approach," *Adolescence* 38, no. 150 (2003): 215.
9   Ibid., 206.
10   David Buckingham et al., "Sexualised Goods Aimed at Children: A Report to the Scottish Parliament Equal Opportunities Committee," January 1, 2010.
11   Jessica H. Baker et al., "Body Dissatisfaction in Adolescent Boys," *Developmental Psychology* 55, no. 7 (n.d.): 1566–78.
12   Eric Strother et al., "Eating Disorders in Men: Underdiagnosed, Undertreated, and Misunderstood," *Eating Disorders* 20, no. 5 (2012): 346–55, https://doi.org/10.1080/10640 266.2012.715512.

In essence, sometime during the middle childhood years, preteens develop an inner voice that sometimes affirms their performance but often criticizes every choice they make. If many of us are honest, this voice is a familiar backdrop to our adult lives as well; it is a hard companion to shake.

Lasting Memories

The preteen years consist of a series of firsts. The first emotional friendship, the first social rejection, the first self-categorization as ugly or pretty. And these firsts can last forever. One of the most intimidating but also exhilarating realizations about working with preteens is that they are forming lasting memories during this stage. Adults typically remember a smattering of isolated experiences from childhood. But the events of our preteen years—home life, crushes, friendships, school work, privileges, and punishments—get etched into our memory banks much more deeply. Most adults can recall with high-definition clarity the formative events of middle childhood.

You may be asking how this is any different from later adolescence, when human beings also order their lives along cultural scripts and make lasting memories, for better or for worse. There are two main differences between the preteen and teenage years in this respect.

1. **Openness**—Preteens are still close enough to childhood to be open to new things. They are inexperienced, not jaded by the disappointments and difficulties that come with growing up. Like children, they can still be persuaded to approach new activities with awe and wonder. Their recourse for handling the overwhelming demands of their imaginary audience might still be to escape by swinging on the playground, playing with Legos and dolls, or watching animated movies. There is a window of opportunity here during these years to set their trajectory, to prepare them for the trials of adolescence, and to speak life and love into this season of learning about cultural expectations.

2. **Inexperience**—Most preteens have not wrecked a car yet, broken up with a serious significant other, or watched friends drink or make out at a party. These and other formative situations are on

the horizon for them, but they don't yet carry the baggage from them. Their anticipation of new privileges and lack of experience with the consequences provide parents and ministry leaders with an opportunity to teach them beforehand. We can prepare them to make wise choices, knowing that they will not always do so. We also can position ourselves and their parents as safe places to land when life gets harder in middle and high school. If young people encounter difficult or even traumatic experiences without any warning or backup plan, they are unlikely to handle it in a healthy way. The time to navigate a young person through adolescent difficulties is before they happen.

Of course, we as church leaders are not always available to witness or pastor our preteens through this season of preparation. That is why we must understand and invest in their parents and caregivers, who will be there for them every day.

Parents and Caregivers of Preteens

Parents and caregivers have as much emotional work to do during this stage as their preteens. While their children undergo a metamorphosis from child to teenager, parents and caregivers become acquainted with a whole new person to raise. This stage can cause grief as well as frustration. For caregivers who understand that their preteen is experiencing huge internal shifts, it can be hard to know what to discipline and what to let slide.

Cultural Scripts for Parents

Most parents have dreams for their children. They agonize over their kids' friendships, hobbies, and academics, always wanting what's best for them. Preteens without a favorite sport or instrument to play could find themselves enrolled in activities by parents desperately wanting to engage them in a fulfilling skill. Playdates may be arranged, when making new friends proves difficult. Parents will watch from the sidelines, hoping that a relationship will stick. If the efforts are unsuccessful, parents can feel even more dejected than their kids.

While parents' dreams for their preteens come from a loving instinct, they also tend to align with the cultural scripts set for parents. Society often unfairly attributes kids' behavior to their caregivers' parenting skills. A preteen who doesn't make good eye contact or has few friends can be perceived to have developed these tendencies because of underperforming parents. Caregivers' efforts to help their preteen fit in often stems from their own desire to follow cultural scripts as parents.

One belief that has become a normalized part of caregivers' cultural scripts is the idea that preteens are entering a typical rebellious stage, and that intervention is therefore futile. This means that while some parents will attempt to micromanage their children's activities, others will throw up their hands in defeat. A study on the retail purchases of parents and their preteens found that parents consider their preteens to be the experts in selecting culturally appropriate clothes and possessions, and even felt incompetent to persuade their kids to consider better choices.[13] If caregivers find themselves hurt or rejected by their preteens, they can sometimes give up and write off any intervention in their preteen's life as needless interference. They may prematurely abdicate the role of counselor, safe place, and listener, which they could have held in the ensuing years.

Approach preteens' caregivers with patience, and be sure to normalize and validate their feelings. Once parents understand that their children are developing an imaginary audience and attempting to meet the demands of cultural scripts, they generally become much more compassionate toward their children and open to hearing strategies for coming alongside them.

Proactive Conversations

The best way to handle conflicts and hurt feelings between preteens and their caregivers is intentional, thoughtful conversations. This is the opposite of withdrawing and leaving preteens to navigate on their own. One of my best friends, Carol, tells how her mom accomplished this practice when she was young. Her mom used to give her hair permanents, a process that took several hours and allowed them to be in close physical contact but avoid eye contact. With Carol facing away from her mom, she found herself conversing about sex, puberty, and other important topics.

---

13   Buckingham.

As she felt her mom's hands methodically working through her hair, she listened to explanations of things that would be appalling if addressed in a formal, face-to-face manner. Now raising her own preteen, Carol finds that car conversations are one of the best times to address important issues with her 6th-grade son, Will. As she drives, she can ask questions and share her honest wisdom while Will enjoys the semi-privacy of being alone and in the background of the back seat. They have used their commutes to talk about friends, music lyrics, sex, and so forth.

Apart from the sex talk, the major proactive conversation that needs to take place early in the preteen years is the Code Word Conversation. The purpose of the talk is to explain to the preteen the changes they are experiencing and the reason these changes are happening. Preteens need to hear that their brains are changing, and those changes require a lot of energy and cause a lot of feelings. All the feelings are normal and expected—it's what we do with them that matters. Once a preteen and caregiver are on the same page about the stress underlying their physical and mental transformation, they can decide on a course of action or a code word to help them signal to one another when they are feeling angry or overwhelmed. Jo Eberhardt, a writer and single parent in Australia, writes that she and her 11-year-old agreed that his brain could equate the anxiety produced by a simple task like giving a presentation at school with the emotional response of facing a sabre tooth tiger.[14] After that conversation, she could say, "Sweetheart, I'm not a sabre tooth tiger," and he would know that his response to her had been uncalled for. That became their code word.

A leader of a preteen small group approached me recently to ask how to help one of the kids in her group rein in his excitement when appropriate. After talking through some options, she agreed that she would talk to him about the importance of settling down to focus when others were speaking. They then would work together to come up with a code word or even a hand signal that would alert him that it was time to exert self-control. Explaining to preteens what is going on in the brain, then collaborating on how to respond appropriately builds trust and teaches them to be responsible for their self-regulation.

14   Jo Eberhardt, "My Parenting Post Went Viral," *The Happy Logophile* (blog), January 7, 2019, https://joeberhardt.com/2019/01/07/my-parenting-post-went-viral/.

The Church's Role with Preteens

As ministry professionals, the first step in leading preteens is to try to understand them, their stage of development, and their needs. By reading everything in this chapter up to this point, you have begun the process of understanding! This next section will cover ministry design for preteens, such as small-group discipleship and apprenticeship within the church. Following that discussion is a significant section on protecting preteens in our church spaces, which includes educating them and their caregivers on topic such as faith and sexuality, technology, and marketing.

Preteen Small Groups

There is nothing quite as delightful as sitting in a circle of 4th- or 5th-graders and listening to them grapple with philosophical or theological questions for the first time. The recipe for designing a fruitful small group for preteens includes adults who are willing to encounter big questions, plenty of time for conversation, and, of course, snacks. Snacks are key.

Snacks

In my experience, kids devour church snacks with gusto, as if they had saved their appetites all week. This phenomenon appears even truer for preteens gearing up to go deep in conversation. Sharing bagels with cream cheese or apple slices creates a sense of comfort with one another and their leaders, and fuels them to talk candidly and listen well to others. If possible, provide snacks that are healthy, and avoid sugary junk food. Preteens in my ministry have feasted many times on cheese sticks, crackers, grapes, bananas, bread and butter, yogurt, popcorn, or unsweetened cereal. It is not lost on me that I have posited snack foods as the first step in organizing a discipleship process, and I have no regrets. Sometimes the most practical, unimaginative elements of designing ministry are the most critical.

Discussion

Once snacks are out of the way, leaders of preteen small groups can enter into the real purpose of the time together—the asking and answering of questions. Providing a safe place where preteens' questions are honored is the best gift we can give them. Centering small groups on questions is also a gift to the volunteers who lead them, since they do not have to spend their Saturday nights preparing catchy activities or memorizing a script from curriculum. Preteens are ready to flex their leadership muscles, and we should prepare them to do that by talking first. There are many ways to set up discussion times. One is to let the kids decide. Each month or semester, gather your preteens together and ask them to submit their questions and discussion topics. Some guiding prompts are:

- What kinds of things would you like to talk about?
- What Book of the Bible are you interested in learning more about?
- What are words you've heard that you don't understand? (It's best to let them write these words and submit them silently!)
- If you could ask God one question right now, what would it be?
- Name some of the hardest things about being a preteen right now.
- Name some of the best things about being a preteen right now.
- What are some of your favorite Bible stories that you heard when you were younger and would like to study in a new way?

Once the kids submit their ideas, the leaders can decide which one to discuss each week. Note that this system only works if leaders are spiritually mature enough to lead kids through questions that they themselves cannot answer. I would not recommend giving preteens free rein on subject matter if your volunteers are on a monthly rotation or are new to preteen ministry.

Another option for conversation with preteens is to write a set of 5 to 10 consistent questions for them to choose from each week, and use those same questions over and over. The questions should be written in kid-friendly language and designed to help them identify their feelings and open up. Folllowing are some examples:

- How do I feel deep, deep down?
- What was one thing I did really well this week?
- What was one thing I complained about this week?
- Who in my life is having a hard time right now?
- How was I a good friend this week?
- What did I do that made me feel smart, strong, or helpful?

- What did I worry about this week?
- How did I show love to my family this week?
- What made me feel God's love this week?
- What's something I learned recently?
- How am I growing?
- What do I spend time thinking about?
- How would I like others to pray for me?
- Where did I see God at work this week?

It is crucial for leaders to model their faith lives for preteens by answering these questions for themselves as well. Coach leaders about sharing honestly but appropriately—anecdotes from a date gone wrong or a crushing defeat at work may be too overwhelming for preteens to process, and that kind of oversharing would be inappropriate. But adults who can admit that they also have questions about faith, and who share the ways they see God working around them, can make faith come alive for kids.

This is not to say that sitting in a circle and talking is the only option. Service projects, group games, and crafts can be incorporated into these times as needed, especially if those are elements that preteens request. But I believe the asking and answering of deep questions should be the bedrock of preteen small-group experiences. The time they spend in conversation will prepare them for middle and high school small groups, where they will have earned one another's trust and learned how to talk about what's truly important. Taking preteen small groups seriously can bless youth leaders with students who consider church a safe place to be themselves.

Apprenticeship

In all my years of ministry, apprenticeship may be the best idea I've tried yet. It capitalizes on the many different aspects of preteen development—increased mental and physical capacity, lessening dependence on parents, imaginary audience—and creates a sense of belonging and ownership for preteens during a stage that can be disorienting. Connecting with nonparental adult mentors is an important part of preteens' faith development. As Catherine Stonehouse writes,

The faith of children is most likely to grow when they have the opportunity to associate with adults who are growing persons who know and love God. The child's faith is inspired when he or she belongs to an inclusive community that seeks to live out God's love.[15]

An apprenticeship ministry also provides an outlet for preteens to explore their gifts and calling in a safe and loving context. Children in 4th through 6th grade are living in a special period of understanding, ability, and openness. When we ask young children what they want to be when they grow up, we often hear answers such as mermaid, firefighter, or pirate. In middle childhood, kids begin to refine those answers, looking for work that is both glamorous and fun but also achievable in the world they know. What I see as a time of calling discernment, researchers have long referred to as a period of career development that they agree begins in childhood.[16]

After spending their early elementary years participating primarily in children's worship and small groups, preteens are ready to give back. You will not find another age group as eager to serve. An apprenticeship ministry places a preteen in an area of service within the church and pairs them with an unrelated adult mentor who will train and oversee their service. The first step in setting up an apprenticeship ministry for preteens is to identify which service areas in your church could be open to them. Possible areas of service for preteens include:

- **Greeter**—open doors as people arrive, greet with a smile, give directions, offer coffee/doughnuts
- **Usher**—distribute bulletins, escort people to seats, straighten sanctuary prior to services, collect offering, take attendance
- **Nursery assistant**—play gently with babies, read stories, help distribute snacks, feed bottles
- **Preschool assistant**—set a good example for children, help with snacks and crafts, tell the Bible story
- **Audio/visual operator**—learn how to operate the mixer, advance slides on cue
- **Liturgist/Scripture reader**—read Scripture for the service, lead in liturgy

15   Catherine Stonehouse, *Joining Children on the Spiritual Journey: Nurturing a Life of Faith* (Grand Rapids, MI: Baker Academic, 1998), 37

16   Erik Porfeli and Bora Lee, *Career Development during Childhood and Adolescence*, vol. 2012, 2012, 11, https://doi.org/10.1002/yd.20011.

- **Acolyte**—light the candles for worship, carry God's light out at the end
- **Personal assistant**—accompany a staff person, run errands, carry supplies, convey messages
- **Behind-the-scenes worship coordinator**—prepare Communion elements, take attendance, distribute water to speakers, ensure worship leaders are in place
- **Setup/Cleanup crew**—arrive early and/or stay late to set up chairs, clean pews, set out worship elements, empty trash cans, turn lights on and off, vacuum
- **Prayer leader**—read a written prayer or lead prayer time for the congregation, collect and record prayer requests, pray with worship leaders prior to service, pray throughout the service
- **Mid-week ministry intern**—attend a ministry program that takes place on a weeknight and assist with childcare or other volunteer needs

Once church leaders have created a list of possible serving roles for preteens, it is time to find trustworthy, loving, mature adults who can mentor a preteen in each of those areas. Ideally, the church will already have such adults serving as sound coordinator or ushers who will agree to take an apprentice under their wing. However, you may be able to use this mentoring request to recruit for your existing adult volunteer needs at the same time! If the church is short of greeters, approach an adult who would be a worthy mentor for a preteen and ask if that adult will join the greeting team in order to mentor a preteen with an interest in that area.

With mentors available in each of these areas, preteens (with the help of their caregivers) can now apply for their preferred areas of service. On *cokesburykids.com* you will find printable worksheets for parents and preteens to complete that will help them to identify talents, abilities, and preferences. Make it clear to families that the final placement decisions rest with leadership, although all requests will be taken into consideration.

Once leaders have assigned preteens to areas of service and matched them with mentors, encourage mentors to get to know their apprentices both during their serving times and outside of church, if possible. Help mentors and apprentices decide on the frequency and schedule of their serving together. Consider your church's safety policy and advise parents and mentors to work together to create safe ways for mentors and apprentices to get to know one another. Conduct safety training and background checks on all mentors before they begin mentoring.

In my church of 150 members, we have seven apprentices who are between 4th and 6th grade. Five of them serve weekly in the areas of nursery assistant, preschool assistant, and worship coordinator. The other two serve at least twice a month in the sound booth, and on their off-weeks they assist with babies and preschoolers. A few weeks ago, a mentor had to miss a Sunday morning due to a medical emergency. She offered the assurance that her apprentice would still be there, and that apprentice could perform almost all the duties of a worship coordinator independently. Last week, after caring for an influx of babies in our nursery, the nursery staff person told me she did not think we needed to recruit more adult volunteers as long as preteen apprentices continued to help. Our children are not the future of our church, but the present.

When the typical preteen arrives at church, they wonder how they will be treated by peers, and whether they will sit alone or among friends. In contrast, when an apprentice arrives at church, they get to work. The question of belonging is settled by their ownership of the job they have been given and the mentor who will be by their side. There is still plenty of time with friends during small-group time or after services, but their sense of belonging comes, in part, from serving.

Protecting Preteens

Just as in every other life stage, the preteen years come with their own special package of risks and necessary precautions. Preteens make discoveries about their personhood, feelings, preferences and attitudes all the time. They begin to categorize themselves as pretty or ugly, masculine or feminine, smart or dumb, popular or uncool, just to name a few areas of self-discovery. It is during this stage of formation and inexperience that preteens need comprehensive faith and sexuality education. If they do not understand sex and their bodies before being confronted by sexual language and experiences, they will be unprepared to make wise choices.

Additionally, preteens who are gay, lesbian, bisexual, transgender, or questioning sometimes begin to express themselves in new ways during this stage, and our churches must prepare in advance to shepherd and love them and their families through that process. This section covers research and strategies for offering faith and sexuality education to preteens, and for discipling preteens who are forming their LGBTQ identities.

Faith and Sex Education

The best time to teach a young person about sex is when they are still ignorant of it. Preteen ministry in your church is the last opportunity to make a first impression on kids who are daily moving toward greater exposure to sexual language, images, and experiences. In my experience, by the beginning of 6th grade, kids have already learned enough language and concepts about sex to make them less interested in learning the truth from trusted adults. While it may seem like teaching comprehensive sex education endangers our kids' innocence, it's actually quite the opposite. Knowledge is the best protection.

The Guttmacher Institute published a fact sheet about adolescent sexual health in 2017, and these were some of their findings:[17]

- On average, young people in the United States have sex for the first time at about age 17.
- About half of adolescents aged 15 to 19 report having had oral sex, and one in 10 report having had anal sex.
- People between the ages of 15 and 24 account for half of all cases of sexually transmitted infections in the U.S.
- About 11 percent of abortions in 2013 were for adolescents.
- The most common reason given by adolescents for not having sex was a moral or religious belief.

I share these somewhat overwhelming statistics to demonstrate that sexual activity is a realistic part of life for preteens and adolescents. They will almost certainly be exposed to sexual behavior or have a close friend involved in sexual activity during these years. If we fail to teach them God's

---

17   Guttmacher Institute, "Adolescent Sexual and Reproductive Health in the United States," Guttmacher Institute, September 2017, https://www.guttmacher.org/fact-sheet/american-teens-sexual-and-reproductive-health.

good creation of their bodies, the healthy and unhealthy ways to express their sexual desires, and the need to prepare for future sexual engagement, we leave them defenseless when other, less loving, and less gracious peers or adults become their teachers.

Church Is the Best Place

Preparing our preteens for the questions and pressures they will face in middle and high school is worth confronting as adults. We must face our own fears and brokenness around sexuality. And not surprisingly, many academics have suggested that the church may be uniquely positioned to convey this education to young people. Religious beliefs are an integral part of a person's life, and all religious groups teach some understanding of sexual ethics and expectations. The way a church communicates with families about sex can have a profound impact on those families' experience of and beliefs about sexuality.[18] Pastors who understand the need for sex education commonly express willingness and even eagerness to provide it in their contexts, but they stop short of implementing programs because they do not know how or where to start.[19]

Other reasons churches may hesitate to offer sex education are fears of conflict or the false conclusion that faith-based sex education is just not a vital offering for their communities.[20] The responsibility to campaign for a faith and sexuality program may lie with family ministry leaders who can draw upon their own expertise with families to convince other congregation members of the importance of this issue. Many scholars who study family life tend to see religion as a negative influence on sexuality development, believing that most religions convey shame in areas of sexuality.[21]

18   Monica McGoldrick, Nydia A. Garcia Preto, and Betty A. Carter, *The Expanding Family Life Cycle: Individual, Family, and Social Perspectives*, 5th edition (Boston: Pearson, 2015). 122–23

19   Alexa Hach and Susan Roberts-Dobie, "'Give Us the Words': Protestant Faith Leaders and Sexuality Education in Their Churches," *Sex Education* 16, no. 6 (November 1, 2016): 629, https://doi.org/10.1080/14681811.2016.1151778.

20   Heather D. Boonstra, "Matter of Faith: Support for Comprehensive Sex Education Among Faith-Based Organizations," Guttmacher Institute, March 5, 2008, 21, https://www.guttmacher.org/gpr/2008/02/matter-faith-support-comprehensive-sex-education-among-faith-based-organizations.

21   Camille Garceau and Scott T. Ronis, "The Interface between Young Adults' Religious

Since most public schools are restricted by legislation to only the most basic, often abstinence-only approaches to sex education,[22] churches have a moral responsibility to change the prevailing opinion that they back the unsubstantiated dependence on abstinence-only education. Ministry leaders must use what influential channels we have to teach a holistic, faithful approach to sexuality.[23]

Empowering Parents as Sex Educators

While the church can play a powerful role in teaching preteens about sexuality, its influence pales in comparison to the impact caregivers have on their kids' beliefs and behaviors concerning sex.[24] Studies show that adolescents in religious families with healthy connections to their parents and religious peers are less likely to engage in early or unsafe sexual activities than those without these supports in place.[25] The church can provide annual programs or consistent preaching on faithful sexuality, but parents can demonstrate those principles to their children on a daily basis.

The trouble here is the persistent fear and discomfort most adults feel about discussing sexuality, even with one another![26] They fear that others will disagree or judge their beliefs and practices around sexuality. When it comes to talking with kids about sexuality, parents often abdicate this responsibility because they feel they lack the resources or underestimate the influence they really have on their preteens.[27] Just because peer relationships have increased importance during this stage does not mean that the values and modeling of parents and guardians are unimportant.

Our task as ministry leaders is to equip and encourage parents to first

---

Values and Their Sexual Experiences before Age 16," *The Canadian Journal of Human Sexuality*, July 31, 2017, 142–50, https://doi.org/10.3138/cjhs.262-a6.

22   Boonstra, 21.

23   Ibid., 22.

24   Jennifer Manlove et al., "Pathways from Family Religiosity to Adolescent Sexual Activity and Contraceptive Use," *Perspectives on Sexual and Reproductive Health* 40, no. 2 (June 2008): 105, https://doi.org/10.1363/4010508.

25   Ibid., 114.

26   Cherie L. Wooden and Frances R. Anderson, "Engaging Parents in Reproductive Health Education: Lessons Learned Implementing a Parent Designed, Peer-Led Educational Model for Parents of Preteens," *American Journal of Sexuality Education* 7, no. 4 (October 1, 2012): 464, https://doi.org/10.1080/15546128.2012.740963.

27   Ibid., 462.

practice healthy sexual behaviors themselves, then to draw their preteens into regular conversation about sexuality. If we teach the caregivers, they will teach the kids. Effective, faith-based sex education is a partnership between parents and the church for the benefit of the kids.

One way to get parents' attention is to offer a faith and sexuality education event for preteens. Truly, one of the best ministry strategies is to address a developmental need of children that also can be emotionally challenging for their parents. Connect with parents over their deepest insecurities, and they will listen. This ministry strategy will be fully covered in Chapter 7.

Faith-Based Sex Education Strategies

In my five years of researching and providing faith-based sex education to preteens, I have found a few principles to be helpful:

- **Teach one grade level at a time.** Preteens change so fast and so dramatically that combining 4th-, 5th- or 6th-graders in this conversation is ineffective. Hearing a 4th-grader's questions can turn off a more knowledgeable 6th-grader, and vice versa. If you must choose only one age group for this program, choose 5th-graders. They are old enough to have an idea of what sex is, but they have not yet experienced middle school, with all its inherent tribulations. They are still eager to hear what you have to say, and even the most sheltered among them are able to understand.
- **Recruit skilled, professional, loving leaders.** Look for the medical professionals, teachers, therapists, and youth advocates in your congregation. Sex education involves a lot of talk about anatomy and reproduction, and pediatricians, obstetricians, doctors, and nurses tend to take these discussions in stride. It is also important to cover material about marriage, relationships, puberty, intercourse, abuse, pornography, and everything else. Draw in leaders who will talk about these topics with love and grace.
- **Create a weekend event.** While it is possible to stretch a sex education program over several weeks (and may be preferable for those in youth ministries), this structure is a last resort for preteens whose schedules make it difficult to achieve perfect

attendance. Sex education builds sequentially from one concept to another, and it is best implemented as one intensive event followed by ongoing conversations in households.

- **Provide parent and caregiver education.** If parents are to accept the gift of entrusting their children's education about sexuality to church leaders, then they also must agree to be educated. Require caregivers to participate in meetings before, during, and after the event for preteens. Use those meetings to teach them some of the same principles the preteens learn, and give parents opportunities during these meetings to ask their own questions and learn from one another. These gatherings for parents help to normalize their fears around this issue. They realize they are not the only ones filled with anxiety, and they appreciate hearing other parents' strategies for teaching about sexuality in the home.

Faith-Based Sexuality Resources

There are many excellent resources available now to churches who desire to offer faith and sexuality training for families. Following is a list of options to consider. When choosing a curriculum, insist on a comprehensive approach that covers contraception, sex on the Internet/apps, sexual identity, anatomy, physiology, and relationships. While it is important to teach preteens about abstinence, research has demonstrated that programs such as Focus on the Family or True Love Waits, which rely exclusively on abstinence, are not effective for preventing pregnancy or affecting teens' decisions to be sexually active.[28]

Wonderfully Made

Leigh Meekins, Tanya Eustace Campen, & Mark Huffman

Abingdon Press

www.abingdonpress.com

This resource helps children ages 10-12 understand their bodies, the changes they are going through, and how God loves them now and

---

28   Carol R. Freedman-Doan et al., "Faith-Based Sex Education Programs: What They Look like and Who Uses Them," *Journal of Religion and Health* 52, no. 1 (March 2013): 247, https://doi.org/10.1007/s10943-011-9463-y.

always. It explains sexual anatomy as well as the different aspects of puberty. The book also discusses the influence of social media on sexual desire and decision-making.

Our Whole Lives: Lifespan Sexuality Education
Unitarian Universalist Association
www.uua.org/re/owl
OWL is a comprehensive, life span sexuality education curricula for use in both secular and faith settings. This resource includes interactive workshops and lessons that engage participants, as well as step-by-step instructions for program planners and facilitators. Curricula speak to participants' needs through six different age levels: K-1st, 4th-6th, 7th-9th, 10th-12th, young adults, adults.

Shepherding Preteen Sexual Identity

While it may be more common that youth ministry leaders encounter opportunities to shepherd sexual identity development, the beginnings of those identities take shape during preteen years. Gender identity development can begin at any stage from childhood to adulthood.[29] Even though sexual orientation can be determined in children as young as 10, it is clearly manifested during the ages of 12 to 17.[30] In 4th or 5th grade (or between the ages of 9 and 11), kids begin to think about their bodies and attraction in a memorable way. That is, gay and lesbian adolescents have reported that this middle childhood stage is generally when they remember first realizing they were attracted to the same sex.[31] This is before secondary sexual characteristics such as chest hair or breast buds are common. Internal sexual awareness precedes external sexual growth.

All good leaders desire to treat each person in their ministry as the unique and wonderful individuals they are. That means actually preparing

29   McGoldrick, Preto, and Carter, 140.
30   Gu Li, Karson T. F. Kung, and Melissa Hines, "Childhood Gender-Typed Behavior and Adolescent Sexual Orientation: A Longitudinal Population-Based Study," *Developmental Psychology* 53, no. 4 (2017): 764–77, https://doi.org/10.1037/dev0000281.
31   Gilbert Herdt and Martha McClintock, "The Magical Age of 10," *Archives of Sexual Behavior* 29, no. 6 (December 1, 2000): 587–606, https://doi.org/10.1023/A:1002006521067.

for the conversations and protocols that we may one day need to have in place in order to protect and guide a preteen with questions or assertions about their sexual identity. It is not unheard of for a preteen to come out as lesbian, gay, bisexual, transgender, questioning, or asexual. The stress of forming an LGBTQIA identity during preteen years can be greater than if this recognition comes later because of the heightened reliance on conforming to perceived cultural expectations and the total dependence on family and others for basic necessities.[32] Preteens cannot easily move away from home, choose their own church, or get access to affirming communities all on their own. They rely on family and sometimes also on trusted adults at school and church to see them through this stage.

LGBTQIA persons come out repeatedly over the course of their lives because we live in a heteronormative culture in which people are presumed straight until they express themselves otherwise.[33] In the words of Monica McGoldrick, "It is the role of the family to provide nurturance, unconditional support, and acceptance as their children discover who they are in the world, and how to name and present themselves."[34]

It is important to agree on principles of acceptance and support in advance, but also to be willing to apply these principles flexibly, knowing that there is no one-size-fits-all standard that works for every preteen. For example, put into place an inclusive policy for sleeping arrangements on retreats or bathroom assignments in your church building, but be ready to update those policies if a preteen or their family informs you that the policies make them feel unsafe. Imagine if a preteen living in a different gender identity than the one assigned at birth were to begin using a different bathroom at your church. After conversation with the preteen and their family, you may choose to un-gender bathrooms altogether. Or you may choose to communicate clearly with those who will use the bathroom with them in the future how to show support and ensure everyone's safety at the same time. Let's be open minded enough to make church as safe as possible for all preteens and their family members.

32   Heather L. Corliss et al., "Age of Minority Sexual Orientation Development and Risk of Childhood Maltreatment and Suicide Attempts in Women," *The American Journal of Orthopsychiatry* 79, no. 4 (October 2009): 511–21, https://doi.org/10.1037/a0017163.
33   McGoldrick, Preto, and Carter, 140.
34   Ibid., 147–48.

In short, do not ignore or avoid the conversations that need to happen both with volunteers, parents, and preteens themselves. For more concrete ways to support young people exploring their sexual and gender identity, check out the Working with LGBTQIA Youth section in Chapter 5.

Final Thoughts

There is no other stage quite like preadolescence. Lasting memories, cultural scripts, and imaginary audiences emerge in preteen minds while their bodies begin to show the first signs of reproductive development. With so much changing in their bodies and their minds, preteens thrive in ministries that provide mentoring, belonging, and meaningful work such as apprenticeship. Parents of preteens are equally flummoxed by this stage and may benefit from assurances of understanding and support from the church. One way to both support parents and protect preteens is to offer education in matters of faith and sexuality, engaging both groups in conversations that will continue for years. Before we know it, these wild preteen years morph into full teenagerhood, or as we in the church world like to call it, youth ministry.

CHAPTER 5

YOUTH MINISTRY

There is a reason that the first autocompletion offered for the search engine phrase "youth ministry is…" turns out to be "…hard." Can you picture in your head the 20-something youth pastor finishing up a 50-hour week that was supposed to be just 30 hours, pulling up a laptop and typing in those four words? I can.

In any youth ministry survey I read, I feel joy and concern in equal measure. Out of all of the church's ministry areas, youth ministry is the most misunderstood by leaders, participants, and outsiders. Students in middle and high school live complex lives, and we cannot serve them well without intense study and thoughtful practice. Unfortunately, youth ministry leaders often serve short tenures on their way to other career paths, and youth parents are frequently too burnt out to pick up the pieces.

There is a wealth of troubling and incorrect information about adolescents. Youth are more than the assumptions we make. While generalizations will be made in this chapter about adolescents, remember that broad strokes fail miserably when applied to the individuals in our ministries. The developmental principles of adolescence must not become limits that we place upon our youth. Just when we least expect, youth will defy our expectations by rising above them, becoming the leaders and positioning us as the students. We should always be ready to learn from them.

This chapter will reframe common obstacles to effective youth ministry and explore some of the mysterious features of the adolescent brain and body. Understanding adolescent development leads to different ministry designs for middle school and high school students and families. The chapter will conclude with an overview of best youth ministry practices, including leader skills, small groups, camp ministry, and faith and sexuality education for teenagers.

Adolescent Development

Perhaps more than any other age-based ministry in the church, youth ministry requires a tandem emphasis on theology and social science.[1] The social sciences have taught us that the adolescent years are packed with emotional, physical, and spiritual changes. One result of all this change is that adolescents are newly able to ask and answer deep theological questions. This section will begin by reviewing insights from social science and continue into the theological implications for youth ministry.

What Is Adolescence?

While there is still some debate about the exact age group encompassed by adolescence, many experts today agree that this period begins at age 13 or 14, then gradually evolves into emerging adulthood between the ages of 18 and 24.[2] The continuum of adolescence is one of dependence to independence.[3] Young teenagers enter this stage still dependent upon adults for food, transportation, homework signatures, and so forth. The end of adolescence is often associated with the ability to be self-sufficient and take responsibility for paying bills, maintaining housing, holding a job, and so forth. Those achievements are not tied to any particular age—for some, independence happens before age 18, while others require assistance into their 30s. For the purposes of this book, the words *adolescent, teenager,* and *youth* will refer to people in middle or high school, ages 13 to 19.

---

1   Mark H. Senter III, "A History of Youth Ministry Education in the USA," *Journal of Adult Theological Education* 11, no. 1 (2014): 46–60.

2   Karen Gilmore and Pamela Meersand, T*he Little Book of Child and Adolescent Development,* 1st edition (Oxford: Oxford University Press, 2014), 125.

3   Ibid., 130.

The Experience of Adolescence

A whirlwind? A roller coaster? A maze? It can be difficult to find a metaphor for adolescence that doesn't have negative undertones. That is unfortunate because there is much to celebrate about this period. A high school educator once used the metaphor of an orchestra rehearsal to explain adolescent brain development. He knew that the prefrontal cortex, the part of the brain responsible for reasoning and judicious decision-making, develops much later than other areas of the brain. When all the musicians in a symphony are practiced, prepared, and experienced, the orchestra produces harmonious music. During adolescence, some sections of the orchestra greatly outpace others, resulting in a cacophony that plays continuously and out of sync.[4]

A child therapist commented to me recently that in terms of brain development, adolescents and toddlers have a lot in common. Their brains are undergoing a rewiring process that can throw everyone for a loop, including family members and friends. This reconstructive process makes their brains extremely impressionable and malleable. All this brain development happens at the same time as the physical and emotional changes that accompany sexual development.[5]

The purpose of spelling out these developmental changes is to inspire empathy for this age group. Our youth deserve to be given the benefit of the doubt. As adults, we often forget the deep stress of choosing an outfit that will accurately portray the person we are trying to be, or the impossibility of laughing off an ill-timed voice crack in front of a classroom of peers. The power of these problems has shrunk for us, but teens are at the apex of it. While it may not be fair that everyone else in their lives gets the scrappy seconds (or thirds) of their personality, we are called to look past their rough surfaces and meet them with encouragement. Whether or not we see much evidence of it, we must accept by faith that, for the most part, youth are truly doing the best that they can, just like we are.

The development that takes place from 6th to 12th grade is monumental. The continuous internal transformation of adolescence stretches over

---

4   Susan Eva Porter, *Relating to Adolescents: Educators in a Teenage World* (Lanham, MD: Rowman & Littlefield Education, 2009), 4.
5   Gilmore and Meersand, 131.

the entire period, and in that sense a 6th-grader is much like a 12th-grader. However, schools and churches arrange youth into separate age groups for a reason—there are unique considerations for young adolescents and older teens.

Middle School Ministry

While high school is an experience to be anticipated with excitement—an invitation to all sorts of life-defining moments, such as going to the prom, obtaining a driver's license, and graduating—middle school does not have quite the same allure. It is rather a gauntlet of social situations that youth must negotiate, sometimes with limited guidance or encouragement. The drive for identity and individualism that kicks in during middle school can put young adolescents in direct conflict with the expectations we have for them in the church.[6] A youth who is questioning long-accepted rules can frustrate a small-group leader who would simply like everyone to sit in a circle so they can have a meaningful Bible study. Young people obsessed with figuring out who they are can have a hard time focusing on a service project to benefit others.

Regarding middle schoolers, Kara Powell and Chap Clark assert in their book *Sticky Faith* that their identity formation is happening almost under their noses, without their conscious recognition of it. They are asking questions about who they are, but they cannot put them into words yet. Parents and loving adults in their lives should provide affirmation and loving boundaries during this stage. Powell and Clark assert that "our job is to know that all of this conflicting, inconsistent, and confusing behavior is actually our kids' way of discovering who they are and making the commitments toward who they want to be."[7]

Rewards are as real as risks for this age group. There is a 200 percent increase in the morbidity and mortality rate among teenagers compared with elementary schoolers, and 8th grade is the peak age for the onset of mental health disorders.[8] Statistics about middle school could easily lead us to think of this stage as a necessary evil—but that conclusion would be

---

6   Ibid., 159–60.
7   Kara E. Powell and Chap Clark, *Sticky Faith: Everyday Ideas to Build Lasting Faith in Your Kids* (Grand Rapids, MI: Zondervan, 2011), 53–54.
8   Gilmore and Meersand, 124.

a failure of faith and imagination. Do not tuck tail and run from middle schoolers just because their lives are exploding into a million different awkward directions. This age group is ripe for meaning-making in ministry.

In middle school, church and faith are still experienced as part of the family's life. Middle schoolers cannot separate their faith from their caregivers' quite yet, but they are starting to wonder why. Thus, the roller coaster takes off, with middle schoolers loving church one week and complaining about having to go the next.[9] Middle schoolers are beginning to seek separation from authority figures, but they are still usually willing to admit that they like and need adults in their lives.[10] While their executive functioning skills are still in early development, they are beginning to think abstractly, a developmental gain that makes them perfect candidates for a confirmation process or a study of creeds, history, and theology. Leaders of middle schoolers must hold sacred space for this kind of conversation.

In Exodus 17:8-16, Moses sent the Israelite army into battle against the Amalekites while he watched the battle scene from a nearby hill. As long as Moses held up his arms, the Israelites triumphed; if he lowered his arms, their enemy gained ground. When Moses grew tired, his helpers Aaron and Hur stood beside him and held his arms high in the air all day. This is how the battle was won. This is a good metaphor for middle school ministry. Youth are the soldiers on the ground, mounting an offensive on the fronts of social life, academics, family, faith, and internal changes. New challenges approach them from all angles. But at church, ministry leaders hold their hands high to provide an open space where middle schoolers can encounter God. Recruit loving, patient adults and train them to see beyond the crusty surface of middle schoolers' facial expressions and snarky talk, to the beating hearts in their chests that genuinely long for truth and encouragement. We cannot fight the battle for them, but we can raise our hands in prayerful solidarity. That is middle school ministry.

High School Ministry

The shift from middle to high school is big. By this point, most adolescents have established self-awareness concerning their sexual

---

9   Powell and Clark, 176.
10   Porter, 12.

orientation and gender identity,[11] and they are ready for all of the different worlds they live in—academic, social, and sexual—to become more sophisticated. According to Powell and Clark, "the brain functions with the concreteness of a child throughout early adolescence and begins the abstraction of adulthood at around age 14 (thus making the shift from early to late adolescence)."[12] These are the years of advanced placement classes, driver's licenses, college preparation, first jobs and internships, standardized tests, dating, and answering the same question over and over: "What are your plans after graduation?"

The most painful moment in puberty has often passed, and these students, although still developing, are starting to look and talk a lot like adults. Along with this adult appearance comes the desire to be treated with adult-like respect. Leaders of high schoolers face the difficult balancing act of allowing them independence and respect while also protecting them from the dangerous consequences of unwise choices.[13]

High schoolers care less about the activities planned for youth group and more about the people they'll be with in the group. It is not so much the experiences as the relationships that will motivate them to attend. High schoolers are beginning to extricate themselves from their caregivers' faith and explore it as something for them to own themselves.[14]

The brain rewiring that takes place during adolescence is ongoing during the high school years, which means that the part of the brain focused on pleasure-seeking is in great shape at this point, while the part that governs judgment and considers consequences is still in process.[15] For this reason, it can be helpful to offer creative rewards for participation. Since sticker charts no longer work, opportunities for leadership, control, and ownership can serve as earned rewards. For instance, 9th-graders who participate in six sessions of a particular Bible or book study then

---

11   Michael Rutter, "Psychopathological Development Across Adolescence," *Journal of Youth and Adolescence* 36, no. 1 (January 1, 2007): 101–10, https://doi.org/10.1007/s10964-006-9125-7.

12   Powell and Clark, 52.

13   Vicky Duckworth et al., *Understanding Behaviour* 14+ (Maidenhead: Open University Press, 2012), 56–60.

14   Powell and Clark, 177–78.

15   Duckworth et al., 59–60.

can team-teach that same content to younger ages. Or they can control the next six sessions and choose the content they will study themselves.

One more unique aspect of high school ministry is the demand for leaders who are friendly. This is one of the most complicated leadership roles. Unlike leaders of younger groups, who are authority figures, or leaders of adult groups, who are peers and friends, leaders of high school groups must be friendly authority figures. High schoolers desire a leader who maintains firm control of the group and keeps their safety in mind, but who also earns their trust by being able to take a joke and showing interest in their personal life.[16] Adults often relate to high schoolers as if they are adults themselves, and mature juniors and seniors often can rise to that expectation.[17] However, leaders cannot count on students to display adult maturity and make adult choices every time, so they must learn to split their identity as both a safe, fun adult and a trusted authority.

High school is a wonderful and yet complicated season, geared toward graduation and the future while still stuck in adolescent development. Leaders who gain insight into the gifts and abilities of the high schoolers they care for will do well to transfer ownership and responsibility to their youth in those areas of giftedness while maintaining a position of guidance. Empathize with high schoolers in the complexity of their schedules, academics, relationships, and understanding, and challenge them to see how God is working in all these areas.

Families and Caregivers of Adolescents

Recently I struck up a conversation with a complete stranger in the customer service line at Target, as one does. Seeing my two young children cavorting around, she fixed her eyes on me and said, "My son is 14, and teenagers are so hard. I really don't know who he is anymore. Isn't that an awful thing for me to say?" This random fellow Target customer is, for me, representative of so many caregivers of teenagers.

If I could choose one word to describe parents and caregivers of adolescents, it would be *worried*. They worry about their kids' friends; their whereabouts; exposure to drugs, sex, and alcohol; their ability to get into

---

16   Ibid., 72–73.
17   Porter, 14.

college, then get a career, marry, and provide grandchildren; and so on. These worries are sometimes coupled with embarrassment and isolation because they do not know whom else to talk to about all this fear.

The developmental changes bombarding adolescents often cause them to lash out at their caregivers or communicate with them only through complaints, requests, shrugs, and sighs. Parents seem to infer from these frustrating communications that they no longer have significant influence over their teenagers—but this is simply not the case. Scholars who study adolescents' spiritual lives have written that parents sometimes can relent and despair too easily because they think their opinions and instruction won't make a difference. These scholars urge parents to continue modeling behavior and communicating with their teens, even if it is hard to tell whether they are getting through.[18] When researchers asked high schoolers to identify the people who had provided the greatest support and deepest relationships with them, they chose parents above friends or any other adult. According to the National Survey on Youth and Religion, 75 percent of American youth self-identify as Christian, and of those Christian youth, about 75 percent state that their religious faith and practices are similar to their parents'.[19] The faith that parents both teach and model is the biggest influence on the faith of youth.[20]

The ministry leader's job is to give parents hope and to encourage them to stay in the race. With our understanding of adolescent brains and development, we can coach parents to see what is going on beneath the surface and to help them set up conversations with their teens based on empathy and boundary-setting. Whether or not their adolescents learn to treat them with respect and become delightful, contributing household members, parents must keep the faith—specifically, their faith practices and relationship with God. A large study found that only 12 percent of youth claim to have regular conversations with their moms about faith, and that percentage drops to 5 percent for dads.[21] This finding is especially heartbreaking for those of us who understand that despite appearances, parents' faith is the greatest influence on the faith of their teenagers. No matter how

18   Christian Smith and Melina Lundquist Denton, *Soul Searching: The Religious and Spiritual Lives of American Teenagers* (Oxford: Oxford University Press, 2009), 56.
19   Ibid., 31–34.
20   Powell and Clark, 23–24.
21   Ibid., 71.

stormy this season can get, adolescents will not forget that their caregivers love them and love God.

Ministry to Youth

No matter what you call them—youth pastor, director of youth ministry, family minister, or something else entirely—youth pastors perform a key role in the ministry of the church. Few other church staff members have the lifelong impact that youth pastors can have as they shepherd an age group that is at once capable and impressionable. While some churches manage to retain youth pastors who view working with teenagers as their lifelong calling and become experts in the field, many rely on young professionals for whom youth ministry is a side hustle or a stepping stone to future ministry areas—and I have all the respect in the world for those young or part-time youth ministers. I also hope this book can serve as a resource for setting up a meaningful, formational youth ministry. While anyone can search Pinterest for great youth ministry games or watch a YouTube tutorial on how to transform your church space on a dime, only those leaders who set a firm foundation of safety and understanding will develop youth and families whose faith stands the test of time.

The first rule for youth pastors is this: you cannot do it all on your own; trying to juggle it all will result in disaster. This rule holds true whether you are full-time staff, part-time staff, or volunteer. If you wear the title of youth ministry leader, the best thing you can do to care for the teenagers in your church is to raise up other leaders, including their parents and other, unrelated adults, to support your youth. Sadly, many job descriptions for youth ministers fail to account for human limitations. If you are currently operating under an overwhelming job description, your best recourse is to work your way out of direct contact with youth and begin cultivating other leaders who can multiply your impact. You can find more details about this strategy in Chapter 10.

In her book for educators, *Relating to Adolescents*, Susan Porter lists five things that teenagers need from adults who lead them,[22] and I will share those along with my own commentary:

---

22   Porter, 66–82.

1. **Distinguish between teenagers' needs and wants**. Teens are more aware of their wants than their needs, and it is our job to focus on needs such as sufficient sleep, mental and emotional health, spiritual practices, and accountability. If their wants are met in the process, that's great! But satisfying desires is irrelevant to our goal.

2. **Respond to them but do not react with them**. This requires leaders who are self-aware and willing to encounter healthy conflict. The key to responding rather than reacting is to enforce a three-second delay between question and answer, allowing time to consider the main thing before choosing a response.

3. **Relate to them but do not identify with them**. Adults should not impose their own needs and backstory on the teenagers they serve. We all have needs and histories, but mature youth ministry leaders know when to share helpfully from their own experience and when to give adolescents the spotlight and focus on their questions and experiences.

4. **Be friendly with them but do not be their friends**. Being friendly is an attitude, an approach that can work for every interpersonal encounter. Being friends involves a relationship built on mutuality. Friendship between an authority figure and a teenager crosses the line of what is appropriate and healthy. Youth cannot and should not be expected to meet your emotional needs through friendship.

5. **Focus on their needs and not on your own**. In order to serve teenagers, we must put their needs before our own. Paradoxically, this priority requires adults to practice true self-care apart from their ministry, so that they have the spiritual and emotional resources to draw from when present with their youth. Before stepping into leadership with youth, adults must conduct their own inventory of trauma and triggers, often in the context of professional counseling, so that they can keep the best interests of youth in mind at all times without causing harm to their own psyche.

Wise youth leaders remember that the teenage brain is different from the adult brain, but it is in the process of becoming more adult every day. Meeting youth where they are developmentally while also challenging them to grow is an incarnational approach, a coming-alongside that resembles the way the Holy Spirit accompanies all of us. Youth will not simply follow an authority figure without question; they need a leader who will protect and care for them in the process of sharing life together.[23] Time spent with this age group is a precious opportunity to create truly new futures for them by building resilience while their brains are in the process of making new connections. It will not happen through just one amazing lesson plan, lock-in, or retreat. It will happen in the context of relationship-building between caregivers, youth, and leaders.

Youth Small Groups

One of the best contexts for building those relationships with youth is small-group ministry. It is ideal to offer small groups at two different times each week, if possible. If your youth ministry meets Sunday mornings and evenings, it is appropriate to set up small groups led by trusted adults during both of those sessions. While some kids will attend both, many will only make it to one meeting option. By providing two opportunities you will reach many more youth with this important spiritual practice time.

The elements that every small group should contain are prayer, guided discussion, and safe space for questions. Prayer is a way to claim small-group time as a mode of discipleship. Without prayer, it is easy to forget that conversing in a small group is a pathway to God. Begin small-group time by inviting the Spirit into your space and opening your hearts to what God would show you during your conversation. End small-group time by sharing with God the blessings of the conversation and the learning that has taken place. Ask God to empower you to walk with grace down the path God has shown you, one step at a time. During prayer time, speak the name of each group participant before God and ask for blessing and transformation for each one. Prayer gives leaders a chance to model conversation with God for the youth who are listening, and it gives youth a safe space to practice talking with our unseen God, a discipline that does not always come naturally or comfortably.

Whether your small-group time is structured around life topics, accountability, or a Scripture passage, it is important to ask open-ended

---

23   Senter III, 57.

questions and allow youth to share freely. At times they will get off track, look to the leader for guidance, or speak some unintentional heresy, and those are moments for leaders to step in with direction. Again, leaders by no means need to provide answers to every question. It is the leader's responsibility to keep the group on track, draw out participants who need an invitation before they are confident enough to speak up, and ask questions that will help the group to think about the topic in new ways. Discussion should be guided but not choreographed.

Creating a safe space is crucial for developing authentic sharing and promoting transformative discipleship. We provide safety by sharing appropriately but honestly about our own discipleship journeys as leaders, including some of our questions or experiences. Youth do not need details about their leaders' foibles or doubts, but it will help them to know that we have experienced enough uncertainty in our faith to be able to relate to theirs. Once youth know that what they share and the questions they ask will be treated with respect, they are free to get real about matters of faith and life—and they can get very, very real. Youth who feel free and safe to talk about their spiritual and philosophical doubts tend to hold onto their faith more than youth whose questions are shut down.[24]

Another way to engender trust in your sharing time is to make expectations clear from the beginning and reiterate them consistently. Agree as a group on what is appropriate to share in the group and what is not, and what group members can expect to have shared with others outside the group. Define what confidentiality means for your group, and before conveying any group admissions to others (such as church staff or parents), be sure the youth know that will happen. Youth should never be surprised by your response to their sharing.

Small groups are the place where we teach our youth how to be in lifelong community with others in a healthy way. They provide chances to practice Christian confrontation (Matthew 18:15-20) or to learn how to actually apply God's Word to our lives rather than simply hearing it (James 2:14-26). Youth small groups are also the right place and right time to encounter some of the big questions of faith such as the theology of the cross and resurrection; answered and unanswered prayer; miracles; doubts; racial and sexual oppression; poverty and wealth; just to name a

---

24   Powell and Clark, 72.

few. Our goal is that our youth can be confident that their questions will be welcomed and treated with dignity in our discipleship groups.

Camping and Camp Counseling

A word about Christian camp attendance and camp counseling for youth is too important to omit. While less than half (39 percent) of today's youth have attended a Christian summer camp at least once,[25] I posit that one week at summer camp each year can be one of the best opportunities available for faith development and calling discernment. Removed from technology and social expectations, surrounded by dirt and bugs, and drenched in sunlight (or thunderstorms), teenagers can connect with God and open their eyes to the work to which God calls them.

Kenda Creasy Dean has suggested that summer camp has an eschatological purpose as a finite experience that ends with hope. The entire week is aimed toward a climax, a spiritual high note where we expect Jesus to show up.[26] Dean compares summer camp to an eschatological pilgrimage. It is a week away that slowly crescendos toward a climactic night where music, preaching, ritual, and sacraments pull back the curtain on God's majesty, goodness, and forgiveness. This God sighting is unusual for teens, who mostly experience religion as a positive but benign outlook without much meaning or direction. Meeting God, however, changes all that. Suddenly our youth realize that if they are to serve a God like that, their life must be imbued with purpose and meaning.

Dr. Jacob Sorenson, an expert researcher of Christian camping ministry, also views camp as the natural place for youth to begin to understand God's call on their lives. Describing Christian camp as a "theological laboratory" or "playground," Sorenson says this ministry has "the potential to provide the new theological language for addressing the present needs of the world as well as emerging adults with a strong sense of vocational identity as Christian disciples moving into the mission field and rethinking church."[27] If we are concerned about the overscheduling of youth, the

---

25 Smith and Denton, 54.

26 Andrew Root and Kenda Creasy Dean, *The Theological Turn in Youth Ministry* (Downers Grove, IL: InterVarsity Press, 2011), 91–93.

27 Jacob Sorenson, "The Summer Camp Experience and Faith Formation of Emerging Adults," *Journal of Youth Ministry* 13, no. 1 (Fall 2014): 37.

dearth of emerging adults pursuing a call to ministry or the identity confusion experienced by so many of the teenagers we lead, sending them to
attend Christian camp for a week and eventually serve in such camps for
entire summers may be the most helpful strategy we can offer.

Youth Leadership

Whether at camp or in the local church, youth gravitate toward leadership roles that allow them to design their own ministry areas and show
others what they are learning. We should involve them in the creative and
decision-making processes inherent in offering a robust youth ministry.
Doing so will help them take ownership of their own context and exercise
leadership skills, meeting a practical church need while also contributing
toward their adolescent developmental needs.[28] Put them on the leadership
team, assign them to assist adults leading younger age groups, and take
their contributions seriously. Making youth a part of your church's ministry teams will benefit them and raise the quality of your ministry offerings.

Safety Strategies in Youth Ministry

While we can offer the most impressive youth ministry in town, led by
experts, with fancy youth rooms and cool evangelistic events, it will all be
for naught if we don't address the risks particular to this age group. Or in
the perspective-shifting words of Dean, "youth workers are in the translat-
ing, growing, and healing business, for we are called to *stop young people
from dying.*"[29] Safety precautions for teenagers can include technology policies, volunteer background checks, and resilience-building techniques for
teens who have experienced trauma or marginalized identities.

Technology Policies

At the risk of insulting your common sense, I will state the obvious:
the Internet, social media, and video games are a huge part of teenage life.

---

28   Monica McGoldrick, Nydia A. Garcia Preto, and Betty A. Carter, *The Expanding
Family Life Cycle: Individual, Family, and Social Perspectives*, 5th edition (Boston: Pearson,
2015), 305.
29   Root and Dean, 9.

Every church should have a plan in place to keep youth and adults safe. Thanks to the research of Monica Anderson and Jingjing Jiang at the Pew Research Institute, we know that smartphone ownership and social media use are ubiquitous among American teenagers,[30] with 45 percent of teens reporting that they are online "constantly," often via their smartphones.[31] Those same studies tell us that most teens feel social media is a positive aspect of their lives and that video games are a popular form of Internet and even social media use, with 84 percent of teens owning and playing a gaming system at home. Although social media is generally seen as a positive thing, more than half also say they have been victims of cyberbullying, most commonly in the forms of name-calling and rumor-spreading.[32]

What do we do when teenagers bring technology to church? While there are times when smartphones can be a helpful tool during a small-group discussion, and video game systems can be an attractive addition to youth ministry spaces, we should approach these things with care. If and when teenagers interact with you on social media or communicate with you via text, never forget that you are the adult, the responsible party. Consider the pros and cons before deciding to accept friend requests from teenagers; it is appropriate to refrain from connecting with youth via your personal social media profiles if doing so makes you uncomfortable. An alternative is to communicate with them through a church-based profile, which has the benefits of a) being transferrable to someone else if you leave your youth ministry position at some point, and b) allowing you to witness their online interactions and know what is going on in their lives.

It is also acceptable to have phone-free times in your ministry. It may not be practical to confiscate phones every time they walk in the door, but there almost certainly will be times during small groups or worship when teens will benefit from putting away phones and focusing on those

30   Monica Anderson and Jingjing Jiang, "Teens' Social Media Habits and Experiences," Pew Research Center, November 28, 2018, https://www.pewinternet.org/2018/11/28/teens-social-media-habits-and-experiences/.

31   Monica Anderson and Jingjing Jiang, "Teens, Social Media & Technology 2018," Pew Research Center, May 31, 2018, https://www.pewinternet.org/2018/05/31/teens-social-media-technology-2018/.

32   Monica Anderson, "A Majority of Teens Have Experienced Some Form of Cyberbullying," Pew Research Center, September 27, 2018, https://www.pewinternet.org/2018/09/27/a-majority-of-teens-have-experienced-some-form-of-cyberbullying/.

right in front of them. Technology can be a friend to youth ministers, and we should avoid an adversarial relationship with it. But we also should be cognizant of the risks and dangers it could bring.

Practically speaking, one of the most important conversations you will want to have with youth and adult volunteers regarding social media is the question of who is allowed to post photos of others during church-sponsored events. Remind youth and volunteers that some people may not be comfortable having their images posted online. Many churches have a policy that only staff are allowed to post photos of church events, and then only on official church accounts. Know what your church's policy is and help youth to live by it safely.

Intergenerational Trauma

Youth pastors have said the training they wish they had received before working with youth is methods for shepherding youth through crisis and trauma. Our understanding of adolescent brain development suggests that previously experienced trauma takes on a whole new meaning during adolescence. Trauma experienced in childhood is often categorized as an Adverse Childhood Experience (ACE). The CDC defines ACE as being any "potentially traumatic event that occurs in childhood (0-17 years)."[33] This could be experiencing or witnessing violence or abuse in a child's home or community, or having a family member attempt or die by suicide. It also includes "aspects of the child's environment that can undermine their sense of safety, stability, and bonding such as growing up in a household with substance misuse, mental health problems, or instability due to parental separation or household members being in jail or prison. A teenager who experienced or witnessed abuse, neglect, discrimination, divorce, poverty, or a number of other forms of trauma as a child will begin to process those experiences anew as their psychological and emotional abilities expand.

Research suggests that 61 percent of people have experienced at least one ACE, and 1 in 6 have experienced four or more.[34] Additionally, trauma affects multiple generations, which means that even if a young person in your ministry has not personally experienced abuse, but their

---

33   Center for Disease Control. https://www.cdc.gov.
34   Ibid.

biological parent has been an abuse victim, that young person can manifest the same or similar effects of their parent's trauma.[35] For instance, Black children who entered school flanked by protestors and police during desegregation efforts in the 1950s and 1960s now may have grandchildren and great-grandchildren who struggle in school for no immediately apparent reason. Traumatic school experiences in one generation can spur intergenerational trauma.

Here is the good news: we can help our youth build resilience to trauma. We do this by being present, offering community, and positioning ourselves as safe, consistent, nurturing adults. Stable relationships with non-parental adults who are willing to talk about the source of a teenager's stress have been shown to interrupt the cycle of intergenerational trauma.[36] The culture in which our kids live and move has taught them that when they screw up, people will abandon them. They expect to watch people walk away after a failure or betrayal, just when they need community the most. Church leaders can defy those expectations by supporting and surrounding youth families when they are in their lowest valley.[37]

Knowing the power of adverse childhood experiences as well as the key to reducing their impact must inform the design of our small-group ministries for teenagers. I believe the most significant role of a thoughtful youth pastor is to design safe groups where teenagers can share experiences, and multiple adult leaders will listen to them and shepherd them spiritually. When youth start talking about things that scare us, such as trauma, risky behaviors, and negative influences, it is easy to react out of fear. If we do react to adolescents out of fear or a need to control, we immediately remove ourselves from their circle of trust. It is impossible to be present and helpful to youth if we are freaking out at the same time.[38]

---

35   Thomas J. Schofield et al., "Intergenerational Continuity in Adverse Childhood Experiences and Rural Community Environments," *American Journal of Public Health* 108, no. 9 (September 2018): 1148–52, https://doi.org/10.2105/AJPH.2018.304598.

36   Thomas J. Schofield, Rosalyn D. Lee, and Melissa T. Merrick, "Safe, Stable, Nurturing Relationships as a Moderator of Intergenerational Continuity of Child Maltreatment: A Meta-Analysis," *The Journal of Adolescent Health* 53, no. 4 (October 2013): S32–38,

37   Powell and Clark, 180.

38   Ibid., 183.

Working with LGBTQIA Youth

For those of us who are straight and cisgender, we might have a strong sense of love and support for LGBTQIA youth, but at the same time feel confused or ignorant about how to show that support. While there are many excellent books available to help church leaders educate themselves in matters of inclusion, this section provides a few notes and best practices to follow when leading youth who are forming identities as a sexual or gender minority.

As Kate Ott puts it, "from a Christian perspective, when one is taught that sexuality is a good gift, it should not just be some people's sexuality."[39] She makes the point that whether or not we can relate to the experience of LGBTQIA youth, it is our responsibility to care for them and to help other members of our youth groups practice welcoming, inclusive, and accepting behaviors as well. One study found that within Christian communities, 12 percent of youth identify as lesbian, gay, or bisexual, but only 36 percent of those noted that any adult leader in their church was even aware of their sexual identity.[40] Our treatment of LGBTQIA people, whether or not we know who they are in our churches, will either position us as safe adults who can be trusted to disciple them or unsafe adults who will neither understand nor accept who they truly are. During this adolescent phase when young people are finding their sexual identity,[41] do not excuse yourself from their lives by ignoring these suggestions, taken from Cody Sanders' *A Brief Guide to Ministry with LGBTQIA Youth*:

- Avoid the term "homosexual," which has a "cold, clinical ring and is now typically used only by those who hold non-LGBTQIA affirming theological positions."[42]
- When talking to youth who have questions about their gender or

---

39   Kate Ott. *Sex + Faith: Talking with Your Child from Birth to Adolescence* (Louisville, KY: Westminster John Knox Press, 2013)

40   Ibid., 128.

41   Renée Perrin-Wallqvist and Josephine Lindblom, "Coming out as Gay: A Phenomenological Study about Adolescents Disclosing Their Homosexuality to Their Parents," *Social Behavior and Personality* 43, no. 3 (January 22, 2015): 467–480, https://doi.org/10.2224/sbp.2015.43.3.467.

42   Cody J. Sanders, *A Brief Guide to Ministry with LGBTQIA Youth* (Louisville, KY: Westminster John Knox Press, 2017), 8.

affective identity, do not push them toward a particular outcome. Just be a supportive presence as they process.[43]

- Avoid gender binary language in general. When talking to a group, address them as "friends," "people," or "y'all," rather than "boys and girls." Don't arrange the group for games based on gender. Instead, arrange them by birthdate, age, or simply by numbering them off.[44]
- Ask questions rather than giving advice.[45]
- Help families of LGBTQIA youth understand how their words, beliefs, and actions directly impact their youth's personal well-being. This is the most powerful way to help families become more accepting.[46]
- Find qualified, affirming therapists in your community.[47]
- Find a PFLAG (Parents, Families and Friends of Lesbians and Gays) or Gay-Straight Alliance in your area.[48]

Last and possibly most important of all, youth do not need us to have all the answers, but they do need us to listen, then ask them good questions that will help them to talk about their discoveries and desires.[49] Keeping silent on the topic of sexuality will communicate to youth that this is forbidden topic to broach with you,[50] and that can be as harmful as an openly non-affirming stance toward LGBTQIA youth. Once again, we are called to help build resilience and wholeness in the youth that we serve, and that calling includes youth of all sexual orientations and gender identities.

Faith & Sexuality Education for Youth

Naturally, a chapter about adolescents would be incomplete without a hefty section dedicated to sex. The average age of first sexual intercourse is 16.9 years old for boys and 17.4 years old for girls. However, the lower

43   Ibid., 20.
44   Ibid., 25.
45   Ibid., 68.
46   Ibid., 72.
47   Ibid.
48   Ibid., 77.
49   Ibid., 86–7.
50   Ibid., 10.

a person's social status and income, the younger this average age tends to be.[51] This does not include oral sex, anal sex, exposure to pornography, sexting, or hooking up—experiences that often precede intercourse during the teenage years. As their bodies develop adult sexual characteristics and the pleasure-seeking area of their brains grow, youth will encounter a host of questions about sex and sexuality, along with situations where they have to choose how to apply the values they have learned from their families and faith communities.

Sex education is just as crucial for youth as it is for preteens (discussed in the previous chapter), but it looks different when presented to adolescents. Whereas preteens need to be educated about the basics of anatomy and prepared for future experiences, youth need to be educated about the sexual messages and experiences they are currently encountering. Sex education for youth is less about preparation and more about debriefing.

It is in the best interest of youth that we preach abstinence, but not abstinence alone. This is a controversial topic, and with good reason—abstinence-only approaches to sex education have done significant harm to evangelical communities over the years and now have been proven ineffective.[52] We now know that purity pledges and abstinence-only education results in only a slight delay in first intercourse, and worse, decreases the likelihood that any form of protection will be used.[53] An abstinence-only approach to sex education implies that a healthy sex life depends on rule-following, and that we can check off a handful of behaviors and beliefs in order to earn God's favor. It leaves no room for grace or redemption when rules are inevitably broken, and it sets up marriages for failure. But that does not mean that we should avoid teaching about abstinence from sex outside of marriage. It simply means we must reclaim the true beauty of chastity, the idea that our whole beings—physical, spiritual, and emotional—are wholly God's and therefore holy.

Another important message to repeat to our youth is that sex is not merely a physical act, but is inextricably linked to their spiritual life as well. Nobody understands better than adolescents the equal intensity of

---

51 McGoldrick, Preto, and Carter, 122.
52 Ott, *Sex + Faith*, 128.
53 Ott, *Sex + Faith*, 128–9.

spiritual and sexual longing, both of which fulfill our God-given need for connection to someone other than ourselves.[54] We cannot stop adolescents from feeling sexual desire. If we disregard the divine beauty of sexual longing, we leave youth with only two choices: suppress their desires and thereby reject a basic part of themselves, or act upon them and live with the consequences of sexual experiences for which they are not yet ready. So, how do we help adolescents celebrate their sexuality without their acting on it?

I believe we accomplish this feat through awkward, loving, ongoing conversations—both the ones that arise unexpectedly during a small-group discipleship discussion and the ones that we plan and lead with intentionality. That is, we must provide formal, guided discussions about sex and sexuality. We must also be ready at all times to respond when teenagers initiate conversations informally on their own. Like all other areas of faith, sexuality is a daily and perhaps hourly consideration, and should be handled with both respect and normalcy.

Professionals caution youth workers to approach conversations about sex with some fear and care,[55] and there are materials available to help us do that. Kate Ott provides materials and guidance for a short-term parent and teen study at *http://kateott.org*,[56] and the *Our Whole Lives* curriculum discussed in Chapter 4 provides materials for adolescents and adults. Regardless of whether or not they are using a curriculum, leaders who plan to engage youth in these kinds of discussions have preparation to do—learning the correct terminology, studying the doctrine and philosophy of their church, and talking honestly with their own supervisors and accountability networks about what they are about to do. It would not be a bad idea to sit down with a therapist or medical practitioner to learn from them how to comfortably share, how to ask the right questions, and how to respond appropriately to questions. Once the leaders are ready, they should prepare

---

54   Root and Dean, 85–88.

55   Robert C. Dykstra, "Ministry with Adolescents: Tending Boundaries, Telling Truths," *Pastoral Psychology* 62, no. 5 (October 1, 2013): 639–47, https://doi.org/10.1007/s11089-013-0509-9.

56   Kate Ott, "Using Sex + Faith as a Parent and Teen Sunday School Curriculum," </Kate> (blog), September 19, 2014, http://kateott.org/using-sex-faith-as-a-parent-and-teen-sunday-school-curriculum/.

the teenagers by setting clear boundaries and expectations. Get everyone on the same page when it comes to confidentiality so that no one is surprised by your response to what they share. Remember that your silence speaks volumes. Regardless of how eloquently and confidently (or not!) you can speak to the complexity of sexuality, speak you must.

Final Thoughts

Youth ministry is…hard, yes, but also one of the most hopeful, potential-filled, and life-giving places to work. The first step toward offering a fruitful, lasting, and meaningful youth ministry is to understand how the brains of adolescents work. Knowing the extent of the neural and hormonal activity going on under the surface of our youth cannot answer all our questions about these changing and challenging people, but it can help us get started. Youth leaders should collaborate with and support parents and guardians as they model faith at home while also creating safe small groups at church. It's also a good idea to offer opportunities for church camp and church leadership to youth.

Effective youth ministry is a ministry where teenagers learn resilience through relationships with safe, trusted adults and peers. Youth leaders who educate themselves to better support LGBTQIA youth in their identity formation, and who create space for honest conversations about sex and sexuality, will position themselves as safe adults who will not disappear or overreact when teens approach them with difficult concerns. The teenage years are way too important for us to spend simply playing games. Understanding, mature youth leaders are the solution to many of our churches' problems today.

CHAPTER 6

INTERGENERATIONAL WORSHIP & SERVING

A friend leads an Anabaptist congregation. Every Sunday, members of all ages form a large circle with their chairs. Worship consists of praying, sharing, and taking Communion together. This is intergenerational worship.

Another dear friend structured her church's Wednesday night ministry around the idea of family service projects. Families baked cookies and delivered them to fire stations during the week, wrote notes to hurting church members, and planned a party to celebrate a beloved volunteer together. This is intergenerational service.

Many churches have family worship services, which are specially designed corporate gatherings where all the worship leaders have chosen songs, Scriptures, sermon topics, and rituals that entire families could participate in fully. This is intergenerational worship.

Members of my church coordinate a ministry in the fall and winter that provides a hot dinner and safe place to sleep for men who need it. When our family cooked the meal and ate with the men a year ago, my six-year-old remarked contentedly (and loudly) that the best part of his day was "eating dinner with these men who don't have homes." This is intergenerational serving.

A few years ago, my church took the summer off from meeting in a sanctuary. Instead, we gathered in groups of three or four households in one home each week for prayer, Bible study, sharing, and blessing. This is intergenerational worship.

The hard part of intergenerational ministry is that it requires worship and service to be age-inclusive. This chapter focuses on the ins and outs of intergenerational worship, including the importance of corporate worship, what makes worship age-inclusive, and the value of ritual and liturgy for all ages. The chapter also reviews intergenerational service, both its impact on discipleship and the kinds of service opportunities that are appropriate and meaningful for all ages. But before we can explore any of that, we must understand the monumental difference between intergenerational *ministry* and intergenerational *programming*.

Ministry Versus Program

It is easy to confuse ministry with programming. Programs do good on the surface of people's lives. Ministries reach the deepest spiritual places. Far too many of our churches approach age-level ministries programmatically, with church staff serving as event planners rather than pastors and spiritual guides. I admit that I myself waffle between these two approaches frequently. It's easy to get caught up in others' expectations for events, performances, and visuals. But the burnout that comes from planning events that don't lead to spiritual growth always drives me back to the basics.

Program Approach

A program is an event that serves as an end unto itself, an activity that not designed with any purpose in mind other than what is accomplished between its start time and end time. Programs are church gatherings that fill time or provide a fellowship outlet. Programs allow people to put churchy things on their calendars to fulfill an expectation of Christian behavior that fits nicely into our overscheduled culture. Anything can be programmed, including staff meetings, vacation Bible school, adult Sunday school classes, preaching, and the middle-school mission trip. On the other hand, any of these events can be part of a ministry approach—the difference is in the intentionality of the leaders.

There is a reason we do not refer to the Gospels as the stories of Jesus' program on earth. Jesus is the supreme model of a ministry approach, never falling for others' expectations or allowing followers to stay on the surface. That is what ministry is all about.

Ministry Approach

Approaching church work as ministry means keeping the big mission in mind. A ministry mindset ensures every event and activity helps our people to become more holy, more honest, more loving, and more courageous—more like God. Ministry does not get distracted by trends or suggestions/complaints from the most generous givers. Ministry keeps the deep needs of humanity at the forefront of our mind as we set the church calendar and plan our worship services and discipleship environments. Ministry positions church staff and volunteers as the servants of God and others, there to take people by the hand and bring them into the presence of God.

There is an abundance of Scriptural backing for a mission-focused approach in our churches. One of the clearest examples is the story of Jesus' conversation with a rich young man who asked how he could be sure to qualify for eternal life (Matthew 19:16-30; Mark 10:17-31; Luke 18:18-30). When Jesus told him to obey all the law, the young man asserted that he already knew and obeyed God's laws. This response would satisfy a programmatic approach to discipleship; the young man looked and acted the part of a decent, righteous person. He would be a valuable chair of a finance team and probably do a great deal of good there, to be honest. But Jesus was not satisfied, knowing that the young man's truest, deepest, God-given needs would never be met by rule-following and fitting in. So Jesus told him to sell all his riches, give the proceeds to those in need, and come and follow Jesus. This high price of discipleship was the best gift Jesus could give; Jesus not only told the man the truth, he invited him to *join him in ministry*. He said follow me, learn from me, enjoy my company, learn to serve as I serve. In a ministry approach, we tell the unvarnished truth, then invite others to pursue it along with us. Later in the New Testament, the Book of Ephesians gives a clear job description for "pastors and teachers," whom Christ appoints in order to "equip God's people for the work of serving and building up the body of Christ until we all reach the unity of faith and knowledge of God's Son" (Ephesians 4:12-13). This is our calling.

A ministry approach is essential for a church that wants to offer worship, discipleship, and serving for multiple generations at once. Intergenerational ministry does not fit in the context of a programmatic approach because it is too messy and too unwieldy to be programmed. Programs limit the audience in order to maximize the effectiveness for that one target group. Ministry asks us to expand the audience to include majorities and minorities, young and old, anyone and everyone. Approaching our work as ministry makes space for generations to collide, building a church that is truly inclusive for all.

Intergenerational Worship

Think about the typical church worship service you have attended. How were you welcomed? What kind of written instructions or on-screen guidance were provided? What music was chosen, and who led it? What was the space like—pews, chairs, pulpit, decor? With all of this in mind, ask yourself: *Can you identify the audience the planners had in mind when they designed this worship time?*

Does your church's time of worship work for kids? the elderly? those with graduate degrees and/or those without much education? Are aspects of the service designed for children? Are the bulletins legible for someone with poor eyesight and the sanctuary accessible for someone in a wheelchair? How many different kinds of people fill the seats in your church?

Every church can and should pursue inclusion to the best of its ability. An individual church cannot be all things to all people—but every church should be age-inclusive. Before we explore strategies for intergenerational worship, let's examine the purpose behind worship itself.

The Audience of Worship

Who is the "audience" of worship? Most of the sanctuaries and auditoriums in which we worship give the wrong impression. It appears that those on the stage or behind the altar are the presenters or performers, and those sitting in the pews or chairs on the main floor are the audience.

This structure has led many to hold inappropriate expectations of worship, believing that it is a place to be emotionally fueled or have one's spiritual energy tank refilled before another week in the real world. Sitting passively in a pew positions us as the audience of worship.

In fact, God is the audience of worship. Our position in the pew is more like the witness chair in a courtroom than a stadium seat at a concert. We are there to agree together that God is good and that God's Word is true, and to submit ourselves to God. We are the actors in worship, and God's Spirit inhabits our praise. Worship is an act of surrender, more about giving than taking. And yes, in that giving, we do benefit, no doubt. But there is nothing passive about it.

People's belief that they are the audience of worship can create barriers to intergenerational worship. I have lost count of the number of times families in my congregations have received scowls or even harsh words from other worshipers because their kids were too noisy or active. A man once told me that it would be nice if the young guy whose disability caused him to make constant noises would find a different place to worship. Another man wrote a lengthy and biting Facebook message to a dear friend of mine claiming that their 4-year-old had ruined worship for him by brushing up against him in the Communion line. A first-year seminary student who started to help plan and implement worship lamented soon after that worship just wasn't the same anymore; now that she knew what went into it behind the scenes, it was not enjoyable.

If we are committed to welcoming every generation into worship together, then we absolutely must remember that God is the recipient of worship. That way, if things do not go according to plan or someone gets in our way, we are able to take a deep breath and remind ourselves that worship is not about us. Intergenerational worship means that sacrifices must be made. Inclusion is not a light endeavor or just a feel-good word. Those of us who are white, able-bodied, straight, cisgender, and between the ages of 20-60 will experience some pain and discomfort in the fight for inclusivity—not nearly as much as those we so easily exclude have felt, but still, we should prepare for some sense of loss as we make room for the others. If your church is not currently planning worship with young children or the elderly in mind, then prepare to provide comfort but remain firm as you introduce intergenerational worship to your congregation. Start small, but start.

Unity

One argument you may encounter as you pursue intergenerational worship is that the needs of each generation are better met in their own spaces. There is some truth to this—not every group or gathering in your church must be intergenerational. But the church's primary corporate worship offering should be age-inclusive.

This will sound obvious, but here is the simple truth: we cannot be together if we are not physically together. If older adults cannot navigate the sanctuary or hear the speaker, they are not a part of worship. If children are dropped off in a separate location for the entire service or largely ignored during it, they are not a part of worship. Just as you would not plan a family reunion and fail to invite Grandma and Grandpa, so we should not plan a worship service and neglect to include them in it. Every corporate worship event is a family reunion, and every family member needs to be there. Some may come and make their own place without our providing it for them, and God bless them. But many families with young children and senior citizens will find more comfortable places to be on Sunday morning if we have not prepared a place for them.

Ritual and Liturgy

Ritual and liturgy are not just stodgy high-church trappings. These practices are unfailing entry points for intergenerational engagement. There are several points in corporate worship when the congregation can be exposed to something new or unanticipated, including the sermon, songs, announcements, and testimonies. These less predictable elements need to be balanced with predictable, familiar rituals. Most people need some degree of certainty and structure in social, public settings such as worship. That need is especially felt by the youngest and oldest generations. Worship should be a combination of old and new, expected and unexpected. God's Spirit can move through ancient words today just as freely and meaningfully as through spontaneous and fresh words. Using ritual and liturgy in worship gives people of all ages a chance to breathe in God with a sense of safety and assurance.

Liturgy refers to corporate, religious worship of God that includes reciting creeds, the sacraments of baptism and Communion, and other forms of worship.[1] When I think of liturgy, I first recall some historical creeds such as the Apostles' Creed or the Nicene Creed. These creeds tell the overarching story of Scripture in a succinct way. The words we say in baptism, marriage, and membership vows, and Communion are all examples of liturgy as well. For the purposes of this book, liturgy refers to the words of worship, based upon Scripture and agreed upon by the church, that express our faith. Liturgy and ritual are vital elements of intergenerational worship because they are:

- **Memorable and memorizable**—There is a familiarity to liturgy and ritual that invites everyone to participate. After just a few weeks of hearing a creed or watching a worship ritual, people of all ages can join in. When my family visits a different church on vacation, I look for one that will practice a similar Communion ritual or recite the Lord's Prayer or Apostles' Creed, because I know my children will remember and be able to participate fully in those parts of worship.

- **Accommodating**—Many children and older adults experience sensory overload in public spaces, and this feeling can be exacerbated by not knowing what to expect next. Any seasoned children's Sunday school teacher will tell you that going over the plan for the hour and setting expectations helps everyone to engage and relax. Ritual and liturgy help people to know what is coming next, which frees them from anxiety and encourages participation.

- **Symbolic**—Everyone can connect with a symbol. Symbolic language is like a wave or a smile exchanged with someone who speaks a completely different language than you; it connects you without using words. There is a great deal of mystery and possibility in our faith. We cannot explain everything about God in human words. The closest we can get is a symbol, a wordless and

---

1   Brett Scott Provance, *Pocket Dictionary of Liturgy & Worship* (Downers Grove, IL: InterVarsity Press, 2009), 79.

boundless image that expresses what language cannot. Symbols are accessible in ways that words cannot be. Everyone can focus on a symbol, such as an empty tomb, a cross, a dove, water, an altar, a pitcher and basin, or other visuals employed by ritual and liturgy, and see God in it.

Ritual is a form of liturgy that serves as a ceremonial rite or practice.[2] Even modern worship services contain elements of ritual. An example of ritual is the particular method by which your congregation takes Communion. Do ushers pass the elements for you to consume in your seats, or do you walk to the front of the church to receive bread and dip it in a communal cup? What about altar calls—are people invited forward to pray at a railing during your service? That is a ritual of prayer and surrender. Ritual often involves some outward sign of inward spiritual transformation. For example, every Sunday, we set a bowl of water on a stand at the front of the sanctuary to symbolize the waters of baptism, both Jesus' and our own. As people approach the Communion table, they are encouraged to dip their fingers in the water and make the sign of the cross on their foreheads as a reminder of the spiritual transformation that takes place at baptism.

Including Children in Worship

Catherine Stonehouse makes the point in her book, *Joining Children on the Spiritual Journey*, that while children should be included in our main worship offerings, this only works if we actually plan the service with them in mind.[3] Simply expecting them to be present for a service directed at adults is not inclusive worship. There are literally gobs of Pinterest boards, blog posts, and Facebook groups filled with ideas for including kids in worship. I will offer only a few ideas here, along with some guiding principles to help you discriminate between quality inclusion tactics and mere gimmicks that pretend to consider the needs of children but keep worship aligned for adults.

---

2   Ibid., 110.
3   Catherine Stonehouse, *Joining Children on the Spiritual Journey: Nurturing a Life of Faith* (Grand Rapids, MI: Baker Academic, 1998), 40.

Children's Message

Children's messages often involve calling children up to the front of the sanctuary and presenting an object lesson or devotional version of the sermon topic. From an intergenerational ministry perspective, there are pros and cons to children's messages. On one hand, they are better than nothing. At least they give the congregation a way to acknowledge children and dedicate some time to them. However, the implication a children's message conveys is that once the 3- to 5-minute moment for children is over, it is adult time again. The kids had their time, and now they should keep quiet and let the adults worship. Another problem with this practice is that it puts our children on display for the enjoyment of adults. A child who asks a question or shouts out an answer is often met with laughter, an experience that can feel like public shaming to them.

If given the choice, rather than having a children's message, make the entire worship service inclusive of children and understandable to them. However, many children or family ministers do not have the power to opt out of the tradition of children's messages. If you must lead these messages, following are some pointers to make them as affirming of children as possible:

- **Speak to the whole room, not just the children.** Engaging in an amplified conversation at the front of the room turns the children into performers. Greet the children, but share your message with everyone. After all, everyone is listening! Do not allow the children to become a comedy show.
- **Capitalize on this opportunity to introduce a multiple intelligences approach to worship design.** Make visuals as big as possible so that everyone can see them. Use music, nature, art, or drama to draw people into the Scripture in a way that the preacher or worship leaders may not feel empowered to do. Be the creative worship leader.
- **Avoid asking the children leading questions**. Do not exploit their lack of inhibition or curiosity by setting them up for a cheap laugh. Frame all your questions rhetorically so that children are engaged but do not have to speak a response into a microphone.

- **When possible, connect messages week to week with a theme, especially during Advent or Lent.** For example, during Advent introduce a different piece of the Nativity scene each week, talking about the roles of the shepherds, the angels, Mary and Joseph, and even the animals from week to week. This gives folks something to look forward to each following week.

These strategies are not foolproof, because there is nothing easy or simple about giving a children's message. But they may help you to share the gospel in a way that respects the children and the flow of worship.

Children's Worship

For years I have watched the debate over whether or not to offer a separate worship experience for children. Although I understand and celebrate the desire to keep kids and adults together in fully intergenerational worship, I believe that offering a short, separate time of worship for young children is a gesture of hospitality. Our children certainly should be welcomed into our sanctuaries, at least for the first half of worship. But providing a more relaxed, interactive worship space for them during the sermon allows guests, families of children with disabilities, and families exhausted by caring for young children to experience a moment of sabbath and focus within worship. Parents and caregivers are the best worship coaches, and they should be encouraged to actively model praise, prayer, singing, and listening for their children. But it is not wrong to give families the option of parting for a portion of the service if they choose, as long as families are also fully accepted if they opt to stay together in the sanctuary.

Quiet Worship Activities

Sometimes having quiet activity for our hands helps our ears to listen better. Offering some quiet worship activities for children is another gesture of hospitality. Fill canvas bags with lace-up toys, dry-erase boards and markers, felt boards with felt shapes, yarn dolls, coloring pages, quiet fidget toys, or tiny stuffed animals. Make snacks such as cereal bars, bananas, mints, or water bottles available for families to pick up. Put noise-canceling headphones and weighted blankets in a special spot for families to check out as needed. Search the Internet for simple kids' sermon note pages and set them at the welcome station for kids to pick up, fill out during the service, and return to you for a prize drawing each month. Avoid giving out balls or anything made of metal or plastic that can crinkle or clang.

Calm Room

If your space and budget allow, set up a room near the sanctuary for parents to nurse a baby and/or for children feeling overwhelmed to play quietly. Caregivers should still be able to hear the service in this space. Equip the room with a rocking chair, hooks for diaper bags, a changing table, sensory-friendly lighting, a sensory swing, cushions, bean bags, weighted blankets or stuffed animals, a sensory wall, lava lamps, an out-of-reach aquarium, fidget toys, or any other calming, quieting items suggested by families who use the space. If the kids in your church are anything like the kids in mine, this room will be an attractive play place that you will need to guard in some fashion so that it is reserved for families who truly need it. I consider that a win.

Pastoral Language

One of the best ways to make children welcome is to watch the language used around and about kids. Avoid phrases such as, "the kids are now dismissed," which implies their window of welcome has closed and they are no longer recognized as intended worship participants. Instead, invite kids to their worship time with language such as, "Children may now continue their worship next door if they would like." The best-case scenario is pastors keeping children in mind whenever possible. When using a sermon illustration only adults will understand, preachers should take just a moment to explain it to the younger crowd. Even better, look for references and metaphors that make sense to all ages.

Worship Leadership

The Milestones chapter of this book will delve into the details of incorporating children into worship leadership, but it is an appropriate point to make here as well. Kids sense they belong and have some degree of control if they are given a task to accomplish. They are capable of performing so many worship tasks, such as greeting, distributing bulletins, collecting offering, reading Scripture, processing a candle in and out of worship, serving Communion, and more. Kids who serve alongside adults make powerful team members, and that visual could be the most hopeful and life-giving element of worship for everyone else.

Including Older Adults in Worship

There is certainly some overlap between including kids and including older adults. Both groups benefit from some accommodations, some environmental planning, and opportunities to serve.

Worship Leadership

The number one, tested and true, best way to make worship inclusive of our oldest generations is to involve them in its planning and leadership. Listen to the wisdom of the elderly as you plan—chances are they have attended a good many more worship services than the rest of us, and they know what works and what doesn't. Let them tell us what is lacking. Make them a part of the solution. Offer them opportunities in leadership: reading Scripture, preaching, singing and playing music, serving Communion, and praying with others at the altar. Prove to all attendees that your church places a high value on its oldest participants by recognizing their gifts of leadership in these upfront ways. One of my favorite opportunities afforded by a corporate worship service is that of pairing older adults with children in service. Invite the older adult who leads the ushers to recruit children to collect the offering, or pair the child who wants to hold the Communion juice with the senior citizen who dispenses the bread. That's heaven right there.

Accommodations

While not all senior citizens are physically frail, it is still important to be attentive to any physical accommodations you can provide to make worship more meaningful for them. If a church member loses their hearing, purchase a hearing device that will amplify the sound equipment directly into the ear. If you find that someone has trouble reading the bulletin, provide a large-print edition for them. Make aisles as wide as possible so there is room for walkers or wheelchairs. The needs will vary according to your own community, so discover what they are and seek to meet them.

Service Times

Sleep patterns vary from person to person, of course, and in my experience some older adults are up with the dawn and arrive early to the sunrise service, while others need extra time in the mornings and would be quite content to meet at noon. Offering both early and late service times is an accommodation for older adults. Many older adults feel uncomfortable driving in the dark, so planning evening events that end before sundown is a way to welcome their attendance. In our church, where just 120 or so souls attend every Sunday morning, we offer services at 9 a.m. and 10:45 a.m. We could possibly fit everyone into a 10 a.m. service, but doing so would exclude people we cannot even anticipate at this point. The more worship opportunities we offer, the more people will participate overall, and this is especially true for older adults.

Listen

It's simple, really. Kids may not be able to verbalize their needs or take ownership of a worship area, but older adults can—we just do not ask them very often. In your planning for intergenerational worship, do not leave out older adults. They are some of our best and most qualified leaders.

In the beautiful prayer of Psalm 71, the writer declares:

You've taught me since my youth, God,

and I'm still proclaiming your wondrous deeds!

So, even in my old age with gray hair,

don't abandon me, God!

Not until I tell generations about your mighty arm,
tell all who are yet to come about your strength,
and about your ultimate righteousness, God,
because you've done awesome things! (Psalm 71:17-19a)

Create times and spaces for the older generation to be involved. Let them tell the younger generation of God's mighty acts.

Thus far, this chapter has explored strategies for making worship intergenerational. But there is another realm of ministry where every generation can be together: service.

Intergenerational Service

For many churches, serving or mission work occupies a significant position in the overall discipleship plan. Service is an inherently external endeavor. Serving can be one of the most exclusive areas of church ministry, because it often relies on financial contributions (which children often are not equipped to supply) or physical labor (which can be problematic both for children and older adults). Travel to other countries, construction work, use of power tools, mentoring, and much other popular and important service work is not ideal for every generation. It is our responsibility to find ways to invite all generations into this important area of discipleship.

Importance of Serving

In *Sticky Faith*, Powell and Clark make a strong argument for the importance of serving opportunities in our churches. In a survey conducted by the authors and distributed to youth, mission trips and service projects were voted second only to "time for deep conversation" as the most valuable experiences.[4] They explained that "family projects and service opportunities, even if just for a few hours, give families common experiences and common memories." It is important to remember that the work of justice is more than just an event; it is a process in which individual service opportunities may play a part. But those events are only effective as part of an ongoing conversation about justice with families.

4   Kara E. Powell and Chap Clark, *Sticky Faith: Everyday Ideas to Build Lasting Faith in Your Kids* (Grand Rapids, MI: Zondervan, 2011), 129–36.

Serving draws us out of our own concerns and opens our eyes to a bigger world, a practice that is especially eye-opening for young people who are often preoccupied with simply figuring out life and identity. It is helpful for them to realize that their experience is limited. Participating in a missional endeavor, then debriefing it afterward reshapes the way they see the world. Both young, old, and in-between folks need these opportunities to see others the way God sees them. The question is how to accomplish these service projects with people whose abilities are limited.

Service Project Ideas

Intergenerational service projects must meet two criteria: they must be appropriate for the age, skill, and ability of the participants; and they must produce meaningful change for the ones served. To determine if a project is appropriate, look for these characteristics:

- **Safety.** Be sure the project follows your church's safety policy in terms of background checks, permission slips, and supervision. If you are partnering with another group, learn their safety requirements. For example, Habitat for Humanity may allow older teens to handle power tools under supervision, but they will not allow younger children to be on site at all. If the project requires transporting people from one site to another, obtain signed permission forms for anyone under the age of 18 and run driving record background checks on all drivers. As with any other ministry in the church, safety is the first and most important consideration.

- **Sensitivity.** Think through any sensitive subjects or interactions that require extra training or maturity to handle. If the mission involves interacting with a group of people who have suffered sexual trauma, incarceration, homelessness, or other forms of abuse, you may not want to bring along young children. On the other hand, some sensitive situations still can be made appropriate for young people with a little preparation.

- **Superiority.** Another way to assess appropriateness is to ascertain whether your group can minister *with* and not just *to* others. I find it much easier to recruit people to ladle food onto another's plate or distribute school supply backpacks than to get church folks to mentor a troubled child or share a meal and conversation with a survivor of trauma. There is nothing superior about serving. It is not a matter of swooping in as fixers but working alongside people. If building relationships with those you seek to serve is not on the table, the project is inappropriate for your church.

If you have determined that a project fits these criteria for appropriateness, ensure that it is also meaningful by looking for these signs:

- **Listening.** We can only know if an area of service is truly needed if we first hear from those affected by it. Serving must start with listening. If you wish to serve your neighborhood, first ask the neighbors what their needs are and pull together people and resources for those specific areas. If you plan to go on an international mission trip, first talk to the people who live there to discover what they need and develop your trip accordingly. It is not possible for a project to be meaningful if it meets only an imagined need and disregards the real ones.

- **Lasting.** Mission work should always have a lasting impact upon both groups, those who serve and those you hope to serve. Often, all that is required to ensure the service has a lasting impact upon those serving is intentional training beforehand and debriefing afterward. Go over expectations, proper language and behavior, and relationship building. It is a little more difficult to ensure that the service has a lasting impact upon those you are serving because so much of our serving opportunities are one-time events with no continued interaction. Whenever possible, incorporate some kind of follow-up into your project design, like setting up pen pals, designing a worship event within the served community a few weeks afterward, or praying with people before departure.

- **Loving.** Every service project should be designed to increase our capacity to love God and love others. If there is a group of people in your community that your church finds hard to love, they would be ideal partners in a ministry project. Have you noticed your church finds it hard to greet those with special needs? Do people with severe financial need receive a cool reception in your church? Then find another church or organization that has figured out how to love these folks and join with them. Learn to love the people who you don't understand.

The projects that are appropriate and meaningful for one church may not work for another. The following list is merely a starting point for ideas. Take some of these possibilities and run them through the rubric already provided to determine if they will work for your community.

Service Project Possibilities

Each of these service projects can be accomplished by people of all ages, but not necessarily all budgets or localities. That is for you to discover!

Weekly

Blessing Backpacks. Partner with a local school to provide backpacks filled with food for children to take home on the weekends. This project requires weekly volunteers to collect the backpacks from the school, shop for food, fill the backpacks, and return them. Funds for this program can be raised by asking church members to make a one-time donation to cover the cost of one child's backpack for a school year.

Teacher/Classroom Sponsorships. Adopt the teachers in your congregation or in your local schools. Send them notes of encouragement and gift cards for school supplies. Help decorate the classroom for each season. Provide chaperones for field trips, or whatever else the teacher may need.

Senior Center. Obtain permission to spend time with residents of a local senior center. Visit regularly to read together, talk, sing, hold a worship service, or do crafts. Develop relationships and learn from one another.

Community Garden. If your church has the green space, plant a community garden each year. Recruit volunteers to tend to the weeding, and invite neighbors to plant, weed, and harvest as desired. Set up an arrangement with a local food pantry to receive unclaimed produce.

Host Recovery Groups. Open space in your church to organizers of Alcoholics Anonymous, Narcotics Anonymous, Al-Anon, Overeaters Anonymous, or any other group that provides recovery care. Provide coffee and a safe space.

Quarterly

Respite Care. Recruit and train volunteers to care for kids with disabilities. Then invite caregivers to drop off their kids for three or four hours of supervised, care-filled fun while they shop, go on a date, or simply enjoy quiet. This kind of event is especially great around times when parents need to Christmas shop, and during the summer when there are fewer outlets and activities for kids. Organizations such as Buddy Breaks or Autism Speaks can provide resources for training.

Family Nights. Provide supplies and instructions for families to do a service project together. Examples include packing meals for Kids Against Hunger; creating brownie and lemonade stands for families to set up in their own neighborhoods to raise money for missions; making housewarming gifts for new homeowners; making invitations to church events that can be distributed at school; filling blessing bags to give to people in need on the street; and the list could go on! Remember always to discuss the purpose of the project beforehand and debrief it afterward.

Annually

Neighborhood Gathering. Invite neighborhoods around the church for a free party at least once a year. Grill burgers (with vegetarian and gluten-free options available), rent a bouncy castle, play cornhole, and sit down to talk with one another. Advertise with a yard banner, an inexpensive postcard, and ads through radio, newspaper, and social-media outlets. Solicit attendees' contact information for a door-prize drawing and use that information to send them information on your next worship series.

Daytime Vacation Bible School. Evening VBS is for families already in your church. But a daytime VBS meets the ever-present need for safe and affordable childcare. As such, it is a perfect outreach opportunity. Whether or not families opt to try your church on Sunday mornings, a quality VBS will introduce children to Jesus in a way they will remember forever.

Mission Trips. There is nothing quite as humbling as traveling to a new part of the world and realizing how little you know. Pair youth with adult mentors for every mission trip. Help participants with fundraiser ideas and possibly with some funding from the church budget.

Endless Ideas

Ask church members how they can serve. Solicit ideas from all ages. If an idea sounds impossible at first, brainstorm ways it could work along with them. Again, while specific ideas for church outreach projects are all over the Internet, the best place to start is your own church's DNA. What do you do well, and what are ways you need to grow? We are all called to be in mission, and we need everyone to be a part of living out that mission.

Final Thoughts

Intergenerational means everyone. Perhaps your church is predominantly older, and you are tasked with attracting a younger generation. Or maybe all ages worship separately at your church right now, with older folks in an early service singing hymns, younger adults in a later service with a praise band, and kids nowhere to be seen outside the children's wing. Pulling everyone into the same rooms of worship and service together will not happen overnight. If some of the ideas in this chapter sparked alarm or defensiveness in you, imagine how crazy they will sound to those who haven't heard them yet. Let these thoughts rumble around in your own psyche for a bit before championing them widely in your church. Consider what your first baby step might be toward intergenerational ministry.

For those of you who are already sold on intergenerational worship and serving, this chapter gives you language to talk about it with others and concrete strategies to continue bridging generational gaps. Always maintain a perspective of ministry, not programs. Even the most innovative and organic ministry initiatives can become stale and institutional in time. Look to the early church in the Book of Acts, to the Psalms, and to Jesus' own life and ministry when you need inspiration. Incorporate rituals into your worship, and respond to participant's individual needs for accessibility. Honor the older generation and raise the younger one with a commitment to inclusion in both leadership and learning.

CHAPTER 7

MILESTONES

During most visits to a pediatrician for a wellness check-up, someone hands the child's caregiver a list of the physical, emotional, cognitive, and social milestones they should be seeing—things like "speaking in 2-3 word sentences" or "can alternate feet going up the stairs." These milestones don't occur at exactly the same time for every kid. But if a child's development falls outside the typical time range for a large number of milestones, the caregivers know to pay attention.

Pediatricians do not include spiritual milestones on their handouts, and that is OK because it really is the church's job to guide families in this way. There are appropriate expectations for spiritual growth that coincide with a child's physical, cognitive, social, and emotional development. This chapter defines milestones and their purpose, breaks down the components of a milestone celebration, and provides a multitude of helpful suggestions for celebrating milestones from cradle to grave.

What Are Milestones?

In *Sticky Faith*, Clark and Powell tell of a church near their research center that accomplishes intergenerational ministry by walking people through spiritual rites of passage.[1] For example, they hold an annual first Communion service for 1st-graders and their families. Similarly, 5th-graders and their families participate in an annual Passover dinner together. At the start of senior high, students hike to the top of a mountain along with the youth ministry leaders and their senior pastor. There, they experience a literal mountaintop moment, which younger kids look forward to for years before they are eligible to participate. These are all spiritual milestones.

A milestone is a figurative stepping stone on the discipleship path, a marker of continued faith development, a rite of passage coinciding with physical, social, and emotional development. As children learn to read (a cognitive milestone), they also unlock the ability to read God's Word for themselves. Thus, the cognitive milestone prompts a spiritual one. When a teenager leaves home for good, this social milestone connects to the spiritual milestone of taking ownership of their spiritual practices. Attending church and practicing spiritual disciplines are now an individual responsibility, independent of the family's expectations. Milestones allow us to track and celebrate our spiritual growth, turning the nebulous realm of spiritual development into a series of celebrations. Most churches already incorporate some ministry milestones, whether or not they know them as such. But it is unlikely that a church will make the most of this ministry structure without an intentional approach that invites the individual, the family, and the whole congregation into the process.

Milestones have the power to organize all of the church's family ministry endeavors. A milestones ministry can draw everyone into the life of the church at regular, anticipated, and affirming moments in their lives. The perfect attendance family and the Easter and Christmas visitors can be motivated to show up to receive a Bible and a blessing for their young reader.

Why Milestones?

This chapter will discuss each piece of a milestone celebration. But first, allow me to convince you that organizing your ministry around a series

1   Kara E. Powell and Chap Clark, *Sticky Faith: Everyday Ideas to Build Lasting Faith in Your Kids* (Grand Rapids, MI: Zondervan, 2011), 118.

of milestones will enrich your family ministry. Celebrating spiritual rites of passage accomplishes a whole range of purposes. Following are some of the most compelling.

Identity Forming

As we know from our study of child and adolescent development, the kids in our ministries are focused on figuring out just who they really are. This process of self-assessment continues into adulthood, with many of us adding to and subtracting from our sense of self over and over as we are exposed to new people and ideas. Rituals and celebrations are the way we process this growth. Physical development is marked by annual birthday celebrations, complete with traditions such as singing a particular song and blowing out candles on a cake. Cognitive development is measured by grade levels and graduations. If a child completes the academic achievements expected of a 4th-grader, that child then becomes a 5th-grader. Those identities of age and grade contribute to our sense of self. They help to put us in context and provide expectations to which we can compare ourselves.

Emotional and spiritual milestones, unfortunately, are not marked by nearly as many traditions. Perhaps this is because we understand so little about growth in these areas, or perhaps because emotional and spiritual growth cannot be neatly confined to a series of stages the way physical and cognitive growth can. But just because emotional and spiritual development are not perfectly linear does not mean we cannot celebrate them. It just means we must get more creative. It is hard to figure out who we are emotionally and spiritually without any key moments, community feedback, or cultural expectations. Milestones are wonderful expressions of pride and support for one another's spiritual development. They allow people to work out their spiritual identity in the context of community, relationships, and some tangible signs.

Empowering

Most discipleship of children and youth happens in the home and during daily life, not during their limited time at church. Our constant question is how to provide the tools and motivation for parents and caregivers to lead their children spiritually. While church leaders cultivate those skills and have educated themselves in discipling children, it can be hard to convey that knowledge to caregivers, who can put it to the greatest use. Parent meetings are notorious for being either poorly attended or turning into uncontrollable gripe sessions that do more harm than good.

Enter: milestones. As you'll see in the next section, every proper milestone includes a parenting component. The celebration is the carrot that will get parents to come—they are attracted by the celebration you are planning for their child and sometimes also by the answers you offer for the new and unfamiliar season their child is entering. Once parents and caregivers are in the door, we have a platform for building in-home discipleship skills and offering practical, time-tested strategies for teaching faith on a day-to-day basis. If we do our jobs right, parents leave each milestone experience with the ideas and the desire to shepherd their children's faith in the home and everywhere else.

Intergenerational

Milestone celebrations bring the entire church together. While it may be appropriate for some milestones to be celebrated within the ministry area of youth or children, you may find families will often invite grandparents and mentors to enter that space to cheer, take photos, and be proud with them. The majority of milestone celebrations can and should take place before an intergenerational church gathering, whether during a worship service or a special event. With kids and their families standing before the church, take the opportunity to lead the whole congregation through a spoken commitment to pray for them, walk with them, be in relationship with them, and encourage them. Use milestones as a reminder to other generations that they also experienced these stages of growth. Milestones are the perfect times to reinforce the idea that the whole church is a great big family. Another intergenerational aspect of many milestones is that they can easily incorporate mentoring relationships between generations, an extra powerful connection we can make for our children and youth.

Inclusive

Every single milestone can be made inclusive of every person in your church. You do not have to have a certain ability or be a certain race, gender, or age to qualify for a spiritual rite of passage. If your milestones are based largely upon age groups or grades, make it clear to families that they can opt into the milestones that fit their child. Last year, a 1st-grader in my church participated in the 2nd-grade Bible milestone because he was already a strong reader, and his parents wanted him to begin reading his own Bible. I have also welcomed a 5th-grader to participate in that same milestone, because her autism made her parents more comfortable placing her with a younger age group. Milestones become less and less linear as spiritual development continues. For the purpose of inclusion, I do not recommend offering a college graduation milestone, since so many emerging adults choose not to attend college at all, and many who do begin college do not graduate. But celebrating new jobs or new home/apartment moves are appropriate because they can apply to almost anyone. Assess your congregation with inclusivity in mind when you design milestones, and commit to being flexible for the purpose of inclusion.

Resilience Building

The meat of milestones is found in the rituals, covenants, and commitments they are made of. For example, students who complete a confirmation milestone can make a commitment to join the church at the end, including a statement of faith. When we send high-school seniors on to whatever is next for them, their parents and the congregation weep their way through a covenant to pray for them, support them, and remember them in this next stage.

These milestone rituals and covenants are powerful resilience builders for families who have experienced trauma in the past. Trauma and crisis often lead people to feel like they are isolated and broken. Milestones counter that belief by surrounding people with a community that promises to stand by them in God's name. Furthermore, milestones position children and youth as God's image-bearers who are called to do good and important work in God's name. Milestones offer a normalizing, equalizing experience in which everyone is celebrated and honored, regardless of their past, personality, gifts, or needs.

How Are Milestones Done?

There is no better way to guide families through spiritual development than by offering these empowering, inclusive, resilience-building, identity-forming, intergenerational rites of passage. How do you begin a milestones ministry? The first task is to choose between a series of physical, age-based stages or a series of life-season celebrations. There are pros and cons to each option.

Milestones Based on Physical Stages

This option is the most popular, probably because it is so much neater, cleaner, and simpler than the alternative. Most churches who talk about milestones describe them as a pathway, a chronological process where people celebrate milestones based on their age or grade in school. This design for milestones makes it easy to talk about them and put them into a linear graphic. This design also communicates an intentional plan for each person's discipleship by setting the expectation that every student will experience the milestones in a certain order.

This method's biggest downside is that not every child progresses through each stage at the same pace. We run the risk of appearing judgmental if we attach certain ages or grades to milestones, even if we are up-front about our willingness to be flexible and allow families to opt in or opt out of celebrations based on their child's maturity and needs.

When students finish high school, age-based milestones naturally merge into achievement-based milestones. Life after high school no longer follows a common trajectory, so churches that offer milestones throughout the lifespan must switch gears after high school, regardless.

Milestones Based on Achievements

Structuring your milestone offerings around achievements is a more inclusive strategy, which also means that it is messier and more confusing than the age-based alternative. This is more of a choose-your-own-adventure structure, similar to the list of merit badges that children in scouting choose to earn. In this design, you may find yourself celebrating the same kid in four different milestone celebrations in one year, then none in the next. You may have a lineup of 15 children, representing four different age levels, during any given milestone ceremony. It is possible that some milestone celebrations may even include multiple generations, depending on what achievements you choose for them.

This method also forces church leaders to get a little creative when deciding what to call each milestone. When designing a spiritual corollary to starting middle school, you may want to choose a milestone such as completion of a service project, changing to a new school (for any reason), or entering the church's small-group ministry. It's likely that many middle schoolers would fit into one of those achievements, and it's possible that members of other age groups would as well.

Choosing Milestones

If you know which milestone structure will work better for you and your church, then it is time to identify the exact celebrations you want to offer. This is the most fun part! First, think about your church's own DNA—size, demographics, attendance patterns, mission statement, goals. Does your church prioritize families? If so, you may want to include more milestones for young people than for older people. Is your congregation aging? Be sure to plan milestones for later life events, such as grandparenting, retirement, and caring for aging parents. Is your church on a mission to reach your neighborhood? Design milestones that are attractive to folks outside the church, such as achievements by local business owners or attendance at a daytime vacation Bible school. There is no set rule for which milestones to include in your church's plan. Do what makes sense for you.

When you start thinking about it, there is a good chance you will realize your church already celebrates a few milestones. Do you have a ritual in place for providing meals for families with new babies? That's the beginning of a milestone. Do you offer infant baptism or dedication? You are on your way. Are you already blessing teachers or service members in some way? That's a start! Is Promotion Sunday a thing at your church? Boom! You've been milestoned.

Create a map or a list of the rites of passage that will work best for your church. If you need more ideas, the second half of this chapter is full of creative options. Once you have chosen the milestones you want to offer, the next step is to plan the way you will fulfill each component of a complete milestone. Let's take a look at what those elements are now.

Components of a Milestone

These milestone components have emerged from my ten years of leading families in ministry and searching for the most effective ways to guide faith in intergenerational settings. They work together to accomplish two common goals in ministry: 1) pulling families more deeply into the life of the church, and 2) equipping people to follow God more closely outside the church walls.

Corporate Celebration

The first and most obvious element of a spiritual milestone is the actual celebration! This is the party, the ritual, the ceremony that everyone thinks of when they hear of a milestone. Most of the time, this celebration will take place during a primary worship gathering and involve the pastor or church staff along with the people being celebrated and their families. For some celebrations, you may decide that it is more appropriate to perform them outside the primary worship service. Perhaps there is only time or openness to offer a certain number of milestone celebrations during congregational worship. Or perhaps the tenor of a particular milestone lends itself to being celebrated by a smaller group, such as a blessing over new drivers in the youth group or a special prayer time with preschoolers during their Sunday-school hour. Maybe one of your milestones is a mission trip or sleep-away camp, and the milestone ceremony takes place on the last night before returning home.

The most critical point to remember is that every milestone should take place in a community setting. Milestones are meant to strengthen community ties within the church, and that purpose cannot be fulfilled if the whole ceremony takes place in someone's home or a private meeting with the pastor. One of the great benefits of a milestone is that it invites people who are otherwise unrelated to join together with the purpose of loving and nurturing one another. Define the best audience for the corporate celebration, and make it clear throughout the ceremony that God is calling everyone present to be family to one another.

The corporate celebration can take many forms and be as personal or impersonal as you want it to be. If you recognize 20 new parents at once, for example, you may not want to introduce each one in detail. However, if you are baptizing just one child, it might be appropriate to share a little bit about the child and their family. There are some celebrations that the senior pastor may be the best person to lead, while others could involve several church staff or volunteers. If planning worship services is not your forte, I highly recommend meeting with worship planners in your church to plan logistics such as timing, which words to put on the screen or in the bulletin, how to invite people forward, staging, and so forth. Do not assume that everyone will know what to do—in fact, assume the opposite. Give clear instructions before and during the ceremony so that participants and leaders do not have to guess where to stand and what to say.

Tangible Symbol

Every milestone should be represented and remembered by a tangible item given to each participant. The high point of the corporate celebration is the giving of this tangible symbol. This symbol can be a tool that helps the person continue maturing in faith, or it can simply serve as a reminder of the celebration.

Just about anything can serve as a tangible symbol. You could take a photo of a confirmand with their mentor, frame it, and give it to them during the confirmation ceremony. Sometimes churches give seashells or a ceramic dove at baptism to remind people of the water and the Spirit at work in that sacrament. Every year I order small crosses shaped to fit easily into a person's fist. I give them to rising kindergartners, so they can carry them into those first weeks of school and remember that their church is praying for them. There is no need to break the bank with this element of the milestone. Sometimes homemade or simple items work best! The point is to cement the ritual in people's understandings and memories.

Congregational Support

Milestones are not just for kids and parents; they are meant to bring everyone together. The people in the pews must not be let off the hook during milestone celebrations. In the ceremony, give the community a part to play. In the United Methodist Church, we encourage infant baptism as a way to situate our youngest family members as invaluable members of the church family. During the baptism liturgy, the congregation vows to watch over that child and model Christ-like faith for them. I revisit this baptismal commitment during almost every milestone celebration in my church. This reminds the congregation of their role in raising all the children and youth of the church to know, love, and serve God.

When we give Bibles to young readers, we instruct the whole congregation in the preceding weeks to bring their Bibles to church that day. After the children receive their Bibles, they can see the entire congregation raising their own personal, dog-eared, highlighted copies of God's Word high in the air in solidarity and commitment. This is a powerful visual to accompany the congregation's promise to read God's Word—powerful not just to the young people standing up front but to all generations as they agree together that studying Scripture is essential to our faith.

When we introduce new preteen apprentices to areas of service and leadership in the church, we first present them from the front, then usher them into the aisles to stand among the people. The congregation is then instructed to hold their hands out in the direction of the apprentices and to pray quiet but audible words of blessing over them. This low rumble of prayerful support rises up and hovers above the apprentices, filling everyone with a sense of togetherness in fulfilling God's mission and calling.

Caregiver Gathering

Parent meetings often are not especially appealing to caregivers who already have too much to fit in their schedule. But one way guaranteed to get parents to show up (and invite extended family and friends) is an award ceremony for their kid. If trophies, recognition, and free stuff are involved, most parents will make the time. Milestones offer all of these things.

Another reason parents might find a milestone gathering appealing is that milestones often occur when families are transitioning to a new stage of physical, academic, or social functioning. These transitions bring with them feelings of fear and uncertainty, and those feelings may prompt caregivers to look for guidance with more vulnerability than usual. The prime example of this is a faith and sexuality event for preteens. The church offers parents the gift of explaining to their children the details of puberty, sex, and all that comes with those things—but only if parents and caregivers participate in mandatory meetings before, during, and after the event. Teaching the kids the right words for body parts is helpful, but helping caregivers overcome their own stigmas and fears of those words is life-changing. And the discomfort of talking about sex with preteens often serves as a huge motivator to get parents into the room and ready to listen.

Honestly, it is easy to overlook this element of a milestone celebration. If we omit the parent gathering, probably no one would complain. But without this opportunity to speak to caregivers and allow them to share with one another, the milestone becomes simply a token event with little impact on the family's future. By bringing parents into the mix, we empower them to be stronger, better disciples themselves and thereby to disciple their family members long-term.

The Faith Markers curriculum published by MennoMedia sums up all of these components nicely:

> A ritual of blessing reminds children that they are an integral part of the faith community. Faith recognition reminds parents of their role in shaping faith in their children at home. And the church community affirms its promise to be partners in forming faith in all ages.[2]

The remainder of this chapter consists of milestone celebration suggestions for all kinds of ages and stages. You will want to pick and choose the ones that work for your church, incorporating tweaks or blending some together as you go.

2   MennoMedia, "Faith Markers: Marking Each Child's Faith Journey" (MennoMedia), 2, accessed July 23, 2019, https://www.faithandliferesources.org/Curriculum/FaithMarkers/pdf/FaithMarkersMin.pdf.

Milestone Ideas

This is a long list, but not a comprehensive one! Following the principles of milestone design covered before, you can create any number of new faith milestones from scratch. Tweak, mix and match, and use any ideas in this section however they will work best for you and your congregation.

Birth

Ceremony: New babies are an exception to the ceremonial aspect of milestones. It is not practical to produce a corporate ceremony to honor families of new babies, at least not right away. However, if your church solicits prayer requests and praises during worship, it is appropriate to name new babies at that time. If your church has screens in the front of the worship center, obtain permission from families to post photos of the babies as an introduction to the congregation.

Symbols: Gifts might include New Baby Kits with a handwritten note from the pastor and/or children's ministry staff; a Baby's First Bible or book of prayers; a handmade blanket, bib, or baby toy from a congregation member; and typed instructions for the first church nursery visit in the future.

Parents: The pastor or a children's ministry staff person can visit the family to offer support and love.

Congregation: Church members can deliver meals to the family and/ or offer free childcare for older siblings.

Baptism

Ceremony: The baptism itself is the ceremony! Be sure parents know and understand beforehand the baptismal vows they will be making.

Symbols: Tangible symbols could include an open seashell to represent water; a framed photo taken of the baptism; a certificate signed by the pastor and parent(s); and a framed copy of the baptismal covenant, signed by people in the congregation.

Parents: Pastors should meet with the parents and caregivers bringing children for baptism before even putting a date on the calendar. The purpose of this meeting is to explain baptism, go over the vows that will be taken, learn more about the caregivers' own faith backgrounds, and walk through the ceremony logistics. (If the person being baptized is old enough to take the baptismal vows, the pastor will cover these questions directly with them.)

Congregation: The whole church should always participate in baptismal vows as well. Following the act of baptism, lead the congregation in renewing their own faith commitments and promising to walk alongside the newly baptized person, surrounding them with a community of love and forgiveness.

Preschool Prayer

Ceremony: The preschool years can be considered the ideal time to emphasize prayer.[3] While preschoolers cannot read, they often love to learn rhyming prayers and to speak prayer requests to one another. Invite the families of preschoolers to join them in their meeting area one Sunday a few months into the school year. Allow preschoolers to demonstrate the prayer rituals you have taught them, and lead both parents and preschoolers through a time of prayer requests and corporate prayer. Speak a blessing over each family.

Symbols: Gifts might include a book of prayers for kids, prayer beads, or a candle to light during family prayer time.

Parents: Right after parents participate in this special preschool worship time, invite them to gather to debrief with you. Ask about their own prayer practices. Discuss different prayer practices such as intercession, journaling, praying in color, Lectio Divina, praying Scripture, praying through spiritual songs, and so forth. Help parents plan prayer time into their routines, and tell them how excited their preschoolers are to pray with and for them.

Congregation: Solicit prayers from congregation members in advance by asking them to write down a short prayer on behalf of young families. Then compile the submissions and give them to families. Also, solicit prayer requests from preschool families and invite other congregation members to pray for them daily.

---

3   Fraser N. Watts, Rebecca Nye, and Sara B. Savage, *Psychology for Christian Ministry* (London: Routledge, 2002), 77–78.

Worship Welcome

Ceremony: If your church incorporates children into the sanctuary worship service at a certain age, make a milestone out of it! Invite new worshipers to the front during a time of prayer. Introduce them to the congregation, giving everyone a chance to applaud them in welcome.

Symbols: Tangible symbols include a worship bag filled with quiet activities; a pen inscribed with the church's name for journaling, doodling, or taking sermon notes; a letter of welcome from the pastor; and an autograph book for children to collect signatures from other worshipers as they meet and greet them.

Parents: On or before the children's "first" day in worship, invite parents to a gathering where you walk them through the new logistics and explain any worship aids that may be available to their children (snack station, cry room, worship activity bags, children's bulletins, and so forth). Use this time to teach parents how to be worship coaches for their kids, including strategies for answering kids' questions during worship and modeling full participation in worship. Make it crystal clear to caregivers that children are 100 percent part of the worshiping community, including the noise and distraction they sometimes bring with them.

Congregation: As children are introduced during the ceremony, take the opportunity to communicate your church's approach to intergenerational worship. Name the noisy questions and squirming bodies as joyful noises unto the Lord. Ask that parents be encouraged and lauded for coaching their children in worship.

New School Year

Ceremony: Blessing of the Backpacks—on the Sunday prior to the first day of school, ask children to bring their backpacks to worship. Line up the backpacks at the front of the sanctuary and pray over them during worship. Ask teachers of all kinds to stand during prayer time for a blessing.

Symbols: Gifts might include identification tags for the backpacks, with the church logo and a Scripture verse or short prayer on one side and space for the child's name and contact information on the other side.

Parents: Send written instructions for parents before their children transition to new classes or teachers. Give specific drop-off and pickup information, and tell the parents how to reach you with questions. Invite them to share prayer requests with you throughout the school year.

Congregation: While backpacks are lined up in front of the sanctuary, invite congregation members to approach and pray over them before, during, or after the service. Provide note cards in the pews and ask congregation members to write prayers, advice, and encouragement on them and to drop them inside backpacks as they pray. Ask teachers to provide wish lists of needed supplies for their classrooms, and post those supply lists in the gathering area for congregation members to claim and provide.

Kindergarten

Ceremony: Invite forward new kindergartners and their parents for a special blessing. If your church expects kindergartners to participate in sanctuary worship at all, use ideas from the Worship Welcome milestone above. Give a special symbolic gift to new kindergartners and assure them that their church is praying for them as they make this big transition.

Symbols: Tangible gifts might include wooden palm crosses that fit easily into a child's hand for comfort; smooth stones with a word or symbol on them; pencil holders with the church's logo; and picture books about church.

Parents: Kindergarten can be a huge emotional milestone for parents. Invite parents to an informal gathering with coffee and snacks after drop-off on the first day of school. Ask them to share what this milestone means to them. Some parents increase their work hours when kids begin kindergarten; others may not know what to do with themselves. Listen and pray over them.

Congregation: Lead the congregation in speaking a welcome and blessing over new kindergartners when they are introduced in worship.

Reading Scripture

Ceremony: Once children are able to read chapter books, they are ready to have God's Word in their hands. Place the new Bibles in a row at the front of your sanctuary, on Communion rails, or an altar table. Invite the readers and their caregivers to the front, and pray a blessing over them. Instruct the parents to pick up the Bibles and hand them to the children.

Symbols: This one is easy—the symbol is the Bible itself! I recommend the *Deep Blue Kids Bible* for young readers—it is engaging, full of help, and written on an appropriate reading level. For youth I recommend any Bible with a concordance and a simple, attractive appearance.

Parents: One practical way to partner with parents is to ask them to fund part of the Bible expense. We give them the gift of doing the research, finding the best Bible available for their children, and completing the purchase. But the most powerful parent component of this milestone is a Bible workshop. Gather parents and their children to walk them through their new Bibles and teach them how to read and study on their own. Provide ideas for family devotions, ways to incorporate Scripture into daily life, and motivation for parents to read the Bible themselves. Instruct caregivers to fill out the dedication page of the Bible, and give them time to write a love note to their child on the inside cover before they hand it over. Go to *cokesburykids.com* to download the Bible Workshop Outline, Bible Story Reference Chart, and I Wonder What to Do When I'm ... worksheets to put on a Bible workshop like this.

Congregation: Bibles can be expensive, especially ones that are graphically illustrated and enhanced with helps for kids. Solicit sponsors in the congregation who will share the cost of a Bible with the recipient's family.

Memorizing Scripture

Ceremony: If possible, coordinate with the worship planning team to review the Scriptures that will be read in worship during upcoming Sundays. Work with them to choose an appropriate Scripture passage for kids to memorize. During the service when that Scripture is the focus, invite those who have memorized it to recite the passage during worship, rather than having someone read it.

Symbols: Tangible gifts could include the memorized Scripture printed on a bookmark or in a photo frame; and a badge or button with the Scripture reference on it.

Parents: Host a Bible study class for caregivers to study the Scripture the children are memorizing. Utilize this time to get parents into Scripture and strengthen their Bible study skills for use in leading their kids at home.

Congregation: When introducing kids in worship, make it clear that they are the Scripture worship leaders of the morning, and are not there to perform for applause. At the service end, let the kids distribute bookmarks with the Scripture passage so everyone can learn this passage at home.

Graduating from Children's Worship

Ceremony: Invite older elementary children who will no longer be attending children's worship to the front to be introduced to the church. The pastor or worship leader should speak directly to them, welcoming them and recognizing their full participation in worship.

Symbols: Gifts might include a hymnal or other songbook; and a framed copy of a prayer, creed, benediction, or common phrase they will hear in worship frequently.

Parents: This milestone warrants its own parent meeting. Folks who have been accustomed to sitting alone for part or all of the service will now have fidgety, needy, questioning kids by their side who are looking to them for coaching. Talk to parents about the importance of having their kids see them worship, and give ideas for discussing worship in the home.

Congregation: During the ceremony, ask the congregation to wave or extend hands of prayer and blessing toward the children who will join them in the sanctuary. Take a moment to pray, and ask the congregation to lift up these young worshipers and their caregivers.

Church Camp

Ceremony: Before kids leave for church camp, pray over them in front of the congregation for safety, transformation, and growth during their time away.

Symbols: Gifts ideas include a compass, a water bottle with the church logo, and a journal.

Parents: Work with parents in the months leading up to camp to encourage them to sign up their kids. It is helpful if a church staff person or family ministry leader has served as a counselor or dean of a camp in the past or present. Help parents make carpool arrangements for drop-off or pick-up.

Congregation: Ask the congregation to write letters to campers and mail them to camp. Give detailed instructions with the address, dates to mail, and camper names. Church members can send jokes, devotions, encouragement, or simple assurances of prayer.

Faith & Sexuality Education

Ceremony: This is one of the most needed milestone celebrations on a practical level, but this one may not require a ceremony in front of the whole church. Rather, at the end of a faith & sexuality education event, walk the children and their caregivers through a blessing of the body. You can find examples of these in *Wonderfully Made* (published by Abingdon Press), or you can write your own litany of love for them to say together.

Symbols: A good gift is a student workbook with a glossary of terms and a review of everything covered in the course.

Parents: More important than teaching kids about sex is teaching their parents how to talk about sex. Require participation in a parent meeting ahead of the event. If possible, conduct parent education simultaneously with student education. Parent education provides the opportunity to talk with parents about what their kids are ready to hear, role play awkward conversations, and discuss matters of sexuality in a safe place.

Congregation: Announce to the congregation when kids are participating in faith and sexuality education and ask for prayers.

New Drivers

Ceremony: This is another ceremony that can take place with the whole church or simply in a youth-group context. Recognize new drivers and pray over them with words of safety, focus, wisdom, and peace. Talk to them about the importance of using this new freedom for good. You can find examples of blessings for new drivers through your denominational worship resources, or you can use Rev. David Hindman's blessing published by Discipleship Ministries.[4]

---

4   David Hindman, "An Order for Blessing New Drivers," Discipleship Ministries, 2013,

Symbols: Tangible symbols might include a wallet card with emergency contact information on one side and a prayer or Bible verse on the other; a church bumper sticker; and a key ring with the church's logo.

Parents: Bring the parents together for conversation and commiseration! Some will be elated that they no longer have to cart their kids around to every event, and some will be terrified. Find information on driving instructors and local driving laws beforehand and print it up. Have seasoned parents share what driving rules have worked for their family and which have not.

Congregation: Post the names of new drivers in a public place within the church, perhaps printed on cards shaped like cars or keys, and ask people to pause there and pray over them.

High School Graduation

Ceremony: This is a big one! Involve mentors, staff, and family members who have watched these kids grow throughout their lives. Write a liturgy that reviews their collective path through milestones up to this point. Call out special relationships they've had along the way in the church. Make this transition about calling discernment, figuring out the life of service God has in mind for them.

Symbols: One possible gift is a custom blanket with the church logo or a symbol of your church on it. Toward the end of the ceremony, invite caregivers to wrap the blanket around their child's shoulders to remind them of all the times they wrapped them in blankets as a baby and to symbolize a final act of protection and nurturing before sending them out to new things.

Parents: Encourage parents to read *Sticky Faith* during their child's senior year, so they might glean strategies for preparing their child to stay close to God after leaving home.

Congregation: Match graduating seniors with congregation members who will pray for them (and maybe send care packages) during this first year. Invite the congregation to write down memories of the graduates' participation in the life of the church up to that point, or let people write down words of life advice (but read through them before publishing!).

https://www.umcdiscipleship.org/resources/an-order-for-blessing-new-drivers.

Church Membership

Ceremony: Most churches have consistent membership vows and instructions for bringing in new members.

Symbols: Provide a membership certificate or an item with the church's mission or branding on it.

Parents: Walk through each section of the membership vows with the prospective member beforehand, explaining the words and making sure parents and young people understand the commitment they are making.

Congregation: As membership vows are taken, remind the congregation that many of them have made these same vows. Ask them to renew those vows from their seats as they hear them. Invite those who have questions to contact the pastor for further discussion.

Home/Apartment Buying

While this milestone doesn't necessarily have all the components the others have, it is still a significant developmental step and should be celebrated. Appropriate recognition of this milestone could include a house-warming party sponsored by the person's small group and a framed Scripture to go on the wall. If furnishings are needed, solicit a list of items and send it to older members of the congregation who may have furniture to spare and want to donate.

Marriage

This milestone is one churches already do fairly well! We know what the ceremony looks like, and the rings are the perfect tangible symbol—but other aspects such as congregational support may need work. While pre-marital counseling is helpful, we should not leave couples alone after the ceremony. Invite newlyweds into pastoral counseling. Encourage them to stay in small-group discipleship, either together or separately. Recommend books on communication, boundaries, sex, and finances.

Retirement

Retirement can be infused with both positive and negative emotions. It may not be appropriate to celebrate it in front of the church, and often church leaders do not even know someone is retiring until after the fact. Instead of a ceremony, set up a coffee or dinner with retirees to see how they are doing and ask about what is next. This is a prime time to ask if there are service areas in the church that the retiree would like to become more involved in. It is also a wonderful opportunity to ask them to write down key lessons learned through their professional lives to share with college students and young adults.

Grandparenting

For grandparents raising grandkids in the absence of parents, include them exactly the same way you would parents and other caregivers. For those who are grandparenting alongside parents or other caregivers, celebrate the birth of new grandkids along with them. Whether or not their grandkids are in your church, offer to send them the same symbol you send to church families with new babies. Many grandparents grieve that their grandkids are not being raised in the church. Offer books and/or counseling for challenges such as prayer, working with parents, and setting and respecting boundaries.

Caring for Aging Parents

Unlike most celebratory milestones, this one is not usually cause for excitement. However, many middle-aged or older adults do find themselves spending long hours caring for their aging parents. Because this life stage often passes under the radar, it can feel lonely and exhausting.

Offer a church support group or find one in your area through the Community Resource Finder of the American Association of Retired Persons (AARP) (*https://www.communityresourcefinder.org/*) or the National Association of Area Agencies on Aging (https://www.n4a.org/). Suggest books on the topic or online resources like Caring for your Parents from PBS (*https://www.pbs.org/wgbh/caringforyourparents/index.html*) and the Caregiver Action Network (*https://caregiveraction.org/*). Mostly, pay attention to the needs of this group and offer pastoral care along the way.

Death

This is another milestone we already know how to celebrate to some degree. If you have ever been involved in planning or leading a funeral, you know what an important role this celebration of life can play in offering closure and helping family and friends grieve.

For grieving kids and teens, ask permission to invite them into conversation with a known church leader. Provide them with hands-on ways to express their feelings by asking them to draw a picture of their loved one or write a message in a sandbox. Light a candle and pray with them.

For adults who are grieving, mark the date of their loss on your calendar and send them a note on that date over the next few years. Invite them for coffee a few months after the funeral and learn how they are progressing through grief. Accept and normalize their feelings, and encourage them to seek counseling whenever appropriate.

Final Thoughts

In a time when many of us spin our wheels each year trying to figure out how to retain families and make church offerings more appealing, milestones provide a family ministry structure that both organizes and rewards participation in the life of the church. It helps families to know what to expect and frames people's growth in an affirming, caring way. Once these spiritual rites of passage become a part of your church's DNA, you will see families begin to experience spiritual identity formation and feel empowered to practice discipleship at home. Through whole-church celebrations, symbolic gifts, parent support, and intergenerational inclusion, you can build resilience and create a common language to talk about faith. It doesn't really matter whether you choose to structure milestones around physical stages, life seasons, or some combination of both, as long as you make them inclusive and affirming of all.

CHAPTER 8

DISABILITY MINISTRY

Moses spoke with a speech impediment.[1] Jacob walked with a limp after wrestling with an angel.[2] Goliath's size and slow movement were likely caused by hormonal and vision imbalances.[3] King Saul experienced symptoms of a mood disorder.[4] Sarai, Rachel, Hannah, and Elizabeth all experienced infertility—considered a disability in their society.[5] Mephibosheth, Saul's grandson, was injured in childhood and paralyzed from the waist down.[6] Zacchaeus may have lived with a form of dwarfism.[7] Jesus healed many people with all sorts of disabilities. In fact, I would suggest that Scripture offers significant representation for people experiencing a disability. Think about it—are there as many people with disabilities in our churches as there are in just the New Testament? I worry there are not.

1   Marc Shell, "Moses' Tongue," *Common Knowledge* 12, no. 1 (January 4, 2006): 150–76.
2   Genesis 32:22-31.
3   Stephen K. Mathew and Jeyaraj D. Pandian, "Newer Insights to the Neurological Diseases Among Biblical Characters of Old Testament," *Annals of Indian Academy of Neurology* 13, no. 3 (July 2010): 164–66, https://doi.org/10.4103/0972-2327.70873.
4   Martijn Huisman, "King Saul, Work-Related Stress and Depression," *Journal of Epidemiology and Community Health* 61, no. 10 (October 2007): 890, https://doi.org/10.1136/jech.2007.066522.
5   Candida Moss, "Biblical Families: Families Have Never Been Just a Mom, Dad, and 2.5 Children," *U.S. Catholic* 83, no. 4 (April 2018): 17–19.
6   2 Samuel 4:4.
7   Amos Yong, "Zacchaeus: Short and Un-Seen," *Christian Reflection: A Series in Faith and Ethics—Disability*, 2012, 11–17.

It can be hard for many churches to figure out how to take the first step toward welcoming families with a parent or child who needs accommodation to truly feel a sense of belonging. This chapter discusses how to take those steps, covering everything from the language we use to the programs we offer. It also covers some of the needs of people with disabilities and their families. At the end of the chapter, you will find practical advice for identifying barriers to participation in your own setting, as well as ideas for providing respite care and a buddy ministry.

Defining Disability Ministry

The Americans with Disabilities Act defines a disability as a "physical or mental impairment that substantially limits one or more major life activities"[8] of an individual. It goes on to explain that major life activities include caring for oneself; the tasks of daily living such as sleeping, walking, hearing, seeing, bending, breathing, and so forth; the working of bodily functions; and social or work activities. Mental illness is one type of disability that deserves its own definition here. The American Psychiatric Association defines mental illnesses as "health conditions involving changes in emotion, thinking, or behavior (or a combination of these)."[9]

Thinking about my ministry as well as my relationships with folks with disabilities, I tend to define "disability" broadly. In ministry, I propose that a disability *is any challenge to a person's ability to participate fully in a ministry area without accommodation.* A few people require accommodation to enter the building due to a mobility disability, social anxiety, visual impairment, or a plethora of other possibilities. Once inside, accommodation needs multiply. The floor plan, doorway sizes, the food being served, the noise level of the worship band, the training of the staff and volunteers—all of these could be barriers to participation for some people. Our definition of "disability" should include physical, cognitive, sensory, or emotional differences that necessitate accommodation.

---

8   United States Department of Justice Civil Rights Division, "Americans with Disabilities Act of 1990, AS AMENDED with ADA Amendments Act of 2008," accessed August 14, 2019, https://www.ada.gov/pubs/adastatute08.htm#12102.

9   American Psychiatric Association, "What Is Mental Illness?," accessed August 14, 2019, https://www.psychiatry.org/patients-families/what-is-mental-illness.

The purpose behind a broad definition of "disability" is to be as inclusive as possible and to help our staff and volunteers approach accommodation opportunities with joy and willingness. Our definition needs to be broad enough to include the allergies that parents record on their children's check-in sheet. The church that learns that a child has a gluten sensitivity and therefore discontinues the goldfish crackers in favor of rice cakes and fruit snacks is fulfilling the spirit of disability ministry. In the same way, a Sunday school teacher who notices that a child covers her ears and recoils every time the class shouts "Amen!" has an opportunity to fulfill the spirit of disability ministry. That teacher might devise a new tradition, such as whispering "Amen," or using sign language for "Amen." This kind of ministry starts small and proceeds one person at a time.

When we hear the word "disability," most of us picture someone using a wheelchair or a person who reads using Braille. It's important for ministry leaders to recognize that disability encompasses these visible manifestations, along with many less obvious or visible forms. Our goal as church leaders should be to make our building, activities, and leaders as sensitive and accommodating as possible. This might mean readily adapting our rules if a practice that works for most participants is exclusive for a few. Sometimes this means changing the whole rule; sometimes it just means altering the rule for one person. For example, you may advertise a class for young professionals but allow a person in their 50s to participate if they relate better to a younger age group due to a developmental disability. Or you may designate the main hallway as the path children take from the sanctuary to their worship room, but allow a child who has difficulty balancing to take an alternate route with assistance. There's no area of ministry that operates so fully on a case-by-case basis as disability ministry.

Attitudes Toward Disability Ministry

The first step in creating a safe, welcoming space for all of God's children is to evaluate the church's attitude and approach toward disabilities. There is an age-old misconception about the cause of disability that unfortunately still appears in some discussions, sermons, and blog posts. It is an idea with which Jesus himself contended. People of able bodies and minds have often made a connection between disability and sin, looking for someone to blame. This false connection has caused incredible pain to people with disabilities, and has made the church feel less safe for many.

This dangerous belief underlies the sidelong glances or outright judgments cast in the direction of parents whose child is having a meltdown. It shows up in accountability groups in which a person with a mental illness is urged to pray more, trust more, and have more faith in order to feel better. This belief is present when a curious child asks in a loud whisper what is wrong with the person using a walker, and parents shush the child in embarrassment, communicating that there is something shameful or off-limits about the topic of disability. The way that ministries and communication with families affected by disability are structured can help to reverse these misconceptions. Church leaders can communicate through their words and actions that disabilities are not necessarily sad, negative, or unfortunate at all. Once we begin to think of disability simply as a need to be met, rather than a punishment or incapacity to suffer through, we begin to see people for who they are—God's children and a part of our family.

Reciprocity

The most important attitude to adopt toward disability ministry is this: reciprocity. Every healthy relationship requires both giving and taking. Too often, disability ministry is perceived as a one-way street in which people without disabilities are the caregivers while people with disabilities are positioned to receive. Sometimes, we reverse direction and envision those with disabilities as the givers and the rest of us as the recipients of life lessons and inspiration.

A reciprocal attitude toward disability ministry rejects the pronouns "me" and "them" in favor of "us." Those of us who have disabilities and those of us who don't are in ministry together. We need to learn to include disability as one of many qualities that make up a person rather than a person's one defining characteristic. We need to recognize the strengths and gifts that people have *because* of their disabilities, not just in spite of them. For example, I have a dear, 5-year-old friend named Josiah who is one of the most relational, personable people I've ever met. Because of his

executive functioning disorder, his brain does not see danger or consequences, or think very far into the future. Josiah lives fully in the present.
There is not a better friend than Josiah, and he makes friends out of complete strangers by simply taking their hand and inviting them to accompany
him wherever he is going. Josiah's actions often disregard social protocols,
but they enable his loving, caring, expressive approach to relationships.

Another example is Adam, a guy who stuck out from the crowd in
his power wheelchair. Adam used a special tablet that could read to him
and speak the words he typed in. After attending for a few months, Adam
let the worship staff know that he was interested in serving in leadership
opportunities. He just needed time to prepare at home for any words he
would need to say through his assistive device. About once a quarter, Adam
served as liturgist in worship. The pastors would send him the Scripture
passage and responsive readings, and he would input them to his device
during the week. Then from the stage, he would play the words through the
tablet into the microphone. Suffice it to say, everyone listened a whole lot
closer to the words of Scripture on Adam's Sundays.

Every ministry that affects people with disabilities must begin with
the understanding that those of us with disabilities and those without can
learn from one another. Plans for disability ministries can only succeed if
they are made relationally, recognizing the image of God in every person.

A Person-Centered Approach

A person-centered approach to ministry understands that every individual possesses unique skills and abilities to connect with God and other
people. Sometimes ministries get caught up in creative, eye-popping events
and programs that cannot be tailored to individual needs. Any church that
is open to people with disabilities will maintain enough flexibility to adopt
a one-person-at-a-time approach. This approach is about recognizing that
we do not know anyone's story just by looking at them, and that the people
we serve are the experts on their own lives and needs. A one-person-at-a-
time ministry asks people what they need from the church, then believes
and acts on their answers. For example, some families in my ministry
have loved the idea of a separate, quiet, intentional classroom where their

children with disabilities can receive one-on-one attention from a trained caregiver during worship. Others have insisted that their children be included in the mainstream children and youth ministries, either with or without a personal helper. Still other families prefer to keep their children with them and sit at the back of the sanctuary or the balcony for an easy exit, if needed. None of these options is right or wrong in itself—it all depends on the needs of the person or family in front of you at the moment.

Here's the uncomfortable truth: this one-person-at-a-time approach can be expensive, both in terms of time and money. There have been seasons of my ministry when I know I have spent 80 percent of my time with one particular family, helping to make church a safe and happy place for their child. There have been times when I have spent 20 percent of my annual children's ministry budget to outfit a room or provide state-of-the-art tools or training geared toward making space for one or two people. When I am in a position to need extra assistance in order to worship, I hope someone will do the same for me. And when overtaxed childcare workers or ministry staff balk at the level of care I ask them to show, we try together to consider how much more exhausting and humbling it must be for folks who are brave enough to ask for our help in order to participate in our congregational activities.

People-First Language

Words matter! Unfortunately, most of us haven't spent much time practicing the use of thoughtful, intentional language to talk about disabilities. But if we can get our hearts into the right place and care about the unique needs of one person at a time, the language we use will start to change, too.

If you have a disability, you know that the words used to describe your needs and care can differ widely depending on context; the words used in a support group might differ from those used in a meeting with an educator, which might differ from those used in a doctor's visit or on a health insurance form. Fortunately, or unfortunately, people with disabilities are accustomed to adapting to whatever language each group finds appropriate or expedient. The main thing for ministry workers to remember is that all of us, with and without disabilities, desire to be treated as equals.

People-first language assumes that a disability is not who a person is but rather a condition that person possesses. It's shocking how much of our language when conversing about disability sounds like name-calling. "He's deaf," or "They're bipolar." These statements prescribe identity and narrow a person to a diagnosis, which can feel dehumanizing and uncaring. "Disability" is not an insulting term. To say someone has a disability is not rude or inappropriate; the problem is if we only see or talk about a person's disability or diagnosis while ignoring their whole personhood. Many disability advocates are reclaiming words such as "disabled" or "autistic," calling for everyone to normalize these terms and accept them as a real aspect of people's lives so that we can actually do something to make the world more accommodating and understanding.

In general, the goal of people-first language is to provide a constant, persistent reminder that people with disabilities are people first, all while demystifying and removing discomfort from the language of disability. "Sandy has schizophrenia" is much more dignifying and appropriate than "Sandy is a schizophrenic." If you find yourself using a disability as a person's primary identifier, stop yourself and first give them a description that fits better—parent, child, student, friend—who also has a disability.

Avoid language casting disability negatively. Saying that someone "suffers from," is "at risk of," or is a "victim" of a disability indicates that disability is a bad thing to be avoided. Some people with disabilities experience feelings of suffering or loss; others experience disability as a different way of being in the world. It is not for others to label someone else's experience, especially negatively. A disability is one need among many. What do we do with people who have needs? We tell them we love them, and that there is room for all of us at God's table. There is always room.

Keep in mind that language is always evolving. The specific words I have cited here may be outdated in a few years, and we will have to learn new phrases and identifiers. It is completely appropriate to ask someone how they refer to their disability so that you can be sure you are using the right wording. If you hear someone using aggressive or inappropriate language to talk about disabilities, be brave enough to suggest that there is a better way to say what they are trying to say. And if someone corrects your language, thank them and make that change.

One final note about language: I have frequently caught myself, when talking about disability ministry, saying some version of, "Well, when you think about it, everyone has some kind of special need." My intent was to engender empathy and bring equality to the conversation. The problem with this kind of statement, I have learned, is that it can easily discount the barriers to inclusion that people with disabilities experience. Disability often means not belonging. It is our job as ministry leaders to make the church a place where everyone can find belonging.

What Disability Ministry Looks Like

Most ministers want their churches to be more inclusive, more pre-pared, more understanding. The question usually lies in not knowing where to start. I'd like to share some ideas to help a ministry leader start designing and implementing a disability ministry. If you already offer ministry op-portunities to families affected by disability, that's great! You may find some new ideas to incorporate. If this is new territory for you and your church, use this section as a place to develop your mindset for disability ministry and adopt a few first steps on your way to becoming more inclusive.

Grief and Timing

The first thing to consider is the process of receiving a disability diag-nosis. We cannot walk alongside families in the process of acceptance if we do not have some idea of how adapting to a disability happens. Sorrow often accompanies a disability diagnosis, with several possible reasons for this reaction. One is that the bedside manner with which diagnoses are delivered is apologetic. In *Scoot Over and Make Some Room*, Heather Avis bemoans the most common statement doctors make when conveying a diagnosis of Down Syndrome to a pregnant woman: "I'm sorry."[10] When a disability diagnosis is treated as a cause for grief, it causes grief.

Another source of grief that might accompany a disability diagnosis is changed expectations about the future. People receiving a diagnosis en-vision the changes they will have to make to their daily lives. We all have

---

10 Heather Avis, *Scoot Over and Make Some Room* (Grand Rapids, MI: Zondervan, 2019), 105–12.

a specific vision of our future that we are constantly revising and embellishing. A diagnosis—whether learning your parent has cancer, your child has schizophrenia, or you need glasses—serves as an abrupt, surprising challenge to that future. This is not an easy, familiar update. Some may even believe (or be led to believe) that the entire future they had planned for themselves is impossible now.

Yet another source of grief is the fear and anxiety around social barriers to full inclusion and acceptance. Lack of accessible spaces, job discrimination, social isolation, lack of funds for healthcare or medical technology—all of these stressors can overwhelm a family facing a new diagnosis. These challenges would be so much easier to handle if we were more culturally and institutionally affirming of folks with disabilities.

I can say from experience and honest conversations with close friends that it is possible and even common to move past this grief stage into advocacy and hope. Many people figure out how to reconstruct a different but beautiful future for themselves or their children. But because grief is an extremely common part of the initial stage of diagnosis, it is important for ministry leaders to know at what point a diagnosis was received.

A disability can be *congenital*, meaning the person has had the disability since birth, or *acquired* sometime after birth.[11] An acquired disability is sometimes *temporary*. A person with a congenital disability has never known life any other way. Therefore, it would be inappropriate to treat their disability as a form of suffering, a condition to be pitied. It is simply a part of the way that person lives life. However, we may need to be sensitive to how that person's caregivers received the disability diagnosis, knowing that they may or may not have completed their adjustment process.

Someone who acquires a disability later must adjust to new limitations and will likely have some sort of grief process. For example, a teenager who is diagnosed with an eating disorder might have to participate in therapy, follow an eating plan, and possibly receive inpatient care. They also must confront peers, caregivers, and other adults at church—many of

11   Kathleen R. Bogart, Nicole M. Rosa, and Michael L. Slepian, "Born That Way or Became That Way: Stigma toward Congenital versus Acquired Disability," *Group Processes & Intergroup Relations* 22, no. 4 (June 1, 2019): 4, https://doi.org/10.1177/1368430218757897.

whom have opinions about their illness or wellness. The mental, physical, and social changes caused by the diagnosis (which could go on for months or even years) can extend the grief process.

A temporary disability may cause frustration, heightened needs, pain, and loss. An adult who breaks their leg will recover, but in the meantime, they will experience difficulty leaving the house, caring for a family, cooking, and so forth.

I hope this discussion of the timing of a disability diagnosis gives a helpful perspective on walking alongside someone who has received a diagnosis. It is important we acknowledge the changes, challenges, and grief that can accompany a diagnosis, while refraining from casting the disability itself as negative. It is one characteristic among many that make up a person. It is appropriate to talk about disability with the same attitude we adopt toward personality, bodily functions, or physical characteristics. Understanding disability as a neutral or even positive characteristic can help ministry leaders begin removing the barriers to participation that many people with disabilities experience.

Removing Barriers

We begin to find practical ways to serve and support people by identifying the barriers that can keep them away from church life. For adults with disabilities, those barriers include accessibility, bad experiences, and lack of invitation.

Accessibility

Churches have an ethical obligation to provide ways for people with disabilities to enter the building and participate on a basic level. Basic accommodations include installing wheelchair ramps, offering assisted listening devices and large-print bulletins, and ensuring adequate parking spaces for people with disabilities. These are the most simple, obvious ways to open the church to adults with disabilities. They also can be the most expensive. However, considering that 25 percent of American adults live with a disability, we close our doors to a huge number of people if we do not make such accommodations.[12] Perhaps this is a good time to conduct an accessibilty audit.

Attitudes toward Disability

Back in April 2017, a Christian leader sent a request via Twitter to parents of kids with disabilities to share what they wish churches knew about their experiences.[13] People used the hashtag #disabilityinchurch to share their responses. People discussed a plethora of barriers to their full participation, including theological stances that imply that they need to be healed of their disability in order to be spiritual whole or to reflect God's image.

Having worked in the church for ten years, while carrying in my heart people living with all sorts of disabilities, I can tell you one thing: the church has been a source of stress as often as a place of support and belonging. Even well-meaning people who would love to be helpful sometimes fail to understand what support for people with disabilities really looks like. When I bring up my own or a loved one's mental health in conversations, folks often shut down. When a family does not conform to the expectations the church has for other families, it does not just feel different. It feels bad.

For some (or most) of us, it doesn't take very many experiences of rejection or social discomfort for us to avoid those situations altogether. We anticipate it even when it's not even there, so when the slightest twinge of judgment or misunderstanding shows itself, we flash a peace sign and make a quick exit.

Embarrassment and feeling misunderstood lead to secrecy and avoidance. Because we live in a society designed only for people with minds and bodies that function a certain way, people with disabilities and their families are constantly in advocacy mode. Pursuing education, sourcing the right diet, seeking employment, and obtaining appropriate medication and therapy can be real battles. Finding a church can easily feel like one more

---

12   Catherine A. Okoro et al., "Prevalence of Disabilities and Health Care Access by Disability Status and Type Among Adults — United States, 2016," *Morbidity and Mortality Weekly Report* 67, no. 32 (2018): 882–87, https://doi.org/10.15585/mmwr.mm6732a3.
13   Sandra Peoples, "Reflections on the #disablityinchurch Discussion," Key Ministry (blog), accessed October 28, 2019, https://www.keyministry.org/church4every-child/2017/4/27/disability-in-church.

battle, one that there is not enough time, energy, or wherewithal to fight.

How can we remove this barrier to participation? One way is to extend personal invitations and accompany people throughout their church experience. Another way is to talk about disabilities openly and affirmatively. Develop reciprocal relationships with folks you know to have disabilities, including them in committees, worship leadership, and service. Create safe groups for people to share about their lives with one another, knowing they can expect prayer and acceptance. Be sure your ministry spaces are accessible with ramps, wide entryways, soft color tones, and minimalist décor. Most of all, remove the barrier of bad experiences by personally creating good experiences, one person at a time.

Lack of Invitation

The most effective act we can take is that of invitation. While you may contend that your church is not yet set up to welcome anyone with a disability, do not let that stop you! Allow the people who need accommodation to guide the process of providing it. Invite people, then ask them to tell you how to make your church more welcoming to them. Include them in your accessibility audit. Ask for their input and give those ideas a try.

Invitations are powerful, whether they are extended by church staff or church members. Create awareness that adults with disabilities may be even less likely than other adults to do the brave work of forging into an unfamiliar church environment. Encourage church members to issue invitations to anyone they think may need a church family.

Listen and Believe

It astounds me how often I catch myself thinking that I know what is best for the people in my life better than they do. From what I hear from families affected by disability, they encounter this phenomenon almost daily. Disability ministry looks like listening and believing. When we know or suspect that someone has an unmet need, we invite them into conversation about it. We ask how they are, and we really listen to their answer. We ask what they need from the church, and we believe their answers.

A few years ago, a woman approached the executive director of my church to say that she wanted to attend, but she could not handle strong fragrances. Walking into a sanctuary filled with people wearing perfume or cologne was not an option for her. No one on staff at the time had any experience with this kind of disability; it was a first for us. Because we had a leader who was willing to listen and believe a person brave enough to express her needs, we brainstormed ways to help. In the end, we designated the balcony of our chapel, the location of our smallest worship service, as a fragrance-free zone. The balcony steps were right inside the church entrance, so this attendee could proceed directly to the safety of the balcony when she arrived. She could only worship at the 10:05 a.m. service, and she could not sit where most others did, on the main level near the worship leaders, but there was a place for her in worship. We wouldn't win any awards for our response to this need, but at least we were able to listen and believe her.

I'll always remember opening my e-mail one day to read a message from a woman named Shawn. She introduced herself as the mom of Cole, a 3rd-grader with a rare genetic disability called CHARGE Syndrome, which caused him to walk, see, and eat differently than his peers. Shawn said they wanted to visit, and she wanted to be sure we were prepared to welcome Cole. He could easily lose his balance when walking on uneven ground, so an adult would held his hand when walking down our sloped hallway. Cole ate through a feeding tube, so we offered him a book or toy during snack time. Friends, if you receive an e-mail from someone like Shawn, telling you exactly what to expect and asking helpful questions, thank her and the Lord Jesus, and consider what a great honor it is to be able to welcome and serve them. It is not often that an inclusion plan comes together this seamlessly, but when it does, we have the parents to thank for it.

Mainstreaming Versus Segregation

This practice of asking honest questions and believing people's answers is especially critical when working with parents to identify the best experience for their child with a disability. In my experience, the majority of parents advocate for full inclusion for their child, and it is our job to make that happen, if at all possible. Honestly, the only justification I have found to separate a child from the group against a parent's wishes is if the child communicates through aggression and needs some time apart for the safety of the group. If children have difficulty communicating their needs, sometimes they will bite, hit, or kick as a way to say, "Hey! Pay attention—I need some extra help over here." If a child shows aggression at church, often a temporary separation from the group (a couple weeks or months) will give you time to pair that child with a loving adult who can learn to communicate with them and help them re-enter the group comfortably.

When caregivers desire for their child to be a part of the main ministry group, it is tempting to judge them as misguided or unrealistic. I have been there, listening to parents insist that their child be included equally, while I inwardly balked, believing that the child would receive better care and deeper discipleship without the distractions of the whole group. I have seen myself as more objective than the parent, who may not recognize the extent of their child's disability or have an idea of the amount of work I'd need to do to make the group more inclusive. Perhaps you have had this same reaction, too.

I'll say it again: we must listen to and believe parents. They know their child's needs. The more I get to know caregivers of children with disabilities, the more I am convinced that no one perceives or worries over their children's needs more than they do. Ever aware of whether their children are behaving "normally" or "socially," the parents I know tend to overemphasize the extent of their children's disability, not the other way around.

Parents of children with disabilities spend every waking moment advocating for their child. At school, on the playground, with relatives, at the pediatrician's office—all they do is try to make the world a safe and welcoming place for their child. The world we've created is not accepting of differences, which means parents must pave the road for their children to walk on and create the space for them to exist in. After all this uphill battling for the sake of their children, it is not too surprising that many of these parents do not feel up to the task of fighting for their child's place at church. And if they do—if a parent brings a child with a disability to your church—you can bet that they do so with their guard fully up, anticipating that they may meet resistance. Imagine what a relief it can be to a parent in fight-or-flight mode to hear, "There is a place for you and your child here."

The place may not be perfect—it may not even exist yet—but it can. With caregivers' input, who know their child better than we ever will, it can.

It is fully, completely OK not to know how to create the right space for every child who may possibly come through the church entrance. Once we acknowledge our uncertainty, we are able to rely on people with disabilities and their family members to lead us. Ask questions such as, "What would make your church experience better?" or "If you could create the perfect space for your child to worship, what would it look like?" Then do it.

While many parents advocate for their children with disabilities to be included within the larger group, I have worked with some parents who are able to relax and worship more freely if their child is in a separate, safe environment designed with their specific needs in mind. This is not common, but for some families this is an attractive option. If a parent expresses a desire for a safe room (and loving adults) where they can drop off their kid upon arrival and pick them up at departure time, think creatively about how to make that work. I have at times hired staff specifically to care for just one or two children so that their parents can worship for that one hour a week without fear or guilt. You may need to ask the family or other church members to chip in financially to make this arrangement work. You may need to rearrange some rooms.

I cannot help but think of James and Annie, a brother and sister who came to church at their neighbor's invitation. Both children had autism, which meant we had to learn different ways to communicate. James communicated through actions rather than words, with those actions generally tending toward escape and destruction of property. I am laughing as I write this, remembering the time he got ahold of my coffee while I was across the room, looked straight at me, and dumped the full cup into my purse. No one has taught me more about staying attentive than James.

For the mom of James and Annie, being able to drop them off in a safe, separate room where experienced staff and volunteers cared for them was exactly what she needed. We connected with a student pursuing her master's degree in occupational therapy and recruited her as an intern who would care for James and Annie on Sundays. They learned from each other, finding creative ways to share Bible stories and practice communication away from home. We rearranged the room based on which activities the kids enjoyed most, and we put a new childproof system on the door to prevent James's escape attempts. That room where James and Annie played on Sundays became sacred space in our children's ministry, a ministry not just to them and their mom, but to every staff member and volunteer who got to know them as well.

Whether mainstreaming or separating a child or youth with special needs, it is essential from the beginning to set clear expectations with the family. They understand that accommodations for their child affect your budget and volunteer numbers, and it is appropriate to uphold boundaries as long as the intention is to honor their family's needs and be inclusive. One boundary I have insisted upon in the past is for the family to notify me by a certain point in the week if they plan to miss church, thereby freeing staff, budget, or volunteers that week. Of course, sometimes families do not know they will miss church until they are walking out the door that morning and the baby has a diaper blowout or someone (possibly even the parent) has an emotional meltdown. In those cases, we can ask that caregivers text or call us as soon as they are able to let us know their plans.

Once more, the overwhelming preference of both parents and kids with whom I have served in the past has been full inclusion in the primary worship and discipleship groups the church offers. Sometimes inclusion means making changes that affect everyone, such as redesigning the room to be less crowded, switching fluorescent lights for warmer lighting options, or only offering allergen-free snacks. Other times, inclusion means making changes that will only affect one or two people, such as recruiting and training an adult to accompany a child or teen at church, or providing a communication board or feelings chart for one person to use. If the person or their parent has a request or suggestion, try it out! If not, then ask educators, therapists, and friends to give creative suggestions. Be content with an ongoing process of becoming more and more inclusive in ministry. You might not have it all figured out by the first Sunday, but when you look back a few months or years later, you will be able to track the growth of your ministry. The key is listening to families, believing them, and accepting their help in designing ministry for their family.

Hallmarks of Inclusion

In this last section I would like to present some of the hallmarks of inclusion. These are the most disability-friendly ministry elements that churches can offer, and families rarely find them anywhere else. They are sacraments, mentoring, and respite care.

Sacraments

By sacraments, I mean Communion and baptism primarily. But another important sacramental act is anointing with oil. It should not surprise us that two of the highest points of Jesus' ministry—his own baptism and his offering of the Last Supper—are remembered in the most sensitive, stimulating, and open practices thousands of years later. Sacramental acts in the church are the most inclusive worship elements we can offer, because they are sensory rituals.

Sacraments as Sensory Experiences

In Communion, we drink the juice, and smell, touch, and eat the bread. There are pieces for us to hold, to dip, to swallow. Participation is tangible. There are no interpersonal social cues to navigate, no complicated responses, no required attention spans. In many Protestant churches, the liturgy of Communion is itself inclusive, describing the table as "open" and inviting everyone to partake. Further, there is something mystical and innately spiritual about remembering Jesus in this embodied manner. No one understands this sacrament fully, no matter what their abilities are. Communion is an even playing field, a place where everyone is forced to confront their human limitations and express their desire for oneness with God. I contend that the most powerful thing a church can do to become friendlier to people with disabilities is to offer weekly Communion as an expected and cherished part of worship.

Just as Communion appeals to our senses through food, baptism literally coats us in the sensory experience of water. Even though most of us only experience the water of baptism once, sometimes during infancy, the knowledge that we are bound together with baptized believers is the epitome of belonging. Erupting into applause when a person is sprinkled with baptismal water, or immersed in a pool, then raised up, is an act of welcome. We are claiming that person as a part of God's family. In my church, we place a dish of water on a small pedestal in the middle of the aisle so that as people approach the Communion table, they can dip their finger in the water to "remember their baptism and be thankful." My 5-year-old basically splashes his hands into the water, and rather than making the sign of the cross on his forehead as most do, he rubs the water all over his face. That is my idea of sacramental worship.

While anointing with oil is not included as an official sacrament in every denomination, it is an age-old and honored practice that continues to give hope, comfort, and support to anyone who needs it. We keep glass vials filled with generic olive oil at our prayer rails to anoint those who request prayer for physical, spiritual, or mental healing. Prayer is such a slippery, cloudy, formless thing—intangible words spoken into space in a beautiful but also sometimes troubling way. But tracing the sign of the cross with anointing oil gives us a visible, felt marker of prayers for healing or commissioning. Making that mark on someone's body stations the prayer in a time and place, making it real in a sensory way. Like Communion and baptism, anointing is available to all.

Sacraments as Rituals

The first time someone is exposed to any worship practice, it may feel new and strange. That is why sacraments are meant to be performed over and over. With repetition comes familiarity, and with familiarity comes confidence. A person with a disability may hang back the first time or two, but as they observe the unchanging ritual, they can more easily participate with confidence. Most rituals are accompanied by beautiful, invitational language that stays the same time after time. It speaks directly to our hearts and minds, calling us into participation in sacred acts.

In many denominations, the liturgy accompanying sacraments remains largely the same in every church across the country and the world. If I were to take my family to a United Methodist Church in another state or another country, we may find many traditions unfamiliar; but when the liturgy of baptism or Communion begins, we would feel at home. The ritual of the sacraments allows us to form expectations and experience a comfort level that is rarely achieved in daily life.

Every week, our church follows the same plan. The sermon ends, and the pastor begins speaking the same words as before, introducing the bread and the juice as the body and blood of Christ, retelling the story of Jesus, and reminding us that God was, is, and will always be God. We then walk to the front, dip our fingers in baptismal water, and cup our hands to receive bread to dip in juice as someone tells us that this food is Christ's body and blood, broken and poured out *for us.*

Every time there is a baptism, we know the drill. We know that the pastor is going to require us to review our own vows, and we get the privilege of vowing to walk alongside this person in Christian love. The baptism liturgy insists that we take spiritual care of one another. We hear the blessing of the water, observe as the water washes over this new church family member, and cheer as the person is literally brought out into the congregation. When the person being baptized is a baby, the pastor walks the baby down each aisle, presenting the precious child to us and commending them to our care. When the person is an adult, we approach them after worship to hug, high-five, and welcome them. The language, repetition, and renewal of sacraments minister to all and for all. We are never more at one as the body of Christ than when we experience these wide-open sacramental acts together.

Mentoring

For kids and teens with disabilities, mentoring or a one-on-one buddy ministry can be one of the best strategies to ensure they are at once fully included in every area and also receiving all the care they need. In almost every small group of youth and children I have supervised over the years, there has been at least one child who would benefit from personal guidance. Not only can we not expect one leader to manage every request and need from a whole group all by themselves, we cannot expect a youth with a disability to merge into a large group and fulfill all the social and physical expectations of the group without some guidance.

But that guidance should come in the form of a partnership. Introducing a caring, non-judgmental, consistent adult to the family of a child with a disability is a welcoming gesture. I think of these mentors as extended family members, the church relative who takes a child under their wing and becomes a trusted friend. This adult protects the child and helps them interpret the group activities in a way that makes sense while abiding by your church's Safe Sanctuary policies.

For youth, having a one-on-one buddy mentor may not be an appealing choice. Some youth may feel that a dedicated adult makes them stand out in an embarrassing way. If that is the case, you can either a) assign mentors to every person in the youth group to normalize this arrangement, or b) position an adult as a hands-off buddy for any youth who needs extra care. Introduce this adult as an ombudsman, a person available to anyone in the group who needs a confidential listener, someone to pray with them, or someone who can answer questions. This adult is never given the task of leading the Bible study or organizing the activity; they are constantly available in the background for anyone who needs them. And they can have their eyes peeled for any youth with disabilities who may find themselves on the outside looking in.

Mentoring ministry is for everyone! The thought of pairing young people with unrelated adults in the congregation can be overwhelming at first, true. But what a great image of what the church should be, to see adults dedicating themselves to the interests of young people.

Respite Care

Respite care is free or low-cost care for children, youth, and vulnerable adults with disabilities so that their caregivers can take a break. Usually respite care happens on a monthly or bi-monthly basis for 4-6 hours at a time—enough time for a weary parent to take a good nap or go on a date. A simple online search will lead you to multiple organizations that provide training and materials to get started. Or you can reach out to a professional in your community to lend their expertise and do it yourself.

Respite care must be undertaken only after careful education and planning. It only works with a 1:1 or 1:2 ratio of adults to participants, and it requires detailed knowledge of the needs and expectations of the families who will participate. Start with just a few families within the church, and let them weigh in about activities, timing, and plans. If that works for the first few times, consider opening respite care to the community. It may be one of the best ways to share God's love with a whole world of people out there who find the church unwelcoming, overwhelming, or impossible.

Final Thoughts

I hope this chapter has stirred in you some passion and confidence for making your ministry area fully inclusive, meaning that you see the image of God in every person and seek reciprocal relationships with everyone in your church. Disability ministry simply requires that we pursue mutuality with all members of our church family. The church operates through a unity of differences, not a select few staff and leaders providing a service for those who attend. Disability ministry brings this dynamic into full view. You can learn more from the Disability Ministries Committee of The UMC at *umcdmc.org*.

No one has done this better than Jesus did. Sometimes he responded to people's requests (pleas) for healing; other times he initiated physical healing unasked. My heart has tumbled and twisted, trying to figure out why Jesus would provide healing to so many, but not give us, today, that same ability. My dear friend, Patrick, a pastor, scholar, person with epilepsy and hearing loss, and father of Asher who has Down Syndrome, has listened to my aggrieved questioning. Patrick told me that in Jesus' world, healing was about restoring people to community. Healing gave people a place of belonging, and removed the injunction for isolation.

We can do that. We may not be able to offer physical healing—and honestly, some of us with disabilities wouldn't want it anyway—but we can offer something much more essential to life: Welcome. Belonging. Inclusion. A place. If we have done all we can to ensure everyone has a place at the table, in the pew, in the pulpit, in the Bible study, in the vacation Bible school—then we have done what Jesus did.

CHAPTER 9

CURRICULUM & MINISTRY DESIGN

It was the first Sunday of a new school year. My 22 Sunday school teachers for grades kindergarten through 5th were about to meet with their groups and begin learning together. I walked up and down the hall, looking in and making sure everyone had what they needed.

My joyful calm was disturbed when a teacher emerged from her classroom to ask, "Um, how exactly do you want me to make the story for today child-friendly?" To my shame, I had to admit I did not even know what the story was for that day—yes, I had reviewed this curriculum in-depth and chosen it for the many excellent features that it offered. But I had neglected to look at that first lesson. On the very first day of the fall quarter, our brand-new curriculum told the children the story of Athaliah, the queen who murdered her whole family and would have killed her grandson if he had not been hidden from her (2 Kings 11:1-21). Oops. Sorry, children.

I have a love/hate relationship with curriculum. While I know there are many great curriculum options out there, I have learned that they all come with drawbacks as well. Curriculum in the hands of a seasoned teacher can be a helpful tool. In the hands of an inexperienced or unconfident leader, it can be a hindrance to effective ministry.

This chapter offers a guide for selecting and adapting curriculum for your unique setting and making sure you are implementing a process rather than relying solely on a curriculum. The chapter also covers ministry design as a whole, from Sunday small groups to worship environments. But first, let's discuss some points we frequently misunderstand when it comes to curriculum.

Common Misconceptions

The first misconception is that curriculum *is* our ministry, or that curriculum *does* our ministry for us. This is simply untrue. Rather, curriculum is a *tool* for ministry, and it is only one of many tools we can use to reach our goals. It is so incredibly easy to allow a curriculum to dictate the goals, mission, and theme of our ministry areas. When I hear church staff identify with a curriculum when they describe their ministry area, I know the curriculum has taken over, and the church has defaulted to that identity. Curricula today are graphically pleasing, and like a greeting card, they express our heart's desires better than we feel we could on our own. Curriculum can bring God's Word to life in ways we never imagined. The people who write and illustrate today's curricula are well-educated in human development, religious education, Scripture, and so forth—how can we compete with that?

Yet, curriculum can hamper relationship-building if we are not careful. An unskilled leader can be tempted to rely too heavily on the curriculum, reading from a script, and pushing play on a video without leaving room for discussion, spontaneity, and spiritual connection. Small groups for all ages must involve the participants in the creation of the ministry—there must be room for sharing, discussion, prayer, and speaking truth to one another.

Curriculum also can be too focused on education rather than spiritual formation. The purpose of church is not to teach; it is to worship God. While it stands to reason that the ministry we have often referred to as "Sunday school" would come complete with lesson plans, it is important not to lose sight of the real goal.

The major misstep in curriculum use is when we choose a curriculum that looks flashy and consider our work to be done. Curriculum alone does not lead anyone to Jesus—only people can do that. And curriculum is most effective when placed in the hands of a leader who understands how to adapt it for their own context and goals. We will discuss how to train volunteers in the best use of curriculum both in this chapter and in the following chapter on working with volunteers.

Curriculum Selection

I began my first full-time ministry job as a Director of Children's Ministries for a 3,000-member church at the age of 25. After just a few weeks, the volunteers in my ministry made it clear that they were dissatisfied with the curriculum they were using, so I embarked on a research venture to find a replacement. I searched all the publishers' catalogs, made a chart, compared expenses, and landed on a curriculum I was really excited about. I debuted it to the teachers over the summer, and we started using it that fall. By spring, the bloom was off the rose. I looked again, chose a different curriculum, paid thousands of dollars, and tried again. In five years, I chose and trained teachers on as many new curricula. My strategy wasn't working.

Here is a better strategy, based on a few more years of experience and familiarity with the options that are available. When you are tasked with finding a new curriculum for your ministry, whether for children, youth, or adults, there is a process you can follow to ensure the curriculum you receive could work in your context.

Know Your Context

1. **Define your audience:** What age group/developmental stage is this curriculum for? Seek curriculum pertinent to only those ages and stages. Consider how many people will be in each group—activities that will work for 20 people may not translate to a group of five.

2. **Set your budget:** Know what you are willing to spend before looking at prices. Consider the props, craft supplies, snacks, teacher appreciation gifts, and other expenses this group will require.

3. **Set the goal:** Is this group meeting for the goal of fellowship,

accountability, Bible study/knowledge, evangelism, or training?

4. **Consider your volunteers:** How much time do your recruited leaders have for lesson planning? Do you have a slate of veteran Sunday school teachers, or do these newer volunteers need more guidance? If your curriculum is not a good fit for the leaders who will use it, it won't work, no matter how good it is.

Know Your Theology

Each publishing house offers biblical interpretation based upon its understanding of theology and Scripture, and you can bet those beliefs become apparent in curriculum for all ages. While just about any theological background can be adapted for any setting, using a curriculum that does not align with your church's beliefs simply requires more work and training to make those edits. Find out the theology of your denomination and the belief system espoused by publishers. Factor in the time and effort needed to edit conflicting theology before choosing a curriculum from a publisher with which you disagree.

To discern how well a curriculum aligns with your church's theology, look for its treatment of key stories, such as the story of Adam and Eve or the Crucifixion and Resurrection. These basic stories are generally covered in curriculum for all ages. Reading the lesson plans on these passages with a critical eye will tell you more about a curriculum's theological bent than just reading the company's statement of faith on its web site.

Know the Features of High-Quality Curricula

In addition to knowing your audience and your theology, there are a few design features to look for when seeking quality curriculum.

- **Representation:** All good curriculum represents both men and women, people of all races, and people with disabilities. If the curriculum includes photos of modern-day people, be sure no one is left out of those representations.

- **Accurate depictions of Bible characters:** In your curriculum, if Jesus appears a white American hipster, your kids will only see a whitewashed savior who fits into our small-world narrative. Show

Jesus, Mary, and Moses as they truly were—Jewish Palestinians.

- **Multiple options:** Good curriculum writers understand that every teacher and class will need different things. Look for curriculum that offers you many different ways to apply the message—a low-cost craft, games, creative prayer methods, journaling, activity centers, rituals, discussion questions, and so forth.

- **Consistency:** Look for a curriculum that follows the same pattern every week. As much as kids love excitement and surprises, the most accommodating and welcoming curriculum leads kids through a consistent protocol each week. The kids can learn the system and can anticipate what is coming next. Kids benefit from routine.

- **Low preparation:** Despite our best intentions, prepping a weeknight Bible study or Sunday school lesson usually gets crammed into the five hours leading up to the event. Most of us just do not have time to memorize a script every week, and we should not ask that of our volunteers either. Look for a curriculum that respects your leaders' time and can be easily implemented at a glance.

- **Discussion questions:** Especially when seeking curriculum for youth and adults, discussion questions are the most important tool! Look for open-ended, challenging, relevant questions that will spark discussion and direct participants back to Scripture.

One thing *not* to look too hard for is flashy videos or graphics. Kids may love the videos, but I am not convinced that they are growing in their faith because of the countdown clock on the slide show. Graphics are great—if you can find stellar content and structure that is supported by fantastic videos and graphic design, all the better! But choose content over style every time.

These are just a few basic signs to look for when selecting curriculum. Once you have made the choice, the fun is just beginning! The next mission, should you choose to accept it, is to figure out how to adapt and use the curriculum for your own church context.

Using Curriculum

I have yet to find a curriculum that can be plugged in and allowed to run word-for-word in any context. We all have to adapt our curriculum to fit our context, including factors such as group size, age, activity level, purpose, and leadership. The smaller your group, the more you can customize the curriculum to fit their exact specifications. A small group of five high schoolers can pick and choose the discussion questions and activities, and really get the most out of them, while a large group of the same age has to go more by the book and not dwell too long on any particular point.

If you are the teacher of the curriculum, this is an easy process. Simply look over each lesson plan in advance, decide which features you like the best, and put those into your own words. If you are training or supervising the teachers, you've got a whole other layer of difficulty to breach. Now you must both familiarize yourself with the curriculum *and* teach other people how to customize it for themselves.

Just as when you selected curriculum, your first glance over the lesson should reveal any theological nuances you want to handle. Then look for the basic elements of a small-group discipleship time: read the Bible passage, seek to understand it (discussion, activity, craft, project, video), then seek to apply it (prayer, discussion, commitments, take-homes).

Ministry Design

Throughout this curriculum conversation, I have referred to small-group and large-group environments. Family ministry is often equated with Sunday school. But family ministry takes place in many other environments as well, which is why Sunday school curriculum should not eclipse our vision for family ministry. The remainder of the chapter reviews best practices for creating an integrated ministry vision across various ministry environments, from Sunday school to youth group to special events.

Main Worship Gathering

Anyone caught reading this book, whether or not they realized it, is now henceforth anointed to be a champion of intergenerational inclusion.

The church is moving toward a model of more accessible worship. For years we have considered noise and interruptions to have no place in the sanctuary. Continuing to uphold that misunderstanding of biblical worship will leave our churches dying on the vine. The cutting edge of ministry requires us to include crying babies, fidgety kids, checked-out youth, overcommitted parents, and aging grandparents in our times of worship. Every time we design a worship service, we must ask the same question: *Whom are we leaving out? Which person does this plan not account for?*

Traditional worship is tailored for the needs of adults between the ages of 30 and 60, with the hope that other generations come and keep quiet. That time is over—now we must be willing to make sacrifices to include every generation. God calls everyone to worship, not just the folks in their prime earning and charitable giving years.

Worship for the Youngest Generation

There is a raging, ongoing debate about how best to meet the needs of children in worship. Many of my colleagues have made strong arguments for including our younger children in sanctuary worship, without offering a separate children's worship time. This argument speaks to me, and I see great beauty in it. If a church is willing to do the hard work of making the leadership, music, sermon, and rituals of worship developmentally inclusive of children, I cannot fault them too much for offering no children's worship alternative.

However, when I can I urge churches to offer separate worship options for children through 3rd grade, for the sake of hospitality. Of course, children should be welcomed in *any and all* of our worship environments, and making children's worship an *option* does not let us off the hook from designing inclusive sanctuary worship. However, I advocate for the option of creating intentionally child-friendly environments as a corollary of sanctuary worship. The guest families who visit for the first time and the parents who volunteer in worship leadership deserve the option to commit their kids to the care of loving volunteers dedicated to their well-being.

The worship options for babies, preschoolers, and elementary ages should be presented as extensions of whole-community worship. Avoid words such as "dismissed" and "their own time" to talk about worship for kids. Bless families who participate in that ministry as well as those who stay together during church. To each their own.

By the time a child reaches later elementary years, they can be expected to participate in whole-church worship events. It is important for preteens to rub shoulders with older youth and adults in the congregation and to see their own family members worshiping God. These impressionable years are really wonderful opportunities for them to hear a pastor preach God's Word to them, to see a parent pray at the altar, and even to pass notes to a friend in the pew. Recruit these young and willing leaders into the roles of worship leader, musician, Scripture reader, usher, greeter, sound board operator, buddy to a younger child or older adult, and so forth.

Worship for the Middle Generation

Not many ministry areas can combine youth and adults together seamlessly, but whole-community worship can. Besides the obvious strategies of making sermons, songs, and illustrations accessible to this combined age group, there is one significant practice that we sometimes overlook when designing worship for youth and adults: involve them.

While some people need to be allowed simply to come sit in a chair, listen in silence, and leave through a side door, everyone should be invited to participate in the planning and leadership of worship. While it does not have to be a requirement or expectation, everyone should know that they are welcome to step behind the curtain, that there is a place for them in the room where decisions are made. One Sunday's attendance is sufficient for me to invite someone to distribute bulletins the next week, stand at the coffee table, or pass an offering plate. By inviting folks to serve right from the get-go, you communicate that there is a place for them at every level of church participation. Your church is not a cruise ship where the staff keep things sailing, but an aircraft carrier where everyone has a role to play.

The executive director of a church I once served in had previously owned and run several restaurants. She told me that when it was time to update or redecorate the restaurant space, she did not just talk to interior designers or corporate bigwigs. She called meetings with the wait staff, the folks with boots on the ground and skin in the game, and asked them what they needed. What worked about their point-of-sale system, and what didn't? What were they always having to replace, what did they consistently run out of, what was not working? She never assumed that anyone else could intuit what they needed; she involved them in the design process. We need to do the same in our churches. Our youth and adults are necessary stakeholders in our worship environments. Ask them what is working, and what is not—and make them a part of the solutions.

Worship for the Older Generation

If I have learned one thing through my partnerships with older adults, it is that we younger folks should not make assumptions about them. While it is true that aging is sometimes accompanied by new needs for accommodation, our senior citizens should be allowed to decide their own capacity for and interest in leadership. The biggest rule about working with older adults is: don't assume anything.

For those who serve aging congregations, make accommodations available such as hearing devices, large-print bulletins, and spacious pews and aisles. Let everyone know those tools are available, and allow them to opt in to using them if they prefer.

Worship planning teams should include members young and old. Sermon illustrations that will get a great laugh from young adults may need to be scrapped in favor of jokes everyone can relate to. Speak and preach to all ages from the pulpit. We do ourselves and our church a huge disservice if we discount the contributions and needs of our older generation.

My personal favorite vignette of what God's family can look like is someone over the age of 60 worshipping alongside someone under the age of 20. Pair up those youngsters with older and wiser mentors every chance you get. Invite older adults to pray for young people and vice versa. Ask older adults to share their testimonies and stories from the front whenever you have a chance. Thank God for every generation represented in your worship space every week.

Once you have designed this magical corporate worship environment that is fully intergenerational, it is time to tackle the discipleship ministries that typically take place in smaller groups. This is the context in which curriculum can be a very helpful tool.

Discipleship Groups

Discipleship is the process of becoming more like Jesus, sometimes through private, personal prayer and study, and often through relationships with others who also desire to grow in their faith. The church is the best context to connect people of faith to one another and support their mutual growth. Discipleship groups for all ages promote relationships between individuals to discuss, model, and pray about their faith lives.

By the time a child is in 4th grade, they need to begin experiencing peer-based faith groups. We honestly do not need to wonder if they are ready—they will let us know! It is common in my ministry for 4th- and 5th-graders to see their parents or older youth enjoying the benefits of a small group or Bible study, and to develop their own plan for such a group with their peers. If I do not provide a small group for them, they will often create one themselves! This is one of the purest, most endearing, and deserving ways that our preteens begin to "act like adults." Groups for all ages are appropriate; discipleship groups for ages 4th grade and up are necessary.

It is here, in this conversation about discipleship contexts for all ages, that an old battle continues to rage on: children's ministry versus childcare. In the perception of some pastors, parents, and other church folks, worship and small groups for adults are the real work of the church, and children's ministry is simply a means to achieve adult ministry. We often congratulate ourselves with feel-good declarations like, "Children are the future of the church!" while we stow them away in a separate building or wing, and proceed to pour our time, money, and staffing into ministries for adults. So many children and youth ministry job descriptions read as if we expect Mary Poppins to apply—run Sunday school and kids' worship, maintain the supply closet, recruit and train volunteers, provide childcare for events, keep check-in running smoothly, don't go over budget, and don't work more than 10 hours a week. These kinds of staff roles are indicative of a desire for children to be seen and not heard in church, except for maybe a choral performance in worship a couple times a year.

Children are the *present* of the church. Raising our children to love and serve God is the calling of every member of the worshiping church. The groups designed for children and youth deserve equal or greater budgeting, leadership quality, and planning as the adult groups. When designing a small-group ministry to meet the needs of all ages, shortchanging children and youth in any way is an indictment of our family ministry philosophy.

Know that I am not talking about childcare for one-off events or the Tuesday morning women's Bible study group. There are times when providing simple, quality childcare for an adult meeting is appropriate. But our regular, primary worship and discipleship gatherings should be designed with the least powerful members in mind—children, youth, and sometimes senior adults or members with disabilities—and the offerings for parents and other adults will fall in line on their own. Trust me.

Best Practices for Special Events

Unlike most family ministers out there, I am the world's worst at event planning. I would so much rather counsel a frustrated parent, write a Sunday school lesson, or even attend a staff meeting than do the work of event planning. This is why I surround myself with folks who are incredible at pulling off events—those people with genes for creativity, vision, details, task-lists, deadlines, and decorations. The following are a few lessons those people have taught me about planning events.

First, special events are important. This is a begrudging admission for me, but I have been convinced. Special events offer one of the best opportunities for us timid church folk to extend an invitation to someone not in a church to be touched by the church. Special events become meaningful traditions when repeated at the same general time and in the same general way. A vacation Bible school or churchwide Thanksgiving dinner work their way into our faith stories as we grow older, reminding us of the feasting and celebration of God's people when they gather together in abundance. Kids who grow up attending Jesus' birthday party every December become parents who choose a church based on whether or not that church offers a similar event. Special events, when done well and repeated consistently, serve as celebratory mile markers on our faith journeys.

But they are so much work, money, and time! Following are some of my own best practices to make event planning easier and more successful:

- **Set a goal**—Keep the main thing the main thing. Decide what you hope to accomplish through the event, and plan accordingly. Some events serve as seasonal or nostalgic family celebrations, safe places where families can connect with other families and enjoy time together, like a churchwide movie night or an egg hunt. Other events may be intended to evangelize, to bring people through your doors you otherwise wouldn't meet. When making decisions about food, decorations, and other details, keep this goal in mind.

- **Justify it**—Once you set your goal, or as you are setting it, factor the event into the overall mission of the church. Acknowledge the time, energy, and money the event will cost the church, and be sure you can defend those expenditures for the sake of the mission. Most family ministers have an unending list of worthwhile ministries and projects that demand their time. Do not let event planning hijack your mission. If the event cost is not justifiable, consider changing or removing the event from the calendar—but do this carefully! I speak from experience when I say that making a decision alone to cancel a calendar event without proper communication and support will backfire on you. If you are having trouble justifying an event (or three), talk to your supervisor and to ministry participants to ask them how to help you change it.

- **Create a timeline**—For every big event on your calendar, create a timeline. Start with the event date itself and work your way backward, setting deadlines for every single task along the way. Clearly identify who is responsible for each task on the timeline, and refer to it at least weekly to be sure every important detail is being checked off.

- **Establish setup and cleanup teams**—leaving setup and cleanup tasks to yourself is the number-one cause of burnout and resentment during event planning. I am the queen of this. I have pulled off a plethora of outstanding events for which I decorated every table, created every stage piece, and cleaned every crumb off the carpet afterward. This is just wrong, folks. Our time as family ministry leaders is too valuable to be spent in lonely, privately resentful painting, decorating, and organizing projects. These are the tasks that *anyone* can help with, and our churches are full of people who will gladly lend an hour on event day to set up or tear down. Recruit folks to do this with you. Or even better, without you!

- **Recruit a coordinator**—If you, like me, become stressed by details and long to-do lists, find someone who is the opposite of you and convince them to coordinate the event for you. Once you have an event coordinator, give them all the details and support they need to be successful. Provide a clear budget, and either give them the funding to make purchases or work out another easy way for them to buy supplies. Connect them with vendors and volunteers who can assist them. Show them photos of past events so they have an idea of what you are looking for. Meet with them as often as they need to answer questions. And when they come to you with grand new ideas to make the event better, grin, high-five them, and assure them that there will be extra jewels in their heavenly crowns for the ministry they are doing on your behalf.

- **Pay attention to details**—Record every detail. Do not keep event details in your head. Have a backup plan for your backup plan. Itemize every task related to communication, marketing, food, supplies, volunteers, budget, recruiting, documenting, and evaluation. Put all of this in a folder and refer to it next time.

My last snippet of advice for offering quality special events in the church is to practice a peaceful presence. At some point in any big event, someone is going to approach you with some kind of emotion and a problem to solve. Our job is to recycle panic into peace. Practice phrases in front of the mirror, like, "Got it! We can totally handle that," and "I am so glad you caught this. No problem, let's talk." Event volunteers will need a pastoral presence. They are giving of themselves, sometimes in truly sacrificial ways, and any anxiety they bring to the table comes from a place of caring and devotion to serving well. During events, the role of ministry leaders is to calm, comfort, support, and express gratitude. On repeat.

Final Thoughts

Curriculum and ministry design are the building blocks of our ministry, and unless we are careful about our philosophy and theology, they can present some rather dangerous pitfalls. The way we set up our ministry and the curriculum we offer affects people's lives, and part of our required preparation for ministry is to be sure we understand how to use these tools. Whether you have used the same curriculum for 20 years or are using something new, you should have confidence that you are using it effectively. Whether you are designing your worship and small groups from scratch for a church plant or inheriting a long tradition of doing things a certain way, you are the best person to determine needs and meet them wisely. That said, pastors, colleagues, parents, and volunteers are in this with us. We may be the best ones to propose change, but we absolutely must not do it in isolation. We will talk more about this in the next chapter where we exult over volunteers—the arms and legs of the church body.

CHAPTER 10

VOLUNTEERS

While I have quite a few favorite volunteers, Ms. Ann is a standout in my memory. Ms. Ann taught theology at a Catholic high school for girls for several years and attended an adult Sunday school class at our church. She loved Scripture, and if you weren't careful, you easily could get stuck for thirty minutes listening to her explain the differences between the two accounts of the Ten Commandments or the cultural connections between the Old and New Testaments. Ms. Ann referred to herself frequently as a "dinosaur," meaning she eschewed electronic communication. If you wanted to communicate with her, you could call her flip phone or send her a letter in the mail. For the two years she volunteered in children's ministry for me, I printed each week's Sunday school teacher blog post and literally sent it through the postal service to her house.

Within five minutes of meeting Ann, I pegged her as the perfect person to teach our annual Bible basics class for the 2nd-graders who had just completed their Bible milestone. I provided her with curriculum, which she graciously accepted, then, I'm pretty sure, chucked into a drawer and forgot about. She distributed printed outlines to our 2nd-graders, then walked them through her lesson plan with the affect of a college professor.

Somehow, it worked. The children adored Ms. Ann. It may have had something to do with her special affinity for kids with differences. Within two seconds, she could pinpoint what she called "problem children," then proceed to lavish so much attention, praise, and affection on them that they became her loyal subjects. I could walk down a row of classrooms on Sundays, watching leaders trying to convince 6th-graders to contribute something to the discussion, or attempt to pry 4th-graders off the walls, only to get to Ann's classroom to see 25 2nd-graders sitting in their chairs, watching her write Hebrew words on the dry-erase board and politely raising their hands to guess the meanings. You can't make up this stuff.

Volunteers Are Everything

Who runs the church? Volunteers. The people of the church. They are the ones who do the ministry. The job of church staff is simply to support them from start to finish in ministry efforts. It is natural for a new staff member to spend the first year on the job simply acclimating and figuring out who the key players are. New children's leaders tend to run the children's worship time from the front every week, while new youth leaders almost certainly find themselves preparing, then leading weekly large-group and small-group times. Uninitiated family ministers can expect to spend a year with their irons in every fire, leading both from before and behind. This period gives ministry staff the opportunity to demonstrate how they want the ministry to run and to prove themselves trustworthy to current and potential volunteers.

But once that initial time of taking over runs out, it is time to start pulling others into all of those roles. A healthy, mature pastor or church staff person will work themselves out of a job. The goal of staff should be to supervise several ministry areas without having to attend every meeting or know every plan, because trusted volunteers have stepped into leadership roles and developed their own skills in those areas.

This is a long process—one full of recruiting, training, empowering, retraining, listening, and supporting. But if you find yourself on the church payroll, or if you identify as the primary leader for an entire age group, that means your congregation is actually much smaller than the number of folks who attend your church. Your congregation is the set of volunteers who lead different ministry teams for you.[1] A paid children's pastor is not truly the pastor to the children; he or she is the pastor to the children's worship leaders, the Sunday school teachers, the VBS director, and the nursery staff. Of course, we should and do develop relationships with the people in our ministries, both parents and family members, and we often find ourselves subbing at the last minute for a leader who couldn't make it. I don't mean to say we exclude anyone from our ministry circle. It's just that the volunteers who take on high-commitment roles often develop closer pastoral relationships with us than with the person who stands in the pulpit on Sunday mornings. And it is a great privilege and joy for us to pastor them however we can.

The best practice I can encourage for church leaders wishing to develop volunteers is to enact partnership expectations with everyone. In the church I serve now, there is an expectation that if you attend more than two weeks, you are fair game! If you're here, you're serving. Every week, we quickly tap five random people to serve Communion at the end of the worship service. It is my goal to pinpoint new attendees as often as possible to place them in this role. My friend, Brian, jokes that he brought his family to our church one summer Sunday, was greeted by name the next week, and was a member of the hospitality team the third week (a perfect early volunteer role, without direct supervision of children or youth). He is now on staff. In an atmosphere of reciprocity, recruiting volunteers is a joy. If you can create an expectation of serving in your church, then finding volunteers becomes a puzzle that you enjoy putting together each week/month/year. Let's go over some strategies for recruiting.

Recruitment Strategies

I am going to guess that recruiting volunteers is one of the top stressors of leaders in children's and youth ministry. We talk about this all the time—the gratitude we feel for the amazing person who has taught our middle school boys for the past 15 years straight, as well as the hair-pulling

---

1   Walter W. Wymer, "Strategic Marketing of Church Volunteers," *Journal of Ministry Marketing & Management* 4, no. 1 (April 8, 1998): 1–11, https://doi.org/10.1300/J093v04n01_01.

frustration of having absolutely no one to teach the kindergarten group on Sunday mornings. Ministries have shuttered over the lack of volunteer leaders, and in many cases, I think that's probably for the best—if the people of the church are not invested in making the ministry happen, we should listen to their voices (or lack thereof) and let things die a natural death.

But with the right approach, I honestly believe that recruiting volunteers can be one of our favorite parts of ministry. It will always require work, communication, thoughtfulness, and planning—which is to say, it's not effortless—but it is totally possible to feel successful and fulfilled by it. Volunteer recruiting does not have to cause the worry and stress that it sometimes does.

Personal Ask

The first and most important approach to recruiting volunteers is to make personal requests of people. Expecting church members to read our minds and take the initiative to fill the holes in ministry is unreasonable. It's the equivalent of the person who wants their friend or spouse to know what they want without having to say it. I get that—the first few years of my marriage were a painful exercise in learning that stating my needs does not, in fact, take all the romance out of having them met.

For one thing, our standards for working with children, youth, and vulnerable adults should be quite high. It is seldom appropriate to advertise in worship or public opportunities to work with these demographics, where we can be reasonably certain not everyone would qualify. Recruiting is more like matchmaking than a marketing campaign. We want to pinpoint who the perfect person would be to fill the ministry role that is available.[2] Our high standards for volunteers with children and youth are another reason I reject parent and caregiver rotation models. Not all people who care for children in their home should have a place caring for them in the church, while many people who do not have children at home make ideal leaders of children and youth in the church. Additionally, senior

---

2   Walter W. Wymer and Becky J. Starnes, "Conceptual Foundations and Practical Guidelines for Recruiting Volunteers to Serve in Local Nonprofit Organizations: Part I," *Journal of Nonprofit & Public Sector Marketing* 9, no. 1–2 (January 10, 2001): 63–96, https://doi.org/10.1300/J054v09n01_05.

citizens are often the absolute best volunteers in the church and should not be overlooked as wonderful potential leaders for kids.[3]

One year, about six months before vacation Bible school, I found myself without a director. Full of anxiety with a side of desperation, I went to my supervisor for guidance, throwing out names of people I thought I might convince to say "yes." He steered me in a different direction by asking the question, "If you could have anyone in the world perform this role, whom would you pick? Who is the best VBS leader you can think of?" Immediately, one of my best and most respected friends came to mind, but she lives an incredibly busy life and is in high demand. When I verbalized this, he said I would be foolish not to go for my first choice. It was at least worth an ask.

Shooting for the stars on this volunteer ask must have been divinely directed. My friend amazed me by agreeing, and she recruited an assistant who partnered with her to create the best VBS I have ever been a part of. The spiritual depth of our planning times and the friendships we curated between ourselves changed our lives. Additionally, that was the year that I spent the majority of VBS week coordinating with the Department of Health and Family Services to intervene in a domestic abuse situation. I was largely unavailable to the 400 kids in attendance and the dozens of volunteers leading them, since I was caught up in documentation, meetings, and caregiving. Without this overqualified, all-star VBS leadership team, I could not have abandoned my regular duties to serve this family in crisis.

I learned from that experience to approach volunteer requests individually and to aim for the absolute best. So when recruiting volunteers to go on a youth mission trip, teach Sunday small groups, mentor a confirmation student, or join the team providing respite care, consider the qualities most needed for those positions. Make a list of qualities, much as you would when completing a dating profile. You may be looking for:

- Experience
- Patience
- Confidence

---

3   Nancy L. Macduff, "Managing Older Volunteers: Implications for Faith-Based Organizations," *Journal of Religious Gerontology* 16, no. 1–2 (January 3, 2004): 107–22, https://doi.org/10.1300/J078v16n01_07.

- Organizational skill
- Outgoing personality
- Contemplative personality
- Reliability
- Love of a certain age group
- Bible knowledge
- Parenting skills
- Expertise in a particular area

The list could go on. Decide what qualities are most needed, then make a prioritized list of the folks who possess those qualities. Start making personal asks, beginning with the person at the top of the list.

When you talk to a potential volunteer, it is crucial to tell them why you are asking them specifically. This is where you can make the ask personal, based on the work you have already done. Explain the needs of the position, the characteristics that will be most helpful for a leader in that position, and how you have seen them display those characteristics in the past. Volunteers should feel seen and known, because if they do, they will see your ask as an invitation to live out their call from God.

Next, go into detail about what specifically you are asking them to do. Outline the expectations for frequency of serving and job responsibilities, giving a clear picture of what you hope they will agree to.[4] It is helpful to know what resources, budget, and curriculum they will have at their disposal, the exact times and frequency they will be expected to serve, how many participants they will lead, who their partner will be, and so forth. We can't dangle a vague job description in front of a potential leader and expect them to sign on.

I recruit volunteers in person, over e-mail, through text, and by phone. There is not just one method that I either use or avoid, because I try to reach out to volunteers in the way that is most comfortable for them. With folks who tend to call me with their questions, or folks who I know will have no problem responding on the spot, I like to use the phone. It's really, really fun to spend a solid minute telling a person the goodness I have seen in them that would make them a great candidate for a serving position.

4   Jennifer Hoffman and Edward Miller, "Engaging with Volunteers," *NonProfit Times* 32, no. 9 (September 2018): 14.

However, many of my volunteers have a tough time saying "no" to me or processing an ask on the spot. For them, I usually send an e-mail and give them a deadline to let me know their decision. I rarely or never ask a first-time volunteer via text—texts are for the person who has subbed for you 20 times before and will definitely step in if they can.

When They Say "No"...

In spite of our meticulous planning and perfect sales pitch, volunteers will sometimes decline. This response is perfectly acceptable, as they know their limits and strengths better than we do. After graciously accepting a decline, there are two follow-up options for you to choose from:

1. Ask if they will serve as a substitute leader or other team position. If they cannot commit to being in a primary leadership role, perhaps they would be willing to serve occasionally when regular leaders are unavailable, or they might participate in planning meetings but not in implementation. Lower the ask, and hit them again!

2. The other option is to ask them where else in the church they see themselves serving. If the person you asked indicates that they prefer to avoid the age group you asked them to lead, or they do not feel equipped to lead in that ministry area, don't assume this is a "no" to everything. God has gifted everyone to serve in some way, and the church offers myriad diverse serving opportunities. Help your other ministry colleagues by suggesting alternative ministry areas. If they do not want to do Sunday morning small groups, perhaps they'd be willing to sit on the board of trustees? If going on a mission trip isn't feasible for them, would helping with the landscaping and grounds crew or reading Scripture in a worship service be more their style? Make it clear that just as there is a place in the pew for everyone in the church, there is a place of service for everyone as well.

You may be shot down multiple times, and that is perfectly OK. The person you are talking to will never doubt that you care about them, that you have noticed them, and that there is a place for them to serve when they are ready and able. Recruiting volunteers is a pastoral ministry, an opportunity to assess someone's spiritual state, pray with them, and encourage them to keep the faith.

My Secret Recruiting Passcodes

I can often find palatable or even uplifting language to package difficult asks so that the person hearing it sees it as a compliment. For those of you who find this helpful, following are some approaches/phrases I often use when recruiting a volunteer. Please make them your own!

- "I have a big ask to make of you. Let me share some of the details of the position, then you can ask me any questions you have."
- "For several weeks, I have been praying and thinking about the best person to lead (insert ministry area), and you come to my mind every time."
- "It is not lost on me that you are in high demand already. I am convinced that you are the best person to lead this area for our church, so I would be crazy not to at least ask!"
- "Of course, if you need to tell me 'no' right now, do not worry—I will gladly wait and ask you again next year."
- "Your background in (fill in the blank) would be the perfect addition to this team."
- "Over the past few weeks, I have observed you doing ministry already without being asked. (Share a specific example.) That is exactly the kind of action I am looking for in a leader for (insert ministry area). Would you be interested in talking more?"

Whenever possible, I spend quality one-on-one time with a volunteer only after they have expressed interest in the position. I do not take people out for coffee to make the ask; that can blow through a budget quickly and also make for some very short or awkward get-togethers. Instead, I try to schedule personal time to give more details to an interested person or talk through their training and go over specifics. You want to demonstrate to your volunteers that you care about them personally, that you're available going forward, and that you want to set them up for success.[5]

---

5   Rebecca Nesbit, Robert K. Christensen, and Jeffrey L. Brudney, "The Limits and Possibilities of Volunteering: A Framework for Explaining the Scope of Volunteer Involvement in Public and Nonprofit Organizations: The Limits and Possibilities of

Big Asks

One final word about making the personal ask in volunteer recruiting. Make your first ask a big one. I have become burnt out (so have most of my volunteer leaders) with the rotation system in which a person commits to serving once a month, give or take. The group participants cannot establish a bond with their leaders within this system, and the leaders themselves have little choice but to view their serving role as someone plugging a hole rather than someone adopting a relational ministry assignment. When we ask adults to rotate into and out of leadership roles with high frequency, we communicate that the assignment is really a drag, and we hope they will sacrifice what they actually want to do 25 percent of the time so that the kids are cared for by someone. Nope. That's not what we're about.

Start by asking your volunteers to serve every week. Ask them to make this a major life ministry, a part of their Christian identity and church life. Tell them you will train and equip them to adopt this work and the participants as their own family. Explain that you will support them, but also look to them to set the tone and agenda themselves, because that's how much trust you have in them. Granted, serving every week with children or youth could prevent volunteers from participating in the main worship service and/or main discipleship hour, and that's a problem. At our small church, this is one major reason why we offer two identical worship services every week, so that our leaders for children and youth can serve during one service and attend the other. The point is, if volunteers' weekly service prevents them from participating in a primary worship or discipleship time for your church, you need to work with them to identify alternative times and places to experience these church offerings. Perhaps they have a weekday Bible study that meets the discipleship need, or perhaps they can attend an evening worship service. Make it clear that the first priority is their own spiritual health, so if saying "yes" to serving means missing out on weekly worship and discipleship for themselves, then the answer needs to be "no."

The only way to make a huge ask like this in good conscience is to

Volunteering: A Framework for Explaining the Scope of Volunteer Involvement in Public and Nonprofit Organizations," *Public Administration Review* 78, no. 4 (July 2018): 502–13, https://doi.org/10.1111/puar.12894.

remember that you are offering the leader something that is in their own best interest. You are not asking them to do something that will deplete them or make their lives worse. On the contrary, finding one's place of belonging by giving and growing in service is a gift that I wish everyone in the church could experience.

Of course, someone who agrees to serve weekly can have as many Sundays "off" as they need! All of my weekly volunteers accept or decline their weekly serving roles in an online communication software. I have a list of possible subs for each serving area that I gladly plug in any time a volunteer has a conflict or is away on vacation. But on a typical Sunday, our children and youth ministries are led by the same two unrelated adults who have been leading them all year long.

Volunteer Ministry Teams

Now that we are on the same page about how to recruit individual volunteers, let's talk about working with volunteer teams! Ministry teams are what it's all about. Think the twelve disciples, the judges Moses recruited to handle smaller matters, or the women who went together to care for Jesus' body at the tomb. Our volunteers do not do their work in isolation, pouring effort into their charges all on their own. We support our volunteers best by surrounding them with others who are also invested in their work. Some ministry teams create deep spiritual bonds, so that their time together accomplishes the work of discipleship as well as any Bible study or accountability group. Have you experienced the ultimate joy of sitting around a table with other leaders as they contribute, suggest, and reject ideas for ministry? It is glorious.

There are manifold benefits to raising up ministry teams. For one, the church staff no longer makes decisions from the top down. With a ministry team in place, a group of people take ownership of the decision. When a parent or fellow staff member takes issue with the direction of your ministry area, you have a team of people behind you who have thought about, prayed over, and debated this issue. Working with a ministry team protects you as the lay or staff leader.

Another benefit of ministry teams is that they help staff members work their way out of a job. By sharing the responsibility for a ministry area, volunteer teams allow the staff member to focus on weaker ministry areas that require more expertise. When I was a fledgling children's director, I led weekly Kids' Worship for both worship services, meaning I rarely worshiped in the sanctuary. After a year, I met Jenna, a parent of three and new attender with a passion for the church. As soon as Jenna met our church's requirement of attending for six months before volunteering with children, she jumped into the children's ministry, agreeing to head a volunteer-led Kids' Worship group. She and I recruited 4-5 trusted adults and formed a team. That team met several times to discuss the right scope and sequence, the proper arrangement of the worship space, appropriate classroom management techniques, and worship elements. For the first year, I led along with members of the team, demonstrating how I wanted things done and listening to their feedback, which was sometimes not that much fun—turns out, when I try to lead a huge ministry area by myself for a year, the quality suffers dramatically. And there's no one like a brand-new volunteer with fresh eyes to pinpoint the weak spots and take initiative to buoy them up.

After a year of co-leading, I stepped out completely. For the next several years until I left that church, I only led as a sub when needed. I still joined the team for all their meetings, and provided direction and affirmation, but it was their ministry. I was just the cheerleader.

The key to developing successful ministry teams is to empower them, then let them go. As ministry experts, we should be able to do the work better than anyone else, but we should delegate anyway. Model and instruct, especially at the beginning. Be prepared to redirect a team that starts to veer offtrack, and set boundaries to keep their work in line with your ministry's overall vision. But otherwise, give them all the power and encouragement they need.

Once someone joins a ministry team, the team changes. It is therefore helpful to establish a system for training new members, which should involve identifying the strengths they bring. Each team member contributes different skills, knowledge, and strengths. Help the team identify and build on their strengths, while recognizing and working on weak areas. I get to work with our hospitality team at church right now. The long-time members of the team have become wonderful trainers. Each time a new team member joins, which is about once a month, they see new ways to improve the system. I recently caught two hospitality team members measuring the backs of our seats in the sanctuary to see if the pen holders they had ordered online out of their own pockets would fit there.

If you are feeling burnt out or overwhelmed with your level of responsibility, or if you simply want to be able to focus on the bigger picture or new ministry ventures, ministry teams are your answer.

Training and Coaching

Of course, once your ministry team is in place, you've just begun. If working with volunteers were like cooking a meal, the recruitment phase would be compared to gathering the best, highest-quality ingredients. Next, you will begin mixing the ingredients together: the training and coaching phase of volunteer work. This is our opportunity to cast a vision for our leaders and get everyone on the same page as far as expectations and goals, a crucial step in achieving high-quality ministry experiences for participants and for volunteers themselves.[6] Training is the preparation and instruction you give to a volunteer to make them successful, and it takes place prior to their classroom work. The most basic and essential training we offer our volunteers concerns safety, both their own and that of those they will lead. I will share with you my strategies for safety training all types of volunteers, then wade into other valuable training topics that should be covered before a volunteer's service starts. After that, we will discuss one of the harder sides of volunteer work: coaching, which includes providing accountability, having hard conversations when they are called for, and being prepared to remove a volunteer from service.

Safety Training

While we can sing the greatest songs, teach the best Bible lessons, and pray the most moving prayers, they honestly matter very little in the process if the ministry participants are harmed physically, emotionally or

6   Stephanie T. Solansky et al., "On the Same Page: The Value of Paid and Volunteer Leaders Sharing Mental Models in Churches," *Nonprofit Management and Leadership* 19, no. 2 (September 2008): 203–19, https://doi.org/10.1002/nml.215.

spiritually. Discipleship cannot happen effectively amid danger—and contrary to how some may feel about church, it is not a safe place for everyone at all times. We must be vigilant in order to keep people safe in our ministry areas. Every new design for a ministry time must begin with safety.

In the United Methodist Church, our safety policy is called Safe Sanctuaries™[7]. The denomination provides basic guidelines for working with children, youth, and vulnerable adults and for protecting staff and volunteers as well. If you are in a United Methodist Church, you are bound by this policy. If you work in another denomination, find your denominational guidelines and become familiar with them! Wise churches will accept and implement all denominational standards, adding to or strengthening them as needed for the context. Your building, location, church size, and types of ministries all need to be factored into a common safety plan.

One safety strategy that seems obvious but is not always implemented is background checks. All volunteers must undergo a nationwide background check before serving. Unfortunately, these background checks are not cheap! Budget the cost of the initial background check for each new volunteer as well as follow-up background checks every 3 to 5 years for volunteers who continue to serve. While this background check is essential, it rarely will give you all the information you need about a volunteer. On *cokesburykids.com* you will find sample volunteer covenants and application forms that you can have volunteers complete as part of the recruiting process. Do not ever place a volunteer in service without first reading their background check report. Decide in advance what criminal charges would prevent someone from serving in your church.

I believe one of the best deterrents to placing a predator in a ministry setting with children, youth, or vulnerable adults is a tenure requirement, a rule that states a person must be known and involved in the life of the church for at least six months before being trusted to lead vulnerable populations. This rule accomplishes more than just the goal of discouraging a person with evil motives from infiltrating your ministry. It also ensures that the volunteers who greet parents at the door or lead a discussion with youth know the church and are known by the people of the church to some

---

7   You can read more about Safe Sanctuaries at *https://www.umcdiscipleship.org/equipping-leaders/safe-sanctuaries*.

degree. The volunteers we recruit are often some of the first people to greet future first-time guests. We want them to be able to answer basic questions about the church and welcome others well, which happens best if they have experienced such a welcome for at least six months themselves. It is a gift to your volunteers to allow them to enjoy a period of learning from the pastor, staff, and other leaders before they are asked or allowed to give back in a high-commitment role.

In safety training, you not only will go over the requirements for service, you also will share the operating procedures you expect them to uphold for their safety and the safety of their group, such as:

- **The two-adult rule:** Two unrelated adults must be responsible for each group of children, youth, or vulnerable adults. Some churches allow one adult to lead the group, with a floater available as needed. When training folks in the two-adult rule, be sure to cover:
  - ° Bathroom break procedures
  - ° Appropriate and inappropriate physical touch
  - ° Confidentiality expectations for each type of group
- **Emergency situations:** Volunteers need to know the emergency and evacuation procedures for your building—where to go in a severe weather warning, how and when to lock doors during an intruder alert, the location of the fire escapes, and so forth.
- **Technology expectations:** Share policies for having and using phones in the classroom, both for volunteers and participants. Pay special attention to policies regarding taking and posting photos of group participants, remembering that most churches require written consent from a parent or guardian before using or sharing the image of a minor in any way.
- **Attendance and check-in/out:** Train volunteers in your system for keeping a written or electronic attendance record and for ensuring that children are picked up by the appropriate adult.

It's a long list! When I lead safety trainings, I operate from an outline and pause several times to receive questions. That outline is on *cokesbury-kids.com* as well, and I welcome you to take it and make it your own.

In addition to all of these basic safety training topics, the volunteer team for each ministry area will require details relevant only to them. For example, a nursery volunteer needs to know the diaper-changing procedure, and special instructions for pick-up and drop-off times. A leader working with youth needs training on how to respond to sticky situations, such as if a student shares very private information or walks into the room spouting a stream of profanity. Volunteers should feel competent to handle these kinds of situations with love and to ensure the safety of the group.

Most of my safety training talks begin with the statement, "This is not going to be the most uplifting conversation you and I will ever have about serving in the church." Not only is safety training full of mundane details and explanations of inconvenient rules, it also absolutely must include a conversation about identifying and reporting abuse and neglect.[8] Your volunteers need to be mindful that there is a chance that someone in their group has experienced some kind of abuse or neglect in their lives. I teach my volunteers the signs of abuse and neglect, and encourage them to speak to me or another staff member if there is the slightest concern. I would rather my volunteers be too careful than let someone in my church continue to experience abuse just because we didn't want to look bad by reporting it. Research some statistics, talk to a social worker or pediatrician, and educate yourself on this topic so that you can educate your volunteer teams. Once you are sure that your volunteers understand how to keep their participants safe, you can move on to the slightly more exciting aspects of volunteer training: the strategies for getting the job done.

Practical Training

This portion of volunteer training is where you really set up your volunteers for success. There is a long, long list of topics you could cover, and you may want to add to or subtract from these basic training requirements. I have found that these topics cover the most frequently asked questions I have received from volunteers on their first day of leading—and it's great if you can answer those questions before they are even asked!

First, look at the roster of children, youth, or adults who will

8   Child Welfare Information Gateway, "What Is Child Abuse and Neglect? Recognizing the Signs and Symptoms" (U.S. Department of Health & Human Services, Administration for Children and Families, Administration on Children, Youth, and Families, Children's Bureau, 2019), https://www.childwelfare.gov/pubs/factsheets/whatiscan/.

participate in the ministry and identify those who may need extra attention. Give the volunteers who will work with those individuals specific guidance on how to care for them. This could mean giving them a heads-up that one of their participants loves to challenge and argue, so they shouldn't take that personally, but be judicious about when to engage. It could mean letting the volunteer know to expect an adult buddy who will accompany a child with a disability. You might want to point out a particularly quiet child, or a person who excels at art, or a participant who has benefited from having access to fidget toys during previous groups. It could mean alerting volunteers, with the family's permission, to an impending divorce or a recent death in the family. Of course, all proper permissions must be obtained before sharing confidential information with a volunteer, and we must ensure that our volunteers can respect that confidentiality. But part of helping a volunteer to be successful is to introduce them to the people they will lead in advance.

Next, have a conversation with volunteers about the use of curriculum. Some volunteers naturally understand how to use curriculum to its greatest benefit, while others need permission and some practice before they are able to tailor it to the needs of the group. Go over your curriculum with your volunteers and help them select the portions of it that will work best, considering their gifts and the group dynamic. Give volunteers permission to make the curriculum their own, within the bounds of your budget, theology, and philosophy.

Additionally, always make the lines of communication clear during training. Let them know your personal preferences regarding phone calls, texts, and e-mails. If you do not answer work calls after a certain time of day, let them know that. If you plan to communicate with volunteers via a separate application or a blog or webpage, walk them through that process. Let them know how to reach you during their volunteer time. Telling volunteers the communication plan assures them that they are not alone and that you have their backs.

A last word to volunteers in training is sharing your expectations for the amount of work you expect them to put in outside of their in-class time. If you plan for volunteers to develop their own curriculum or activities, estimate the time that it should require of them. If you want volunteers to review the curriculum ahead of teaching it, give them an idea of the time that will take. You may have some volunteers who will be tempted to put in too much time outside of class, so set limits on prep time to avoid burn-out. Whether or not your volunteers comply with your expectations, it is incredibly helpful to them for us to share those expectations with them. At least, if they blow them off, they know they are doing that!

And, of course, pray with your volunteers. Pray blessings over them, asking God to pour out goodness on their efforts and to bring redemption and blessing to the people they will lead. Ask God to increase their faith as they serve and to speak words of calling, inspiration, and love to them as they lead. Solicit prayer needs from your volunteers and position yourself as a pastoral presence among them as under your direction they do the work of the church.

Coaching

Once the training is complete and volunteers step into their roles, the coaching stage commences. This is the on-the-job training that never stops—the feedback, encouragement, and explanations that are required in order to strengthen your volunteers. Honestly, coaching is about 50 times harder than training, but it is also exponentially more powerful for impact-ing the discipleship and growth of your volunteers. Providing profession-al development and encouragement is linked to volunteer retention in all kinds of charities and non-profit settings.[9]

As volunteers begin to implement the training you have given them, inevitably they will encounter questions no one anticipated. It's super im-portant to make yourself accessible as they lead. I used to love walking the hallway where the children's small-group leaders were leading in class-rooms, waiting for one to poke their head out the door and ask for some extra craft supplies, a child's bathroom escort, or how to pronounce a name in the Bible story for that day. I also found it incredibly helpful for my own enrichment to step in to observe the leaders at times, making note of par-ticipants who did not seem engaged or volunteers who seemed frustrated.

9   Mark A. Hagar and Jeffrey L. Brudney, "Volunteer Management Practices and Reten-tion of Volunteers," Technical, Volunteer Management Capacity Study Series (Washington, D.C.: The Urban Institute, June 2004).

In addition to being available, it sometimes will be necessary to address concerns or give direction when you see that something is not as it should be. If a teacher is being overrun by a group participant, or a group is climbing the walls for the whole hour rather than sitting down to follow the curriculum, or a group goes completely off topic on a regular basis, you will need to step in to have a conversation with the leader. In these situations, always ask questions first! Whether you are following up with them because someone else reported a problem or because you witnessed something troublesome yourself, ask the leader to share their perspective first. Once you are on the same page with the reality of the situation, share direct, clear, brief instructions for what you expect to change.

When coaching leaders to improve, be content with taking small steps. If a volunteer is completely overwhelmed or frustrated, identify small changes you can make, such as recruiting someone else to assist them, asking a church office volunteer to prep their crafts and handouts for them, or having them arrive five minutes earlier to pray and settle before their group storms in. We all (or if you haven't, you will soon) have found ourselves working with a volunteer who could benefit from loads of improvement! Give them the benefit of the doubt, and set small goals for yourself and for them. Do not try to turn a newbie into an all-star in one week.

When you have a concern about a volunteer's leadership, address it quickly. Do not allow the whole group to suffer, or ignore the problem hoping it will go away, for weeks on end before things get bad enough to spur you to action. If there is a small redirection to be made, have that conversation the same day if possible. If your concern is significant, you may want to talk to a supervisor before addressing it. In that case, have that conversation within 24 hours so that you are prepared to talk to the volunteer at the next possible opportunity.

In-person coaching conversations are always best. Do not—I repeat, do NOT—send a mass e-mail to all volunteers to address a problem you are only experiencing with one or two of them. Everyone is better served when hard conversations are initiated promptly and in person. Ask appropriate questions, state your expectations, then ask your volunteers how you can help them achieve the standard you have set. Assure them that you are in their corner and that you see all their gifts and strengths. Provide real encouragement and commiserate over how challenging it can truly be to serve in a church with other imperfect humans. Let your volunteers know that you are cheering for them, and at the same time, you expect them to do what's right and needed.

Rarely, you may find that you need to remove a particular volunteer from a position of service. If this is the case for you, remember: removing a volunteer from a place of serving is not just in the group's best interest, but in that volunteer's best interest, too. You may recognize the needs of the group first, but I am confident that what is bad for the group is also bad for the volunteer. We are responsible for both parties, and the decisions we make must exhibit pastoral care for everyone involved.

The first step in removing a volunteer from a position is to communicate your intentions and rationale to any church leaders who may be called upon to support you in this act—and only to those people. This could include a pastor, a supervisor, the chair of the human resources board, the chair of trustees, or a lay leader in the church. Ask for their prayers and prepare them to listen and support you if the volunteer reaches out to them in hurt and anger. Ask your own leaders for help finding any policies or principles that will substantiate your decision.

The next step is to identify other areas of service that the volunteer may be more suited for within the church. There is a place for everyone to serve in the body of Christ—if one area is not working out, there are five more that could be a better fit. Removing a volunteer from a position does not mean removing them from serving. It simply means finding another place that will better contribute to their growth and utilize their gifts.

Once you have the support you need and the alternative service opportunities in mind, it is time for a face-to-face conversation with your volunteer. Just like with every other coaching interaction, begin by asking questions. Find out what they really think about their experience so far, and get to a place of mutual understanding about the challenges. Then tell them that you want what is best both for the ministry and for them, and you want to move them to a different role. You may need to share with them specific policies they have violated, or you may simply say that you know their efforts have not played out the way either of you wanted. Take responsibility for any part you played in assigning them to a task that was a bad fit, but do not take responsibility that is not yours. Assure them that there is a place for them in the life of the church and that the last thing you would want is for them to feel excluded, dismissed, or unappreciated. Temper the conversation with encouragement, and be sure to note any successes or good times that have taken place as well. But stand firm in your decision.

If this conversation causes hurt to your volunteer, show them how to find healing. Refer them to appropriate people for them to process this with, give space if needed, and make yourself available for further conversation once they have had time to think. Tell them that you love them and want what is best for them. If possible, pray together about next steps.

Last, take off the rest of the day. Give your body and spirit time to re-energize after this emotionally taxing conversation. Journal, go to the gym, see a movie, meditate, or take a nap. Plan rest and recovery into your day. You worked hard to make this conversation as loving, helpful, and firm as you could—now recover.

Sit Back and Watch

After recruiting, training, and coaching your leaders to strength and wisdom, you get to experience the golden tomorrow, the fun and fulfilling vision of ministry happening at the hands of leaders you have cultivated. While you know that you could lead a lesson, design a small-group activity, or pray a blessing just as well as or better than any of the leaders you have put into place, it is so much better to watch them live into your design and implement it themselves. Multiply yourself by raising amazing volunteers, and thank God for the honor of doing so. Stop and think for a moment about all of the conversations, Scriptures, prayers, and songs that build the body of believers on your watch, not limited to your personal gifts and availability. Relish your place in the body as someone who equips others to do the work God has called them to do. It's a pretty fantastic place to be.

Final Thoughts

If you are in a position that allows you to recruit, train, and empower volunteers, then you are a pastor, whether or not you've been to seminary. You get to introduce people to God's work in ways that can change their lives and change the world. Yes, it can be hard work, but the hard work is also an honor and privilege. Consider yourself a pastor to your volunteers, a caregiver for caregivers, a coach for other coaches.

And if I could leave you with any final thought about working with volunteers, it would be this: appreciate them. Become a broken record of sincere gratitude for these people who run the church. I realize that electronic communication is amazing, but there is really no substitute for a handwritten thank-you note and an intentional, eye-to-eye "thank you." Remind your volunteers that they are the church, and that this big responsibility is also a big blessing. The church literally doesn't exist apart from the people who serve one another in it. Some of you have the gift of pairing a candy bar with a cute pun of appreciation to create a sweet volunteer gift. Others of you have the gift of creating art or writing words that will communicate gratitude to your volunteers. Use what you have! It does not so much matter how you communicate love and appreciation for volunteers, as long as they receive those true sentiments from you regularly. Thank God, and thank them, then repeat. Because volunteers really do run the world. And the church.

CHAPTER 11

MARRIAGE & DIVORCE

This chapter reviews some of my professional experience with marriage and divorce, research from experts in the field, and practical advice for supporting families through marriage and divorce in the church context. The chapter begins with thoughts on how marriage has evolved over time, and the cultural and economic constraints on marriage today. Following that quick history, the chapter explores marriage enrichment and marriage crises we can expect to encounter in ministry. The chapter concludes by reviewing the life cycle of divorce and the support we can offer to divorcing adults, their children, and extended family and friends who are affected.

Both marriage and divorce have huge influences on family and church life, affecting not just married people, but adults who never marry, widows and widowers, and youth who wonder if marriage will be a part of their lives. The church has struggled to espouse compassionate and practical theologies of marriage and divorce, and struggled even more to live them out. Few subjects are more sensitive, more ripe for hypocrisy, or more misunderstood than marriage and divorce. This chapter will attempt to provide some perspective, and equip church leaders to strengthen all families in their churches, whether they are affected by marriage, divorce, or neither.

A Brief History of Marriage

Most books on marriage from a Christian perspective begin in the Book of Genesis, where God brought Adam and Eve together in the garden of Eden. There is a lot to say about that story, about how the first chapters of our Bible describe two people uniting in a lifelong, committed relationship ordained and blessed by God. My own favorite part of the story is this: that God did not want people to be isolated. God made two distinct, separate people who reflected God's image by being in relationship with one another. God created us for community and companionship, affirming the deep desire in all of us for intimacy with others.

While this human union is beautifully illustrated in the Genesis story, we have tended to extrapolate many of the details of the story as inspired, intentional, essential injunctions for marriage, reading into it limitations that are incongruent with the big picture of God's design for human relationships. I am not convinced that the Genesis story is a prescription for marriage. Certainly, God wants us to be in relationships, and marriage is an intimate relationship unlike most any other. I'll simply say I think the biggest and best takeaway from Adam and Eve is that we are not meant to be alone.

According to Diana Garland, marriage has been many things throughout history—a strategic tool to form alliances with other households or countries; a social construct that strengthened and benefited society; and, in New Testament times, a sacred, monogamous, loving union that reflected Christ's love for the church.[1] Christian theology has historically presented a beautiful, sacred view of marriage as a union that teaches us about the depth of God's love. However, for centuries, church teaching on marriage and sex has not aligned with reality for most people. For example, Aquinas saw celibacy as a way to be closer to God, and sex within marriage as only acceptable as a means of procreation.[2]

Fast forward to modern America, and consider that in 1950, 78 percent of households included married couples, a statistic that dropped to

---

1   Diana R. Garland, *Family Ministry: A Comprehensive Guide*, 2nd edition (Downers Grove, IL: IVP Academic, 2012), 70.
2   Ibid., 72.

48 percent by 2016[3]. One reason for delayed marriage is economic—it's just too expensive for young people to form and join households today. American views on marriage have also shifted. Whereas marriage at one time was a business arrangement, now it is more of a celebration of adulthood, a social milestone to achieve. Cohabitation is an increasingly acceptable practice socially, and its practical and financial advantages have contributed to lower marriage and divorce rates.[4]

The United States currently holds the record for highest divorce rate in the developed world as well as the largest number of cohabiting relationships that break up early.[5] We apparently believe in marriage but practice breakups. In 2009, it was estimated that 40 percent of marriages end in divorce. Social scientists believe that the divorce rate will remain relatively stable at 40-60 percent for the foreseeable future.[6]

While I do not want to return to the time when marriage was simply a business transaction involving the trade of a human being in exchange for property or political allegiance, it does not appear that our more romantic approach to marriage is working out very well either. Surely there is another view of marriage that recognizes the goodness and beauty of the individuals in the marriage and their strength as a couple. We have to ask what God wants for marriage and divorce by looking at the overarching principles of marriage in Scripture.

Blessings & Challenges

The New Testament writers clearly believed marriage to be the best metaphor for God's relationship with God's people and Christ's relationship to the church.[7] Over and again, we read in the Gospels and Epistles that spouses are to submit to one another and love each other the way that Christ loves the church (Ephesians 5:22-24; Colossians 3:18-19;

---

3   Monica McGoldrick, Nydia A. Garcia Preto, and Betty A. Carter, *The Expanding Family Life Cycle: Individual, Family, and Social Perspectives*, 5th edition (Boston: Pearson, 2015), 260.
4   Ibid.
5   Ibid., 261.
6   Ibid., 377.
7   Garland, *Family Ministry*, 169.

1 Peter 3:1-2). These words from biblical writers, researched and interpreted through the centuries by theologians, tell us just as much about God's expectations for God's kingdom as they tell us about God's expectations for marriage—both are based in community, in relationships. And therefore, both are a wonderful mess.

The math of marriage is strange, with two people becoming one unit together, retaining their individuality but also comprising a whole that is greater than the sum of its parts. Those who choose to marry commit to living two personhoods—growing as the person God has made them, with their own calling, preferences, personality, and needs, at the same time contributing to a "couple-hood" with its own set of traits and needs. It's beautiful, complicated, and often painful.

Marriage is a process of high costs. As Garland writes, "It costs us all a tremendous amount in terms of our ability to be ourselves, find harmony in our relationships, and support the tasks of family life."[8] A dear friend recently commented to me that he is least like himself in his marriage. He loves his spouse and cherishes their relationship, but the importance and closeness of it infringes on his freedom to express himself. One of the constraints on marriage is the heavy pressure we put on it to be wonderful and successful. No one, from the married couple to those around them, wants to observe any emotion emerging from the marriage relationship other than happiness, which in turn encourages couples to downplay or ignore problems.[9] The church has not always done a great job of acknowledging the pain and sacrifice necessary to blend two lives together in a way that honors and portrays God. The stress of perfectionism and the felt need to put only our best, happiest foot forward in marriage contributes to the failure of many marriages.

Supporting Marriages

There are many merits and beautiful aspects of marriage to celebrate. At the same time, I want to acknowledge that 1) marriage is not for everyone, 2) marriage does not make anyone better or make life itself better or more valuable, and 3) for our LGBTQ friends, marriage has not always

8   Ibid., 259.
9   Ibid., 252.

been an option. Talking about marriage in glowing, elevated terms can disenfranchise many for whom marriage isn't desired, isn't an option, or for whom marriage just hasn't worked. My hope is that the church can find a way to support marriage and those who choose it without glorifying it or glossing over its challenges.

I believe God loves to work on people's hearts through marriage. Saying "I do" at the altar is a commitment to a refinement process. There is nothing cheap, easy, or simple about marriage; its demands and rewards are both high. When I married my husband, John, at the age of 23, I had no idea how small my world still was. I had observed my parents' beautiful marriage my whole life and incorrectly assumed that I could just repeat everything that worked for them and expect John to fulfill all the roles I had observed in my family members. It's actually quite shameful for me to admit how many of my marriage expectations came from Christian romance novels and bridal magazines. I had no idea what I was getting into.

After 12 years of wedded life, I look back on those first few years and just shake my head. Neither one of us was a dreamboat newlywed spouse to the other. We immediately felt pressure to succeed—sexually, emotionally, professionally, spiritually. I started grad school the day after we returned from our honeymoon, and after just a few months John switched careers, hoping to provide better for the big family I wanted. After three years we moved to a new city so I could take a full-time ministry job, and John fully supported me, but also didn't find the right next career path for himself for a couple years. Through it all, we offered very few glances into our day-to-day relationship struggle to others, both because the church never asked and because we barely recognized those struggles ourselves. We glossed over irritations and hoped arguments would go away. It wasn't until we had our second child that we started to get real with each other, five years into our marriage. Thank God for therapy, which we finally tried, and which probably saved our relationship.

I can look back and see so many moments during our preparation for marriage and first years of marriage in which the church could have offered support and help to us. For being so very pro-marriage, our churches often offer very little in terms of practical help to make marriages healthier. Literally thousands of books, curricula, and organizations exist to provide mentoring, retreats, and groups that help strengthen marriages. Offering these kinds of opportunities is great—I highly encourage it. If your role in the church includes ministry to married adults, you have many tested, high-quality materials and events at your disposal.

Emotionally Healthy Discipleship
Pete & Geri Scazzero
https://www.emotionallyhealthy.org/
Claiming to help church leaders develop mature disciples, Emotionally Healthy Discipleship offers two 8-week courses with written and video materials, one on spirituality and another on relationships. Both courses are helpful in marriage ministry, but the relationships course is more pertinent. A free newsletter and sample lesson download are available.

The Daring Way
Brené Brown
https://brenebrown.com/thedaringway/
The Daring Way is a certification program for helping professionals, not intended for lay persons to offer in churches. However, the website lists certified professionals, searchable by state, so that others can find an event happening near them or contact a professional to offer the course within the church. Beyond this specific program, most of Brown's books work as marriage enrichment materials and could be used by any size group as a book study. Many of the books include discussion guides.

Rekindling Desire
Esther Perel
https://www.estherperel.com/
Esther Perel is the daughter of Holocaust survivors and has explored relationships and sexuality through her work with refugees; her therapeutic work with couples; and her books, TED talks, articles, and interviews. Rekindling Desire is her online, 4-hour course intended to help couples connect or reconnect to the erotic in their relationship. It is important to note that Perel does not offer overtly Christian or Scripture-based materials, and some of her beliefs about infidelity and other marriage

issues may not align with all churches, which could be a deal-breaker for some ministries.

The Art and Science of Love

John M. Gottman, PhD

https://www.gottman.com/

A weekend workshop based on John Gottman's 40 years of research into couples and relationships. The website will allow you to find existing workshops in your area, receive training from the Gottman Institute yourself, or purchase the workshop as a DVD set.

Marriage enrichment opportunities can take many forms: retreats, book studies, professional counseling, small groups, lectures, and more. In my personal and professional experience, the two best marriage enrichment experiences that churches can offer are small accountability groups and supportive referrals to qualified professional counselors.

Accountability Groups

You've already heard me humbly brag about my small group consisting of myself and four friends who meet nearly weekly to go deep about our lives. These women know me more deeply than almost anyone else, particularly when it comes to my marriage. But I'll be honest: in our group, where we have sworn confidentiality and unconditional love, it still doesn't feel 100 percent safe to share about the cry session my spouse and I had that week over jobs and financial stress. It's scary. But in the dark, lonely moments when I'm ruminating over an ongoing argument with my spouse or wondering if our sex life could use some therapy, knowing that none of this is a secret to my small group has been a safeguard. I am convinced that every single marriage has mountaintops and valleys, and in both those kinds of moments, we need supportive relationships outside our marriage.

In my experience, creating space for this kind of deep accountability and vulnerability in groups is tricky, both as a member and a ministry leader. When you're going about establishing such small groups, be sure it is abundantly clear to those who join them that honesty and respect are required. Think Alcoholics Anonymous meets prayer team. These groups are akin to an old-fashioned Wesleyan band meeting,[10] a place where people can expect to ask and answer difficult questions. Providing spaces for people to get real about their marriages is a powerful marriage ministry program. When you're designing your accountability group ministry, following are a few guidelines to keep in mind:

1. **Establish expectations through covenant**—A good way to establish trust in the early stages of a group is to form a group covenant, a "pledge to uphold certain standards and expectations."[11] A covenant can include the group's plan for what topics are on or off limits, confidentiality rules, expectations for advice-giving, and even logistics such as attendance standards, meeting times, quorum for meeting, and so forth. Stating expectations clearly, then fulfilling them builds the trust needed to share openly.

2. **Model vulnerability and acceptance**—Willingness to be vulnerable comes when there is trust, and trust is earned when group members demonstrate acceptance and confidentiality. The leader(s) of a marriage accountability group, whether volunteers or staff, should know how to model vulnerability and acceptance. Leaders' openness paves the way for others to be open and honest as well, as research shows that participants closely imitate group leaders in sharing.[12]

3. **Provide a group structure**—Help the groups create a structure that works for them. Consider questions such as: Will the groups use a curriculum? Who will lead the group? Who are the right people to participate, and how should participants be grouped? Will the group be open to new members or closed? These are all important questions; the right people to answer them are the group members themselves. In my leadership roles, I solicit interest from all couples in the church, either through targeted e-mail or personal invitations. Then I invite participants to attend an information session, where they have a chance to share what kind

10   Kevin M. Watson, *Pursuing Social Holiness: The Band Meeting in Wesley's Thought and Popular Methodist Practice*, 1st Edition (Oxford: Oxford University Press, 2014), 72–98.
11   Neal F. McBride, *How to Lead Small Groups* (Colorado Springs, CO: NavPress, 1990), 46–48.
12   Ibid., 94.

of discipleship growth they are looking for, whether they prefer a Bible/book study or open discussion format, and if there are any preferences as to group leaders or participants. I then arrange folks into groups I believe will be compatible. Several of the curriculum options listed above would work in a small group context.

Marriage Accountability for Both Spouses

One question you'll encounter if you seek to implement accountability groups in your church is whether couples can participate in a group together. There are positives and negatives, no matter how you answer this question. An accountability group for married couples offers convenience, as the couples can share childcare arrangements if needed, and they only have to commit one night to attending groups. Members of married couples also can see and hear their spouses differently as they share openly with friends about their lives. Having this scheduled time together can help their relationships grow and increase their communication.

The biggest reason not to allow couples to do accountability groups together is that it can be an impediment to honesty and vulnerability, especially for members whose marriages are struggling. For couples who are experiencing a difficult time in their relationship (and that is everyone at some point), attending a small group can become just another time to push the problems aside and pretend they don't exist. A group full of wonderful couples I know who met regularly to share and strengthen one another's faith was shocked when one of the couples announced unexpectedly that they were separating. You would think that in a group like this, group members would have an inkling of what was happening before any official announcements were made. But the truth is, participating in an accountability group with your spouse is sometimes just not safe enough. Giving individuals the space to share the hurt and struggle of their marriage without their spouse present can result in more encouragement, better communication skills, and greater motivation to make loving choices in marriage.

One last note about accountability groups for married couples is that these groups do not and cannot fill the role of therapy for a marriage in crisis. These groups are an ideal place for someone to hear the loving question, "Have you considered talking to a professional about this?" or, "Let me give you the name of my therapist." Friends in accountability groups should be quick to recognize when someone's level of need has crossed over into clinical territory, and they can help walk their group member to that place. Church-based accountability groups are the right place for prayer, encouragement, listening, speaking hope, and asking questions. They are not the place for one member of the group to bring their weekly crisis. They are also not the place for any psychology buffs to try to diagnose and fix others' problems. For the more serious crises in marriage, pastoral and professional counseling are both wonderful and necessary options.

Marriage in Crisis

Like I said, every marriage hits the rocks at some point, most at multiple points! While there are a few life events that are extremely predictive of marriage stress—career changes, childbirth, health issues—every marriage undergoes unpredictable stress and struggle as well. Let's look at the life cycle of a marriage as well as some recourse the church can offer when crisis hits.

Ron and Jody Zappia have written a book on marriage, and planted churches with thriving marriage ministries, but their story did not start there.[13] During their first year as a married couple, Jody returned home early from a business trip to find Ron cheating on her. The next day, Jody walked into the church across the street, looking for someone who could counsel them and give her permission to pursue divorce. They landed in a church-sponsored marriage workshop, which led to counseling with the pastor, who asked good questions and led them both to recognize their need for repentance and forgiveness. In an interview on the Think Orange podcast in February 2019,[14] Ron urged churches to find a way to

13   Zappia, Ron & Jody. *The Marriage Knot: 7 Choices that Keep Couples Together*, Moody Publishers: Chicago, IL, 2019, pp 27-46.
14   The reThinkGroup, host, "How Transparency Can Save Marriages in Your Church," The Think Orange Podcast (podcast), February 5, 2019, accessed November 11, 2019, http://orangeblogs.org/thinkorangepodcast/081-how-transparency-can-save-marriages-in-your-church/.

communicate to married couples that they are not alone. Gather couples together and give them room to share openly and authentically with one another. As someone who can attest to the church's power to support marriage, Ron's advice holds authority. The ideas I will share here for growing healthy marriages in the church are all some iteration of this primary goal: provide the space and leadership to get couples in the church to talk vulnerably about their marriages.

First Years of Marriage

I would rather relive middle school than the first three years of my marriage. Those years of learning to share a home, a bed, and daily life can be full of friction. We participated in our church's version of premarital counseling before saying our vows, which meant we met with a mature married couple in the church a few times and went through a curriculum together. I found it quite easy to keep our discussions at the surface level, and I regret that now. They did ask us some hard questions, but we glossed over them as best we could. We just wanted to get through it, check the premarital counseling box, and zoom straight toward the wedding day. A former pastor once said that premarital counseling doesn't matter—couples who have gotten that far will rarely be convinced to acknowledge their problems and work on them. What should be required is postmarital counseling! I tend to agree with him.

Most if not all couples experience the first stage of marital dissatisfaction in their first year of marriage. That first year is absolutely critical in terms of helping a couple to form a secure attachment to one another and establish resource security physically, emotionally, and financially.[15] The greater two people's differences are in terms of background, socioeconomic status, age, and so forth, the more difficulties they may face in coupling.[16] Premarital counseling certainly doesn't hurt and should be encouraged, but postmarital counseling, especially during that first year a couple is together, should be required. While clergy are generally the only people who can provide this level of counseling, lay ministers should be quick to refer engaged and newly married couples to either pastoral or

---

15   Garland, *Family Ministry*, 227.
16   McGoldrick, Preto, and Carter, *The Expanding Family Life Cycle*, 264.

clinical counselors. This is true for young 20-somethings embarking on this journey for the first time as well as for older adults who have found new love after divorce, widowhood, or half a lifetime of singleness. Counseling during that first year is critical, yet many blaze through it alone, dealing silently with the disillusionment found by spending unromantic evenings with someone who doesn't really resemble the person they thought they were marrying. Whether married or not, family ministers should remain aware of the particular stresses found in these first years of marriage, especially if a newlywed couple volunteers in ministry or has children in the ministry area.

Beyond the First Years

I recall complaining to my boss about a marital squabble several years ago, and he responded by asking, "How long have you all been married?" I straightened up a little as I answered, "Five years," to which he responded, "Oh, well, that explains it. Y'all are babies." I felt affronted at first—five years didn't feel too shabby to me—but looking back, he was right. That was right around the time that John and I got real with one another. Around the five-year mark, we at least decided that we would rather get over ourselves and express our emotional and mental health needs to one another than continue to act like martyrs and pretend. Getting honest about what was and wasn't working for us in our marriage didn't feel great, but I'm glad we did. We're still figuring it out, day by day, and sometimes crisis by crisis.

When a marriage enters into crisis, family ministers may reinforce the inherent guilt and sense of failure by simply telling the couple to tough it out and hang in there, as if laboring at the marriage alone will save it. Leading up to almost every divorce, couples put great effort into trying to salvage what they have. If hard work were all that were required, we would see many fewer divorces. This experience of putting forth superhuman effort and still ending in divorce is truly traumatic. Believing that hard work is all that is required for a successful marriage assumes that we imperfect people are enough on our own to achieve a perfect relationship.[17]

Systems theory helps explain why successful marriages do not rely

17　Garland, *Family Ministry*, 169-173.

solely on the effort of the partners. A marriage is not a closed system—it is affected by many other factors, such as health, child-rearing, finances, community, jobs, and so forth. Factors and systems outside the couple's control have a bearing on the strength of their union. One of those systems is the church and the beliefs it espouses. Unfortunately, the church often plays host to lovely wedding ceremonies, then ignores the need for marriage ministry afterward. The church can and should be one system in a couple's life that supports and nurtures the marriage relationship. The church's support system for marriage ideally should include accountability groups like the ones discussed previously, pastoral counseling, a strong theology of marriage preached from the pulpit, and the clear and loving inclusion of single and divorced people in events, classes, and groups.

According to one broad study,[18] churches that successfully shepherd and support marriages, both those that are strong and those in crisis, exhibit three key characteristics. First, the pastors and members of these congregations are realistic about the difficulty of marriage but also confident in aiming for marriage to be a lifelong commitment. Second, these congregations empower their members (married, single, divorced, everyone) to see themselves as cheerleaders of intimate relationships and active servants of others. Third, these churches talk honestly both about marriage and the cultural influences upon it, noting the differences between cultural beliefs and a healthy theology of marriage. In short, the church has the power to be a safe, healthy environment for people to enter into, strengthen, discuss, and even exit their marriages.

If keeping marriage vows becomes impossible due to the sin, brokenness, or addiction of one or both partners, then the marriage is undone, whether or not legal divorce proceedings happen. Both adults and children in these broken marriages experience lasting harm from the arguments, abuse, manipulation, and estrangement that ensue. It is not added sin to make the dissolution formal by divorcing; the family needs protection and healing regardless.[19]

18   Mary Ellen Konieczny, "Individualized Marriage and Family Disruption Ministries in Congregations: How Culture Matters," *Sociology of Religion* 77, no. 2 (June 2016): 144–70, https://doi.org/10.1093/socrel/srw010.
19   Garland, *Family Ministry*, 231.

Life Cycle of Divorce

I want to say that I believe divorce is OK. While divorce isn't great or desirable, often, it is the best option available. It is time to stop associating divorce with shame or failure, when often it is the only lifeline available to members of a toxic marriage. There is a push among many therapists and scholars to reframe divorce as a normative social institution just like marriage, an "unscheduled life transition" that can happen to anyone at any point in their journey.[20] That said, marriage and divorce are quite possibly the most difficult existential and interpersonal dilemmas in a person's life.[21]

Perhaps normalizing divorce would help combat the judgment and loneliness many divorced people suffer now because the church often views divorce so negatively. People grow the most during transitional periods such as the ones prompted by divorce.[22] We as ministry leaders must hold space to mourn the need for divorce, strengthen the marriages that have the potential to be healthy, and support and celebrate with those for whom divorce is the best option for safety and freedom.

Garland's model of divorce has three stages:

1. **Anger, hurt, and optimism**—In this stage, the couple begins to recognize the ways they hurt and are hurt by each other, and they are looking for ways to fix the problems. There is still hope that the marriage can improve.

2. **Anger, hurt, and pessimism**—This is the point where the couple continues to experience hurt but begins to lose hope. Change no longer seems within their grasp, and the continued pain of their interactions begins to desensitize them.

3. **Anger and apathy**—In this stage, hurt decreases. The actions that caused hurt continue, but the couple becomes apathetic and hopelessness fully sets in. This is the stage at which most couples finally seek help through counseling, even though divorce is nearly inevitable at this point.[23]

---

20 McGoldrick, Preto, and Carter, *The Expanding Family Life Cycle*, 376.
21 Ibid., 259.
22 Ibid., 380.
23 Garland, *Family Ministry*, 226–27.

Actual divorce proceedings are usually preceded by months or years of unhappiness, separations, and reunifications. These prolonged periods of turmoil keep both the couple and any children in limbo and make the finality of divorce hard to accept. An announcement of divorce clues us into a whole history of suffering and difficult emotions.[24] As a church, when we hear that a couple is struggling, it is safe to assume that we are late to the party, that the marriage problems are advanced at that point, and that there is a history of dysfunction to which we are not privy. Knowing that people rarely reach out for help until the pain in their marriage has become unbearable should quicken our empathy. No matter who is at fault for what, both members of the marriage are hurting and probably have been for a long time. It is appropriate to listen with love, patience, and acceptance if someone shows willingness to open up about their marriage trouble.

Supporting Families Through Divorce

Of all the stressful life events, divorce ranks near the top, in large part because it involves so many overlapping and recurring stressors. All of these ongoing and ambiguous challenges persist in a family system, affecting everyone differently but equally. Arrangements for co-parenting, ongoing communication between ex-spouses, legal processes, and so many other questions are unresolvable for years or possibly forever.[25] In many ways, a marriage never really ends because the interpersonal aspect of it continues through time, especially if there are children to be co-parented.[26] The church can offer resources to each member of the family, depending on their position and needs. Here are some of the ways we can serve the adults, children, and extended family and friends affected by divorce.

Supporting Adults in Divorce

When a parent approaches me to share that they are entering into divorce proceedings, I consider it a privilege that they confided in me, then ask questions about how the church can support them. Who needs a

---

24 Ibid., 227.
25 McGoldrick, Preto, and Carter, *The Expanding Family Life Cycle*, 380–81.
26 Garland, *Family Ministry*, 228.

referral to a counselor or a support group—one parent, both parents, kids? We provide meals for families who have a baby and wedding showers for engaged couples—could we not also provide meals or childcare for families in the immediate crisis of divorce? I ask what the kids' level of awareness is, and whether I can alert their ministry leaders. I also ask if it would be welcome or helpful to have a pastoral presence in court, to provide a prayerful presence before, after, and during proceedings. These are all practical gestures that any family minister can offer to any divorcing family.

There are also specific kinds of spiritual support that divorcing adults might need. Last week, I sat down at a favorite coffee place with my friend Lizbeth, and she shared openly about her experience of divorce and single parenting in the church. Much of what she told me came as brand-new information, truths I wouldn't have realized because I don't have the experience of divorce. While every divorced person is different, I bet many of them would resonate with Lizbeth's experience.

For Lizbeth, divorce felt like a failure, at first. Because she, like many others, had been raised to believe marriage was a necessary and righteous part of her Christian identity, watching her marriage break apart felt like she herself was breaking in the process. Every person who had ever invested in her marriage had feelings about the news of the divorce, and Lizbeth felt responsible for all of those feelings. Because she had fully believed that her marriage was God's plan, the guilt that was part of divorce was overwhelming, even though her divorce was biblically justified and absolutely the right decision for her, her ex-husband, and their daughter. A decision still can hurt even when it's right. Adults who are working through divorce and its aftermath often experience a spiritual crisis along with a multitude of practical stressors, including legal proceedings, family schedules, division of assets, and the process of breaking the news to everyone's teachers/therapists/pastors/friends. It is exhausting and complex. Family ministers cannot resolve all of these difficulties, but they can strive to spiritually support divorcing adults. They can remind folks in the midst of divorce that they are not alone. They can normalize their feelings and offer grace and reassurance in the midst of spiritual crises. Family ministers can offer spiritual direction, prayer, Scripture, resources, and blessings in a way that regular friends usually can't.

Family ministers also can connect divorcing adults to qualified therapists. Any adult approaching divorce needs to establish a relationship with a licensed counselor. Most divorcing adults are experiencing this difficult life event for only the first time, but a good therapist has walked alongside dozens or even hundreds of divorcing couples. Talking to someone can help a person manage triggers, identify signs of danger, and provide context for their feelings. Divorce can feel dangerous; counselors are equipped to provide a safe space, even just for that one hour a week, that will help divorcing adults to make the process just a little bit smoother. Churches can help to get people the counseling they need in a few different ways. They can set aside funding to help cover the cost of counseling, even if just on a temporary basis.

Another helpful resource churches can offer is a short list of trusted, experienced attorneys. My small church is blessed to have an excellent divorce attorney involved in the congregation, and I have watched as many church members have heaved sighs of relief upon being introduced to someone they can trust to lead them through the process.

Many couples who once attended church as a family need to make a decision about which parent will remain at the church. Pastors and ministry directors can help by offering available options depending on the situation. If the church offers multiple services, you could invite parents to claim different times to attend. If they need to find separate worship communities, you may be able to recommend other churches where you know they will receive welcome and care. The conversation about who remains in your congregation and how also should include plans for children's involvement. Whenever possible, keep the church open and safe for every member of the family. If there has been abuse or trauma leading up to the divorce, it might not be possible for some members of the family to worship safely with the others. If that is the case, make a clear plan for who will remain in your church community as well as how those who need to find another place to worship can do so and find care there.

It is our responsibility to consider all different types of families when setting our church calendar. For single parents, events that take place after dinner, especially on weekdays, can be prohibitively difficult. Ask yourself what assumptions are at work in the timing of our events—if Bible study only works for people who can leave kids at home, then consider how to make it open to those who do not have that privilege. Single parents may benefit from events that are structured as playdates, where they can bring their kids along. Or they may be interested in hosting meetings in their home after their kids' bedtimes. Offering quality childcare during ministry times, especially outside Sunday mornings, is no longer optional. Single parents need childcare options in order to fully participate in your ministry—which they may need more than any other adult in the church.

Just as we discussed in the disability ministry chapter, our goal in working with divorced families should be reciprocity. As a divorce's initial shock and crisis subsides, the way we treat divorced parents should also evolve. They should not always be on the receiving end of ministry. Divorced parents have told me that they actually grew tired of always receiving pity, gifts, and time from others, no matter how loving the intention. People on the other side of divorce have gifts and abilities to contribute, and we should allow them to assume a normal, reciprocal position in the church. I recall a church member who is a single mom with two young boys. This woman is a powerhouse, always among the first to volunteer for service opportunities, one of the earliest arrivers at early worship service, and one of the last to leave the churchwide property work day. I am always tempted to fawn over her, exulting over how sacrificial she is as she comes to serve with two kids in tow—but I have learned that for most of us, being allowed to serve and receive just like everyone else is what we need. We all need to belong, and that only happens in a relationship of mutuality.

Most of all, churches can help divorces to happen in healthier, safer, better ways by talking about them openly and honestly. One of the worst things we can do as church leaders is to ignore a family's divorce. Both adults in a divorce need our care, compassion, and honest questions to determine how we can see to their needs.

Supporting Children in Divorce

Recognize that divorce is such a big deal for the adults going through it that it can be hard to consider the needs of the children. Children want to be included, listened to, and given a sense of normalcy throughout the process of marriage dissolution.[27] Kids are affected every bit as much by divorce as their parents, and in caring for divorced families, we want to be aware of the feelings and needs of the kids just as much as the parents. That care looks different for kids, however, because their age, birth order, and maturity vary so widely that there are no simple rules for how they'll process this big family change. And we cannot simply invite them to coffee and ask penetrating questions to determine how best to serve them. In fact, it is important not to interfere with their grief process in divorce by inserting ourselves into the dynamic too much. For kids, often the best thing we can do is to care for both of their parents, then make their spaces in youth and children's ministry as safe as possible.

Upon learning that parents in your congregation are divorcing, one of the best first steps to take is to obtain parental permission to inform the children's church leaders. Explain that you want the leaders to be able to provide protection and extra care for their kids, and to do that, they need to be prepared to respond appropriately if the child behaves differently or references the divorce. Every kid processes divorce differently. Some will talk about the divorce during church, while others will shield themselves from sharing. It is also possible that other young people in the church will hear their parents discussing someone's divorce in the home and bring questions or even teasing into church. We must be ready to interrupt such dynamics, to take any questioning or teasing friends aside to coach them in the right way to show love to their friend. Being proactive means sharing basics with the church leaders who may be in contact with the family and being sure they know to be respectful, encouraging, and alert to needs.

Kids of all ages will often internalize the hurt, guilt, shame, or fear they feel during their parents' transition to divorce. With a parent's permission, it may be appropriate to broach the subject of divorce privately with a teenager and offer to be a listener for them. For young children, however, recognize that they are not nearly as conscious of their emotional process yet and likely would not benefit from having an adult bring up the topic of divorce with them, other than perhaps briefly mentioning to them that they are loved and that you're there for them, if they ever need to talk. Children of divorce can feel immense pressure to give allegiance to one or both

---

27   Ibid., 234.

parents, whether that pressure comes from their parents or is self-imposed. The last thing they need is for a well-intentioned third or fourth adult to position themselves as someone in need of loyalty as well.

On the flip side, kids whose parents have divorced bring a broader, more inclusive perspective to family than other kids. Kids whose families have broken, shifted, and re-formed see family as a broader network, and many of the stories in the Bible of mix-and-match families will make clear sense to kids who have learned to claim friends, aunts, uncles, grandparents, and stepparents as family members themselves.

For children whose parents remarry after divorce, roles and allegiances must shift. They may find themselves trying to maintain the right amount of loyalty for each biological parent and stepparent. If stepsiblings are blended into the household, birth order and age-based roles shift, which can produce identity confusion for both the kids and their parents.[28]

One of the more awkward but essential conversations to have with divorcing parents about their children concerns custodial agreements. Get clarity about who is allowed to pick up the child(ren) and set up a communication plan if there are custodial agreements that affect the church's security procedures. If a parent has lost legal privileges for contact with their child, the church needs to proceed with caution when releasing that child to a parent at pickup. Be sure all childcare staff and volunteers in charge at drop-off and pickup times are aware if there is a specific adult who is not allowed to pick up a child.

A practical and simple gift we can give to children of divorce is to recognize that their attendance pattern at church is subject to which parent's household they are a part of that weekend. Keeping attendance charts, offering rewards for excellent attendance, or making a big deal of multi-week projects can make church a sad place for children who are only there when they're with a certain parent. Emphasize for all kids that when they're present, they 100 percent belong. Offer activities and challenges that can be fulfilled the same day they begin.

One other note to keep in mind when working with kids of divorce is to be sure never to put them in the middle or on the spot. Don't ask them which parent is coming to pick them up or where they spent the night.

---

28 Ibid.

Don't bring up the divorce for them during prayer request time or ask them to share about it. If they want to share, that's great! But that's up to them.

Divorce is often a lifelong relational challenge. Even after the papers are signed, coparenting and custodial arrangements between parents go on. Kids sometimes find that their emotional needs are met by both parents, and sometimes they feel neglected, used, or blamed. Expect kids of divorce in your church to go through a long process of highs and lows. Just like adults in divorce, kids need and deserve quality time with a quality therapist, and it is appropriate to urge parents to connect their kids to a professional counselor throughout the divorce proceedings and beyond. Kids are resilient, and if their parents are able to love and care for them, they will most often emerge on the other side of divorce with all the hope and thriving of any other kid. We as church leaders can be lookouts for these kids, accepting their struggle on hard days and celebrating the goodness of life with them, too.

Supporting Friends and Family in Divorce

One family's divorce can affect many other friends and family within the church as well. We can do a huge favor to divorcing families by putting a stop to rumors and gossip as much as possible. One way to do this is to encourage divorcing adults to speak clearly and openly about the divorce and to clearly communicate their plans for participation going forward. Because divorce requires that two people divide their lives from one another, taking sides is a natural reaction for their friends to have, but not necessarily a helpful one. We can model how to be in relationship with both adults in a divorcing family by refusing to gossip or share confidential information with others, by designating meaningful spaces for both of them to continue to worship and serve in the church where possible, and by initiating conversations with their friends and extended church family members who could benefit from knowing how they can best support and grieve with the family through divorce.

Final Thoughts

Marriage is at once wonderful and complicated, a life event to be celebrated and supported. The church has the opportunity to be a support system for marriages that are healthy and those that are in crisis. At the same time, we never want to put marriage on a pedestal in our theology, elevating it to a status toward which single adults should strive, or a requirement for service or belonging in the church. We ought to love marriage just like we love singleness, recognizing the blessings and struggles of both.

When marriage becomes toxic and harmful to those in it, we church leaders can hold the hands of couples who need to separate and provide safe spaces through pastoral counseling or by diverting them to trusted professional therapists as needed. It is our job to shepherd the whole family and the larger community through divorce, not taking sides or demonizing anyone, but showing the church how to value everyone as children of God. Both marriage and divorce care call on us to exercise our highest capacity for honesty, unconditional love, and checking our judgmental preconceptions at the door. Loving our people, asking hard questions, and setting careful boundaries may never be more vital than in marriage and divorce ministry.

CHAPTER 12

CRISIS & COUNSELING

A few months ago, I woke up planning to lead a weekend retreat for a ministry team and discovered I couldn't move my leg without awful pain. Within a few hours, I was admitted to intensive care with a blood clot that ran the length of my right leg and a bilateral pulmonary embolism. Crisis strikes fast. Reflecting on that sudden hospital stay, I can't help wondering what it would be like without a church family. Multiple pastors from my church visited me every day, and friends quickly filled a meal delivery schedule for the next three weeks. Never did I feel alone.

One of my friends is a single dad with a 15-year-old son. He had surgery to remove cancer earlier this year and had to stay in the hospital for a few days. With no family or church connections, he arranged for his son to sleep in his hospital room and take the city bus across town to school each morning. While lying in his hospital bed, he worried nonstop about his son's safety, wondering what he would do if his son needed him. He was alone in his crisis.

So much of our job is simply to ensure that everyone has a support network, that the families in our church are not alone when they walk through dark valleys. God sends comfort, grace, healing, and peace through the words, actions, and presence of people—through us. This chapter reviews some of the effects trauma and crisis can have on families. The chapter also discusses the particular needs families may experience during crises involving addiction, death, illness, abuse, and so forth. It's not uplifting to contemplate walking through these difficult events; at the same time, it is quite a privilege to be spiritual companions to people experiencing tragedy and heartbreak.

Crisis Ministry

At times, every church leader is called to hit the pause button on the day-to-day tasks of ministry and focus significant time and energy on supporting families in crisis. While this part of our work doesn't show up in many official job descriptions, I venture to say it is one of the most important things that we do. Before we can make a response plan for different crises that may affect our churches, we need a basic understanding of the effects of crisis and trauma. Please let me emphasize the word *basic* here—this chapter will be just enough to whet your appetite for further learning about crisis and trauma.

Not every event or circumstance that you or I would consider traumatic is so for everyone else; the application of words such as "crisis" or "trauma" to an event is based solely on the perception of the individual involved.[1] For example, delivering a baby a month early could be truly difficult for some new parents, while others would consider it expected and take it in stride. In short, we can't assume what constitutes a crisis for someone else. We must trust others to communicate their perceptions of their life events to us.

People define words such as stress, trauma, and crisis in many different ways. For our purposes, we will use the following definitions:

Stress is "a particular relationship between the person and the environment that is appraised by the person as taxing or exceeding his or her resources and endangering well-being."[2] Again, the stress is in the perception of the person experiencing it. Stress also can be thought of as an

1   Catherine N. Dulmus and Carolyn Hilarski, "When Stress Constitutes Trauma and Trauma Constitutes Crisis: The Stress-Trauma-Crisis Continuum," *Brief Treatment and Crisis Intervention* 3, no. 1 (March 1, 2003): 27–36, https://doi.org/10.1093/brief-treatment/mhg008.

2   Richard S. Lazarus, "Puzzles in the Study of Daily Hassles," *Journal of Behavioral Medicine* 7, no. 4 (December 1984): 376, https://doi.org/10.1007/BF00845271.

uncomfortable "emotional experience accompanied by predictable bio-chemical, physiological, and behavioral changes."[3] It is accompanied by ongoing negative changes that wear us out in every way, affecting our physical, mental, and spiritual health.

Trauma is a perceived physical or psychological injury that follows a stressful event, causing anxiety and exceeding a person's ability to cope with the stress.[4] Trauma develops out of stress and encapsulates deep feelings of powerlessness.

Crisis occurs when a person's perception of trauma progresses "to a place of understood instability and disorganization due to an unresolved acute or chronic perceived stress."[5]

Stress, trauma, and crisis operate on a continuum, and we can find families in our ministries at any point on the continuum. Stress is an almost everyday occurrence, and while stressful circumstances have the potential to become traumatic, families are usually able to resolve through the systems and personal resources they already have. Regular, everyday stress can lead to *eustress*, which is the ability to gather the resources needed to meet the increased demands, thereby strengthening family bonds. On the other hand, stressful circumstances also can lead to *distress*, which is the inability to meet the demands of the stressor, thereby weakening family bonds.[6] When a family is in distress, their needs may be greater than the church is equipped to meet. They are also at greater risk of moving down the continuum to trauma and/or crisis.

When stress evolves into trauma, it is because the person experiencing it perceives the stress has caused damage to their psyche or their body that they cannot overcome on their own. Crisis is the natural result of trauma that is not resolved and healed, the state of being that occurs when injuries go untreated. Crisis is an overall state of imbalance caused by trauma.

3   A. Baum, "Stress, Intrusive Imagery, and Chronic Distress," *Health Psychology: Official Journal of the Division of Health Psychology, American Psychological Association* 9, no. 6 (1990): 653–75.

4   Dulmus and Hilarski, "When Stress Constitutes Trauma and Trauma Constitutes Crisis," 29.

5   Ibid., 30.

6   Diana R. Garland, F*amily Ministry: A Comprehensive Guide*, 2nd edition (Downers Grove, IL: IVP Academic, 2012), 259.

Taking Blame out of Suffering

We can only respond to a person's suffering with grace if we have learned to dampen the reflex to look for someone to blame. It is sometimes easier to think of suffering as sin or the effects of sin than it is to accept that bad things happen for many reasons. The tendency to place blame is as harmful as the tragedy itself. When a parent is incarcerated, we can expend more energy speculating about what went wrong than doing everything in our power to support both the parent who is taken away and the family that is left behind. When a child receives an autism diagnosis, we might catch ourselves wondering if the mother smoked during pregnancy, or if there is some family history of disorder that could have caused this. These inclinations to lay the blame somewhere can keep us so preoccupied that we fail to provide grace and support to our church family. Our job is to set aside questions of blame and go about building resilience in one another.

"What Happened?"

A simple change we can make regards the language we use when talking to people experiencing stress. We want to invite people to share their stories truly and freely. An inviting way to begin a conversation with someone who is experiencing difficulty is to ask "What happened?"[7] This sounds ridiculously obvious, but bear with me. When people appear upset, our tendency is to ask, with all the care in the world, "What's wrong?" By questioning with a negative word, we may shut down the storytelling we are trying to invite. People take "What's wrong?" personally, because it comes across as blame—either they or someone else did something wrong to cause the problem. By reframing the question to ask "What happened?" we communicate that we will listen without judgment or blame.[8] When a youth has a meltdown during a group game or a parent approaches with a serious look and asks if you have a minute to talk, avoid

---

7   Lucy Johnstone and Mary Boyle, "The Power Threat Meaning Framework: An Alternative Nondiagnostic Conceptual System," *Journal of Humanistic Psychology*, August 5, 2018, 187, https://doi.org/10.1177/0022167818793289.

8   Cathy Kezelman and Pam Stavropoulos, "'The Last Frontier'—Practice Guidelines for Treatment of Complex Trauma and Trauma Informed Care and Service Delivery" (Blue Knot Foundation (Formerly Adults Surviving Child Abuse), 2012), 14.

asking what is wrong. Ask what has happened. Giving people the chance to tell their story is one of the best healing practices God has given us.

Stress Begets Crisis, Which Begets More Stress

Crises come in multiples; one bad experience often leads to others; the ripple effect can feel overwhelming. Crisis begets stress, which begets more trauma and crisis. A parent who becomes depressed may not be able to get out of bed and get to work on time, which could bring on another crisis of being let go from their job. That crisis leads to financial stress on the family, which can show itself in a change in socioeconomic status, the loss of home or belongings, marital and family fighting, and so forth. And all the while, none of these stresses goes away—they simply build upon each other.

Crises are not neatly contained within family systems, either. According to Diana Garland, "stress is contagious."[9] We see this in a family system, when one member's extreme stress affects the whole household. We also see it in church families, when one person enters into crisis mode and everyone else jumps right in with them. Many communities can attest to this phenomenon when it comes to cluster suicides, or a rampant drug addiction problem, or racially-motivated crimes. Experts have coined the term "contagion" effect to explain the increased likelihood of additional mass shootings following a single mass-shooting incident.[10] Ask your pastor if they have ever experienced a surge of funerals all at the same time, and my guess is, they have. It is important to zoom out from an initial stressful event to ask what ripple effect it may have both within the family of origin and throughout the church community at large. Our first attention goes to direct survivors of crisis, but good leaders will keep a close watch on others who may find themselves in the pathway of an escalating crisis.

Making Church a Safe Place

Church does not feel like a safe place for everyone. Safety is not automatic; it must be cultivated in a given environment. Families often feel that

---

9   Garland, 258.
10   James N. Meindl and Jonathan W. Ivy, "Mass Shootings: The Role of the Media in Promoting Generalized Imitation," *American Journal of Public Health* 107, no. 3 (March 2017): 368–70, https://doi.org/10.2105/AJPH.2016.303611.

their greatest crises are shameful, and therefore, should be hidden from the church. They might see the church as a place to put their best foot forward, even as their lives are falling apart at home. Perceived judgment creates a sad cycle wherein the church cannot support those in the true crises of adultery, mental illness, addiction, or poverty because these conditions are kept hidden.[11]

Safety is established through clear boundaries and expectations. Uncertainty about boundaries breeds fear and anxiety. Naming important boundaries around things such as appropriate touch, confidentiality, codependency, and accountability makes church a much safer place for people to share and grow. The best time to name a boundary is at the very beginning, before people have a chance to cross it. It is possible, but more difficult, to enforce accountability for a boundary someone crossed without knowing it was in place. It is much easier to refer to a safety rule that everyone acknowledged and agreed to from the start. That is why my first session with any small group consists of walking through the boundaries the group will live by and explaining the rationale behind them.

We need to do a better job in general of making church a safe place for everyone. Once people know what the expectations are, they are freed to be more open and vulnerable, trusting that the information they share will be received with respect and care. When a crisis hits, our hope is that the families in our churches will have established care groups with whom they can share and who will provide support.

When people do begin to share about a crisis in their lives, it is important to treat them as the experts in their own lives. After all, the individual sharing their first-person experience is undoubtedly the most knowledgeable and trustworthy source! It can be tempting to try to fix people before they've hardly gotten the words out of their mouths. Jumping to conclusions and stepping in to "fix" someone in crisis are some of the quickest ways to make them feel unsafe in sharing further.

There's one more consideration to keep in mind when creating safe spaces for people to share in small groups: discussing a person's current trauma can cause unknown harm to someone who has had a similar experience in the past. We can re-traumatize people simply by talking in too

---

11   Garland, 12.

much detail about a crisis at hand. As we approach any topic that could bring up difficult and damaging experiences in someone's past, we must acknowledge that and set up safe, healthy places for people to either opt out of the discussion or process their experiences with someone qualified to listen to and guide them.

Ritual and Storytelling

Another way to talk truthfully about stress, trauma, and crisis is through narratives. Storytelling is a practice that can protect people who are stressed out or traumatized by giving them an indirect reference point to help them work through their experience. At the same time, these narratives can help people who are unaffected by trauma to develop empathy. The Bible is well-stocked with trauma stories—we do not have to look more than a few chapters into Genesis to see a couple being evicted from their home (Genesis 3:23-24) and a brother murdering his brother (4:2-9).

Telling the stories of Scripture through a trauma-informed lens is a healing practice for those who are wrapped up in the shame, secrecy, isolation, and fear that crisis can bring. Once people realize that God is no stranger to hurt and pain, perhaps trusting God with their own hurt could be possible. When we read Bible stories in our churches, we should look for the places where God and God's people experienced crisis and trauma, and we should acknowledge that human experiences haven't really changed all that much. In Scripture, we see how God works through it. God doesn't prevent pain, but God does bring redemption, as only God can. Telling the story of God and God's people is one of the most loving, healing things we can offer in the church.

In addition to storytelling, I believe rituals are one of our best tools for delivering healing power. In therapeutic settings, experts use rituals to combine everyday ideas and symbols with new or unfamiliar changes and ideas. Rituals used in this way encourage positive reflection on change and help people to accept what's next in their lives.[12] And if ritual can be put to

12   Monica McGoldrick, Nydia A. Garcia Preto, and Betty A. Carter, *The Expanding Family Life Cycle: Individual, Family, and Social Perspectives*, 5th edition (Boston: Pearson,

reparative use in therapy, how much more powerful could these practices be in the spiritual setting of the church?

A ritual can be anything that utilizes a symbol or metaphor to help people process change—whether the change is spiritual transformation, the loss of a loved one, divorce, or recovery from trauma. Crisis changes us, sometimes trapping us in a confusing, paralyzing, dark place emotionally. Rituals encourage us to repeat the same uplifting practice over and over, using symbols to approach our pain rather than facing it head on. Rituals make the hard changes of life appear less threatening.[13]

If we want our churches to be places of safety and healing, we will install rituals into our worship and discipleship. For someone processing trauma, the weekly practice of taking Communion, lighting a candle, touching the baptismal water, or writing down anonymous prayer requests can bring more peace than a hundred sermons or sympathetic looks. Instituting rituals in recovery and support groups is mandatory, but they don't have to be limited to those environments. No matter how contemporary your church's worship style or old-fashioned your membership, consider what symbolic rituals could work in your worship setting. Perhaps your children could write or draw letters to God each week and put them in a mailbox. Or you could pick up a pair of binoculars or a magnifying glass and direct the kids to share it around as they tell where they have seen God at work in their world in the past week. Give people a tangible item that symbolizes the work of God in their lives.

Ritual is applicable to all ages—adults and kids alike need safe, familiar, repetitive invitations to healing and holiness. It can be intimidating to think of walking alongside anyone in their healing journey, but it's especially hard to contemplate shepherding a hurting child. Keep in mind that spiritual resources are just as needed and just as appropriate for the young as for the old. "Children of all ages have the capacity for spiritual thoughts and beliefs, and very often their spirituality can help them to heal."[14]

Odds are that you have already incorporated ritual into your weekly worship and discipleship routines without even realizing it! Identify the

---

2015), 498.

13   Ibid., 493.

14   Ibid., 159.

rituals you are already using, and look for other places to introduce symbolic language and objects that can invite people into safe processing. One of my children's leaders realized that many children in elementary school shared deep burdens during prayer time, so she introduced them to the Candle of Hope. Even though this was a simple white pillar candle from a big box store, to the kids it contained significance. Anyone who had a prayer request for themselves or someone else who was hurting could ask to light the Candle of Hope, and as they held the lighter along with her, they would speak a prayer for mercy. Each time, a fraction of their grief was transferred to that little flame, taken in by a candle and transformed into hope. That's what the church does; we gather in all of God's hurting people and light a flame of hope inside their hearts. It doesn't fix the pain, but it does give comfort amid the hurt.

Our Own Trauma

Before moving into discussions of specific crises that merit preparation and attention in ministry, I have one final note of great importance: Deal with your own trauma first.

It is possible that already while reading this chapter, your own trauma has been triggered. There is potential for all of us to see ourselves in discussions of trauma and crisis. If there are traumatic experiences in your history that you have not yet worked through, you are in no condition to walk alongside someone else as they make that journey, too. A small-group leader who breaks down or lashes out when a youth shares about an experience of bullying, sexual assault, or drug use because it touches on painful personal history can do infinite harm. None of us is exempt from the hard work of therapy and healing from trauma, and attending seminary or reading this book won't take care of that for us. If there is a chance that there is unaddressed trauma in your life, put down this book and schedule an appointment with a pastor or therapist (or both) right now. No strategies or research-backed suggestions will mask deep-set hurt that we haven't yet given over to God.

Even if we have worked through our trauma, we've still got to stay on our guard when it comes to compassion fatigue, the "natural, predictable, treatable, and preventable consequence of working with suffering people."[15] In other words, supporting someone else through stress, trauma, and crisis has an effect on us. Church leaders, especially pastors and ministers, spend a lot of time with people who need to talk about their stress and trauma. Repeated experiences of listening to others tell stressful and traumatic stories and providing support can result in two different responses.

One is compassion satisfaction, the positive effect of trauma work that has to do with feelings of pleasure and fulfillment in supporting survivors well.[16] You have probably experienced the joy of serving, the confidence-boost that comes from knowing you are making a difference, the pleasure and blessing that come from giving. Those are all parts of compassion satisfaction.

Compassion fatigue, on the other hand, is characterized by emotional burnout and feelings of exhaustion and isolation. If left untreated, compassion fatigue can develop into vicarious trauma, a state that encompasses burnout and secondary traumatic stress, which can lead to post-traumatic stress disorder (PTSD) symptoms.[17] That's right—according to research on vicarious trauma, the person who listens to and guides others as they process a traumatic experience can be traumatized themselves. Therapists and social workers manage this phenomenon all the time, and church leaders are no stranger to it either. We are foolish if we do not acknowledge the emotional and spiritual toll that shepherding can take upon us and upon the volunteers we supervise.

Whenever ministry leaders experience compassion fatigue, they need to take a step back and care for their own spirits in order to continue providing care to others. When it comes to vicarious trauma, however, professional help may be needed. The best way to know if you are

15   Stephen B. Roberts et al., "Compassion Fatigue Among Chaplains, Clergy, and Other Respondents After September 11th," *Journal of Nervous and Mental Disease* 191, no. 11 (2003): 756–58, https://doi.org/10.1097/01.nmd.0000095129.50042.30.

16   Debra Larsen and Beth Hudnall Stamm, "Professional Quality of Life and Trauma Therapists," in *Trauma, Recovery, and Growth: Positive Psychological Perspectives on Post-traumatic Stress* (Hoboken, NJ, US: John Wiley & Sons Inc, 2008), 275–93.

17   Ekundayo A. Sodeke-Gregson, Sue Holttum, and Jo Billings, "Compassion Satisfaction, Burnout, and Secondary Traumatic Stress in UK Therapists Who Work with Adult Trauma Clients," *European Journal of Psychotraumatology* 4 (December 30, 2013), https://doi.org/10.3402/ejpt.v4i0.21869.

experiencing common compassion fatigue or the more serious phenomenon of vicarious trauma is to ask yourself if you are exhibiting the symptoms of PTSD: repeated, distressing recollections of the traumatic experiences you've heard others describe; difficulty sleeping; irritability or angry outbursts; difficulty concentrating; decreased interest or participation in significant activities; feelings of exhaustion and isolation; a negative shift in your self-perception or worldview.[18] If these symptoms apply to you, simple self-care and investment in your well-being is not a sufficient response. Care from a licensed therapist may be needed.

Once we recognize signs of compassion fatigue within ourselves, we must deal with them, and fortunately there are possibilities for relief. There are helpful practices that can make compassion fatigue and vicarious trauma manageable for those of us in a position to help others. Studies show us that receiving quality, loving support and direction from a supervisor is a key protection against burnout and compassion fatigue.[19] The ability to unload on a supervisor and receive affirmation and advice alleviates some of the stress of carrying a burden for a church member. Another protective practice against compassion fatigue is participation in a variety of learning and ministry activities, apart from personal support to people in crisis.[20] In times of crisis we do often devote large portions of our week or month to assisting a family that needs us, but even in the most difficult times it is important to maintain work and life balance. It is more than OK—it is healthy—to set boundaries, even with someone in crisis, if their emergency begins to encroach upon our health, our relationships, and our availability to carry on in ministry. We cannot support others if we are utterly depleted ourselves.

Apart from the research, I will say that from my personal experience, one of the greatest safeguards against burnout and secondary stress is having a separate, unaffected person or group in whom I can confide. While I haven't found this in my research, I know that when someone in my life

18   John P. Wilson, "PTSD and Complex PTSD: Symptoms, Syndromes and Diagnoses," in *Assessing Psychological Trauma and PTSD*, ed. John P. Wilson and Terence M. Keane, 2nd Edition (New York, NY: Guilford Publications, 2004), 7–44.

19   Sodeke-Gregson, Holttum, and Billings, "Compassion Satisfaction, Burnout, and Secondary Traumatic Stress in UK Therapists Who Work with Adult Trauma Clients."

20   Ibid.

is hurting and shares that painful experience with me, I often find that the burden is too heavy for me to carry alone. I need a tertiary presence to hold my hand as I hold the hand of the primary victim. For anyone who loves a trinitarian God and believes in the importance of Christian community, it should come as no surprise that one of the best ways to deal with vicarious trauma is to be in relationship with others.

It does absolutely no good to share our secondary trauma with some-one who is already affected by it. The only people who can help carry our burdens are the ones who are separate from them. If there is a crisis in your church, you need to find someone outside your church to listen. Talking up a crisis to someone who is a part of it does nothing to alleviate the stress from either of you. I realize this practice can easily fall into gossip territory, and I caution all of us to take care to ensure that we are not talking out of turn about those in our care. This is one reason why a therapist or a confi-dential accountability group outside our church's purview is a really good idea. Spouses, colleagues, and church discipleship groups are rarely in a position to help us process trauma that occurs in spheres they are a part of.

There's no cure for crisis. Being aware of it and in relationships is a way to deal with it. Don't perpetuate trauma by only being in relationships with others who are also experiencing vicarious trauma! That is, develop rela-tionships with people who aren't like you, who aren't working in the church or in positions that expose them to other people's crises on a regular basis.

Addiction, Death, Tragedy, and Trauma

This is by no means an exhaustive list of things that can go wrong in families. Some of the options I'll offer below will work in a variety of cir-cumstances. Others are only relevant in a few cases. Of course, there are some supports that are almost always welcome in any situation—those would be providing meals, free babysitting services, and visitation. I have never yet been turned down when offering to set up a meal delivery sched-ule for a family after the birth of a baby, or a hospitalization or death. Always cater to dietary restrictions and preferences, of course, and be sure to ask if any relatives or friends should be included in the number of servings. Recommending babysitters or setting up childcare services must account for background checks, training, and safety. Visitation, whether in the home or in the hospital, is necessary to be sure none of our people can ever feel alone or abandoned in their time of need. (Unless they fail to inform us of their need, which does happen sometimes. All that can be done then is to act as soon as we have any idea there is a need.) In times of crisis, we always visit our people, pray over our people, and seek to meet basic needs like meals and childcare. If budget and support allow, housekeeping services, grocery shopping and other errands are welcome contributions from friends and volunteers. Now let's talk about some specifics.

Addiction

If a family in your church reaches a crisis due to a drug or alcohol addiction, you can better support them if you have a cursory understanding of these matters. Alcoholism is "the persistent and excessive use of alcohol that results in physiological, psychological, and/or social impairment over the course of the life cycle, and this behavior is shaped by family dynamics."[21] (While this definition is specific to alcohol, you could replace alcohol with any other drug and it would hold true.) The most important principle to keep in mind is that addiction affects every person in the family. And the effects of living with someone with an addiction can last a lifetime.

According to the U.S. Department of Health and Human Services, between 2009 and 2014, about 8.7 million (or 12.3 percent of) children lived with at least one parent with a substance-use disorder.[22] What these statistics tell us is that the families in our churches are not exempt from the effects of drug and alcohol addiction; it would be surprising if there were no children in your church affected by alcohol or substance-abuse problems. And these numbers do not even touch on the children and youth themselves who become dependent on drugs or alcohol at young ages.

Because of a tricky little phenomenon called codependency, the "habituated excessive mental and emotional attachment to a partner with

21 McGoldrick, Preto, and Carter, 455.
22 Rachel N. Lipari and Struther L. Van Horn, "Children Living with Parents Who Have a Substance Use Disorder," Substance Abuse and Mental Health Services Administration, 2017, https://www.samhsa.gov/data/report/children-living-parents-who-have-substance-use-disorder.

an addiction,"[23] it is common for the family system affected by addiction to close in on itself in secrecy. Scholars use the term "alcoholic family" to convey the tendency for families to develop patterns of interaction that center around the addiction and the need to cover it up and abet it.[24] Alcoholism should not be considered outside a family systems philosophy, with the understanding that the disease impacts each member of the family and that each member of the family influences the addiction story.[25]

We will not gain any headway in helping families navigate the crisis of addiction if we demonize the person with the problem. People with substance-use disorders often feel shame and helplessness without outsiders piling it on. Still, the church's efforts should prioritize the needs of children, siblings, and spouses, as well as the one with the alcohol or drug problem. As discussed earlier, crisis leads to crisis—drug and alcohol abuse can contribute to joblessness, abuse (physical, emotional, or sexual), mental health concerns, driving accidents, isolation, and so forth. Addiction is not a simple or well-contained problem. While the church is not usually equipped to meet all of a family's needs in an addiction crisis, we do have an important role. First, we can know which warning signs to look for:

- Sudden changes in personality or mood. While it can be easy to chalk up these changes to puberty in our adolescents or stress in adults, if a person becomes suddenly withdrawn, uninterested in the usual activities, or angry, it is worth paying attention.
- Lack of concern about appearance or grooming
- Sabotaging relationships with family and friends[26]
- New friend groups, especially folks who drink or use drugs
- Being unable to stop or limit the amount of alcohol or drugs used
- Observable changes in job, relationships, eating and sleeping habits, mood, or defensiveness

---

23   McGoldrick, Preto, and Carter, 461.
24   Ibid., 455.
25   Ibid., 454.
26   "Principles of Adolescent Substance Use Disorder Treatment: A Research-Based Guide" (National Institute on Drug Abuse, 2014), https://www.drugabuse.gov/publications/principles-adolescent-substance-use-disorder-treatment-research-based-guide/frequently-asked-questions/what-are-signs-drug-use-in-adolescents-what-role-can-parents-play-in-getting-treatment.

- Using alcohol or drugs in unsafe situations, such as when driving or swimming.[27]

The next thing we can do is ask tough questions. If it turns out that our suspicions were unfounded, we can hope that the person we talk to interprets our questions as a sign of care. There are plenty of resources on the Internet with helpful questions to ask someone we worry may have a problem with drugs or alcohol. Because the desire for secrecy is so strong, we may not get straight answers; simply the questions may begin to offer some accountability. If there is any concern that children in the family or a spouse may be at risk for harm because of an addiction, it is our duty to call the appropriate department in our state to report it.

Know that addiction can affect any person and any family. No one is too good, too well-off, or too healthy to suffer from this disorder. Talking openly with youth and parents about our concerns and the warning signs to look for is one way to communicate that you are a safe person to confide in, and that you will always put the safety of the kids and parents in your ministry above your own interpersonal discomfort.

A practical, simple first step in learning about and supporting recovery in your church community is to partner with existing 12-step programs such as Alcoholics Anonymous, Al-Anon and Alateen, Narcotics Anonymous, Adult Children of Alcoholics, or Families Anonymous. These programs are free, already existing, and often open for anyone to attend, including pastors and church staff who simply want to learn from them. Hosting one or more meetings like these at your church is a wonderful way to support 12-step programs and introduce your church to conversations about alcoholism and addiction.

Death

One of the most important ministries the church performs is funerals, which allow grieving family and friends to say goodbye to loved ones. In some aging congregations, this is a regular and repeated ministry of the church, and the pastors there glimpse one of the most profound, life-

---

27 "Alcohol Use Disorder - Symptoms and Causes," Mayo Clinic, accessed September 20, 2019, https://www.mayoclinic.org/diseases-conditions/alcohol-use-disorder/symptoms-causes/syc-20369243.

changing challenges that families confront: dealing with death and loss.[28] While coming to terms with the absence of someone who has occupied a huge part of your world is a long process, the funeral event is a significant moment of closure, much like a milestone of grief that people can look back on for comfort or direction.

When working with grieving families in planning a funeral, our primary goal is to promote healthy grief. The technical term is "adaptive mourning," the transition from seeing a lost loved one as a physical presence and instead focusing on the positive memories, stories, and legacies that honor them.[29] Helping people adjust to a new reality without their loved one can be a messy process. Anger, bitterness, depression, isolation, and irritability are all common feelings in the grief process.

As shepherds of this difficult milestone event, we are called to pay special attention to children and youth experiencing grief. Kids under the age of 5 do not understand the finality of death. To them, death is reversible, and they may ask questions about when Grandma is coming back or what Daddy is doing up in heaven right now.[30] Don't use euphemisms or metaphors for this age group—keep it simple. Tell them that their loved one has died and their body isn't working anymore. Let children know that we can remember them, talk about them, and miss them very much, but we won't be able to see or talk to them anymore. Avoid talking about the loved one going to heaven, going on a journey, passing away, and so forth. Use concrete language as much as possible. But just because they can't fully understand death, don't assume that young children do not grieve. They have great capacity for mourning and sadness, and their grief process should be respected just as much as an adult's would be.[31]

On *The Moth Radio Hour* podcast, a chaplain named Kate Braestrup told a story about how she helps others deal with death.[32] Her story centered on a 5-year-old girl who insisted on visiting her deceased cousin's

---

28   McGoldrick, Preto, and Carter, 360.

29   Ibid., 361.

30   Atle Dyregrov, *Grief in Children: A Handbook for Adults*, 2nd ed. (London, England: Jessica Kingsley Publishers, 2008), 15.

31   Ibid., 17–18.

32   Kate Braestrup, "The House of Mourning," The Moth Radio Hour (podcast), July 21, 2015, accessed November 11, 2019, https://themoth.org/stories/the-house-of-mourning.

body in the funeral home prior to services. The girl's parents were hesitant—wouldn't such a jarring, mournful experience scare her or hamper her ability to cope? But Kate reassured them that human beings can be trusted with grief; we somehow know what we need. In the end, the child sneaked in a meaningful memento to leave with her cousin in the morgue, sang a song over him, lovingly touched his arm, then was ready to go. She wanted to mark his passing in her own way.

Kids ages 5 to 10 have a more developed sense of empathy and justice. They think fairly concretely and, like younger children, benefit from simple, honest, straightforward language about death. Children in this age range sometimes make assumptions in their grief about who is to blame for the death, entertain mystical or magical reversals of death, or develop deep sympathy for others who have lost someone.[33] Funeral planning can be a form of meaning-making for older children, and it provides a way for families to talk about the death together. If you are involved in funeral planning, invite all generations to be as much a part of it as they desire. Coach parents in talking plainly to their children about death. Encourage them to be open to their children's proposals about grief rituals, whether that means continuing to set a place at the table for a deceased family member or developing another ritual for remembering them.

For children ages 10 and up, the death of a loved one is felt to be much more personal. This age group can comprehend the finality and permanence of the loss, so they must confront the relearning process of living life without someone important. For this age group, death is an existential crisis, a demand to reevaluate both personal identity and theology/philosophy.[34] Teens are highly social; peer relationships are significant to them. They may want to process their loss with the youth group, a few select friends, or even the whole of the Internet via social media. Since they are sensitive to rejection and misunderstanding, teens may isolate themselves if their peers are not prepared to sit with them in mourning. A meaningful and practical way to support a grieving teen is to coach their youth-group friends and leaders to listen to and accept them in their grief. Friends can make a remembrance craft, set up a schedule for sending encouraging text

33 Dyregrov, 19–20.
34 Ibid., 20–21.

messages, or sign a sympathy card to show that they are safe people to process and share with.

The long and the short of it is, do not be afraid to encounter grief, and trust those grieving to state their needs and desires for their grief process. Be prepared for hard conversations to come up with kids, teens, or the adults who care for them—but do not force them to talk, especially in public, if they don't want to. Also, don't be surprised if one person's recent loss revives others' grief over past losses. It could be helpful for a peer with a less recent loss to share how they felt and how they grieved, while acknowledging that saying goodbye to a loved one looks different for everyone.

It's important to note that when a death occurs suddenly or due to tragic circumstances, the need for pastoral care escalates. The majority of people who survive a traumatic death will experience awful distress initially but eventually gain resilience. Some, however, do experience post-traumatic stress disorder (PTSD) and need professional therapy to regain a healthy ability to live and work.[35] One of the most common traumatic deaths is suicide. A death by suicide occurs every 13 minutes in the United States, and for each suicide, there are 25 nonfatal suicide attempts.[36]

Suicide causes feelings of shock that can devastate friends and family members. The trauma of suicide has been likened to a grenade exploding inside a community. The effects of this explosion include intense guilt, anger, bewilderment, and the belief that the survivor should have prevented the suicide somehow.[37] The effects of suicide reach all ages; additionally, children who lose a parent to suicide tend to struggle more in their grief than children who lose a parent to other causes.[38]

Besides providing support and help with meals, childcare, and so forth, the best thing to do for survivors is to let them talk. Prepare yourself to accept a wide range of emotions, and do not interrupt. Do not try to explain. Do not try to fix or make them feel better. Hold a safe space for the person to talk, without fear that you will judge or cause them to suffer for it.[39]

---

35   McGoldrick, Preto, and Carter, 363.
36   Connie Goldsmith, *Understanding Suicide: A National Epidemic* (Minneapolis: Twenty-First Century Books, 2016), 6–7.
37   Ibid., 10.
38   Dyregrov, 63.
39   Goldsmith, 11–12.

In ministry, death is a drop-everything-else-and-run-to-help situation. Everyone grieves differently, but the common need for community support is a given. Reschedule the lunch meeting, order pizza for your family at home, turn over the responsibilities you can to others, and go be with the family that is grieving.

Tragedy and Trauma

While it is impossible to list here every type of crisis that will befall families under your care, I wanted to share a few words of comfort and advice when heartbreaking tragedies like abuse, infidelity, incarceration, and large-scale violence affect your congregation.

First, secrets and silence do us no favors in the wake of tragedy. While we always respect the privacy of survivors, perpetrators of evil may not necessarily deserve that same right to privacy. When abuse, crime, and adultery take place in your community, the only way to healing is through public confession and forgiveness. If a member if your church sins in a way that affects the whole body, keeping quiet about that trespass simply enables it to continue.

Second, our job as ministry professionals is to believe survivors.[40] Psychologists who work with children who have been abused urge us to believe their reports, because evidence suggests that children do not allege this abuse falsely.[41] Scholars who study law enforcement practices find that, although police officers and even the general public have a terrible tendency to suspect women of fabricating sexual assault claims, false allegations of sexual assault are no more common than false claims of any other type of felony.[42] I have observed a strange tendency in my own psyche and in others' reactions when abuse takes place—the tendency to protect the abuser. It is a natural, albeit despicable, desire to excuse, ignore, or even enable abusers, possibly because of the power dynamics of race, sex, age,

---

40   Garland, 408.
41   Tommy MacKay, "False Allegations of Child Abuse in Contested Family Law Cases: The Implications for Psychological Practice," *Educational and Child Psychology* 31 (September 1, 2014): 85–96.
42   Philip Rumney, "False Allegations of Rape," *The Cambridge Law Journal* 65 (March 12, 2006), https://doi.org/10.1017/S0008197306007069.

physical ability, and money often lie with perpetrators.[43] Let's be extremely careful not to give too much credit to people in power; instead, stand with survivors, believe them, and advocate justice for them.

Sometimes the tragedy is large-scale, as in the instances of mass shootings or natural disasters. When public, large-scale tragedies happen, our grief is both personal and communal.[44] These events are generally obsessed over by media coverage, which ensures that our exposure to them will be ongoing and extensive. After every mass shooting or act of violence, I see posts from friends and colleagues on social media asking how we can (or if we should) talk to our children and communities about what happened. Instinctively we know that we should say something; leaders in communities play a key role in helping their people through the phases of shock, processing, and adaptation to a new normal.[45]

When an act of terror or violence disrupts the social norm expectations of a community, it is easy to start making enemies of anyone who is different from us. Homogeneity provides a psychological sense safety, even if it is a false one. But trusting our own group and demonizing anyone who looks, talks, or lives differently than we do will cause a community to fall apart.[46] In the wake of this kind of tragedy, leaders need to model unification in the midst of differences, reaffirming God's clear and open invitation to anyone who wants to sit at God's banquet table.

Because mass tragedy affects communities as a whole, it is important to provide a community-wide acknowledgement and olive branch. A prayer vigil, an open funeral, a candle-lighting service, or some other public gathering where the whole community can agree to acknowledge the pain and also claim hope in God's goodness. The church is right to bring people together in prayers that cover our own hearts, the hearts of victims, and

43   Silvia M. Straka and Lyse Montminy, "Family Violence: Through the Lens of Power and Control," *Journal of Emotional Abuse* 8, no. 3 (August 26, 2008): 255–79, https://doi.org/10.1080/10926790802262499.

44   Nancy P. Kropf and Barbara L. Jones, "When Public Tragedies Happen: Community Practice Approaches in Grief, Loss, and Recovery," *Journal of Community Practice* 22, no. 3 (July 3, 2014): 281–98, https://doi.org/10.1080/10705422.2014.929539.

45   Ibid.

46   Matthew J. Friedman and Anica Mikus-Kos, eds., *Promoting the Psychosocial Well Being of Children Following War and Terrorism*, vol. 4, NATO Security through Science Series (Amsterdam: IOS Press, 2005).

the hearts of perpetrators. Whether this time of prayer takes place during Sunday morning worship or a specially-called event, the point is to remind ourselves of two things: 1) that God is present even in darkness, and 2) that we are all still members of God's family, and we are the best channels for God's love, forgiveness, and healing to reach one another.

Counseling Services and Referrals

For every tragic event and challenging situation named in this chapter, professional therapy is an appropriate and available recourse. As church leaders, we should be both participants in therapy and vocal proponents of it. I have personally benefited from the services of three different counselors or therapists since beginning in ministry, not counting the pastoral counseling I have taken advantage of as a church staff person. I am forever grateful for the impact that counseling has had on my development both personally and professionally. I am not confident that my ministry, marriage, or family would be places of fulfillment and joy for me today if not for the therapy I have received along the way.

One of the best relationships we can cultivate as pastors and church leaders is a connection to quality therapists in our area. Ask other pastors, social workers, and therapists for referrals, and when possible meet one-on-one with local therapists to ask about their practices, their rates, and areas of expertise. Some therapists will only treat adults, some only children or adolescents, and some all ages. Some professional counselors operate an openly religious practice, while others are careful to keep religious principles out of their talk—both these approaches are helpful and appropriate, depending on what the client is seeking.

Many times, the first counselor a person meets is not the right one for them, and this discovery can deter them from counseling altogether. It is also possible for someone to go to counseling for the wrong reasons and therefore fail to benefit from it. Either way, encourage your people to keep trying. There is no shame in switching to someone new. The benefits of finding the right therapist are worth the search.

The main point here is that we should be quick to destigmatize therapy by participating in it ourselves and urging others to pursue therapy when needed. And everyone needs therapy at some point! As ministers, we are always equipped to listen to someone's story the first time and to pray with them, but unless we have a license to practice social work or therapy, we have no business getting into the gritty details of someone's marriage, identity formation, abuse, or dysfunction. It is tempting for busybodies like me to want to collect all of someone's confessions and carry them on my back, but that would overstep the bounds of spiritual advising and holy listening.

Final Thoughts

In the end, most of this chapter can be summed up by saying we should listen well to people and hold space for God to work. It is not our job to bring healing or fix problems in times of crisis, but rather to act as a gateway to holy places. We believe that God is good, even when life is bad. We do not suffer as if we have no hope. There is great evil in the world, and it shows up in the lives of our people all the time as trauma, pain, illness, death, tragedy, and personal choices to cause hurt. Without overlooking, excusing, or wishing away the evil, we do our best to believe in the goodness of God and to call it down into the lives of our hurting people.

In crisis, we pray, we talk real talk, and we send people to good counselors. We believe in the powerful combination of faith and therapy, that counselors can be wonderful communicators of God's healing and growth. And as church leaders, both in the everyday and in times of crisis, we remember our most important job is to tend to our own faith lives and nurture our own relationship to God, so that we have the spiritual and emotional resources to help others.

CHAPTER 13

NAVIGATING THE ORGANIZATION

I am pretty sure I held my breath when I received my first ministry job offer. I was sitting in a small conference room, looking at the executive director of Christ Church United Methodist in Louisville, Kentucky, not knowing that she would become one of the most influential forces on my faith and leadership abilities. I just wanted the gig.

After I accepted their offer, unable to conceal my glee, Shannon brought me back down to the ground with words I'll never forget. She peered into my 25-year-old soul and said, "Sarah, what I am going to say next is very important. You are the Director of Children's Ministries now. You are not an intern; you are not the director-in-training. You are the boss of this ministry area, and I wouldn't hire you to do this job if I didn't know you were up to it. Do not go out there and *think* about doing your job. Do it."

Friends, my advice is to get yourself a boss who will mentor you the way Shannon mentored me for the six years I worked under her. But the street goes both ways. Don't just look for excellent leadership to follow. Navigate the organizational chart of your ministry with a humble desire to learn and grow. Shannon told me more than once that she would teach me as much as I would let her, and I was honored to be her pupil. She's the one who forced me to have some of the hardest conversations of my career. She taught me to assume the best of people, and to come prepared to meetings with more than whims and exciting ideas. I interviewed her when crafting this chapter, and many of the beliefs I will espouse here came from that interview. But mostly, this chapter is a product of the last ten years of working with both highly effective and ineffective leaders, distilling advice from them into pathways that make sense for ministry professionals.

This chapter is a guide for how to get a ministry job, then how to do it well. It is about being a great subordinate, a wise supervisor, and a flexible team player. While I hope to share some specific and practical advice, much of this chapter can be boiled down to two mantras: give people the benefit of the doubt (including yourself), and build relationships—messy, hard, complicated, beautiful relationships.

The Organizational Chart

Every church should have an organizational chart that visually represents how staff and lay positions interact with one another.[1] This is one of the first things I ask for in a new job. I want to know who is responsible for whom, and which jobs are intentionally intertwined.

There are all sorts of church staffing structures, depending on the denomination and the size of the church. Whether you come from a small church led by a solo pastor who relies on lay people to run many ministry areas or a megachurch with multiple ordained or highly trained staff leading ministry, you need to know who occupies the top slot(s) in the organizational chart. Some churches differentiate between high-level leaders who supervise and perform relational, pastoral ministry from high-level staff who oversee administrative, financial, human resources areas—and if that is the case for you, it would be helpful to ask questions to find out how those different duties are divided. Titles at the top of the organizational chart often include terms like "executive," "lead," "senior," "pastor," and "director."

These are the people who set the vision for the church and make the big decisions. People in these positions cannot and should not know every

---

1   Robert H Welch, *Church Administration: Creating Efficiency for Effective Ministry.* (Nashville: B & H Pub. Group, 2011), 27–28.

detail of what is happening in all the ministry areas of the church. They have a much broader perspective. They hear and know things that most church members and even church staff are not privy to, from political moves within the denomination to complaints from the top financial giver in the congregation. When they make decisions, they take into consideration information that no other staff member or lay person can know.

Next on the organization chart one might find assistant or associate pastors. These are often leaders with seminary or other post-graduate training who fulfill a pastoral role without as much of the administrative or political attachments. Often these are the staff who are able to provide the most pastoral care to the congregation, often performing many of the hospital visits, leading the prayer teams, organizing grief groups, and serving as a listening ear for people. In healthy churches, assistant pastors enjoy a symbiotic relationship with senior pastors, so they can play to their own strengths while relying on one another.

The next level down on the organizational chart often consists of age-level ministries, where the leaders of adults, youth, and children sit. In some churches, these staff report directly to the senior pastor or executive director; in others, they are supervised by associate or assistant pastors. Either way, these leaders provide expertise for their particular generational group by fulfilling the mission of the church for that group. I anticipate that the majority of those reading this book sit on this rung of the organizational ladder. Many who populate these positions do so on a part-time or volunteer basis, and, in my opinion, their work is every single bit as essential to the life of the church as that of the most senior pastor on staff.

There are other vital positions on the typical organizational chart that I will not detail, such as business officers, administrative assistants, office managers, custodial staff, receptionists, office volunteers, and human resources staff. These folks often make or break the effectiveness of the church structure. A wise pastor or ministry leader will go out of their way to support, value, and show appreciation for the staff and volunteers who manage the details of day-to-day church work so that the visionaries and paid disciple-makers can do their thing.

Knowing the organizational chart is important for several reasons. First, it tells us the appropriate flow of communication. Later I will discuss in more detail my "only vent upwards" philosophy, which involves expressing anger or gripes only to people above you on the organizational chart. It is inappropriate to vent downward or even to the side and doing so can be incredibly destructive. A second reason this chart is helpful is that it clarifies the power dynamics of the organization. Churches are not run by democracy. No matter how great a youth pastor's ideas and energy are, they can be vetoed by a senior pastor at any time. Knowing where the power lies tells us how to propose change and whom to include in our own decisions. A third benefit of a clear organizational chart is that it reveals who needs to be included in our planning. If I, as a director of children's ministry, wish to change the way my Sunday-school hour works, I first need to have conversations with everyone else on my organizational level to get their support and make sure my changes will not derail their ministries. Only then can I move up the chart with my proposal for change.

It's important to remember, however, that all our theories go out the window when we start working with actual humans. Having the flow chart of staff positions on paper is a place to start, but the people who fill those positions come with all their own dreams, hurts, needs, personalities, and fears just as we do. In the end, navigating the organizational chart is simply a matter of building relationships and putting the best interests of God's church front and center.

Ministry Interviews

Before we can begin to work the church structure advantageously, we must first get hired! Having been on both sides of the interview table, I firmly believe that interviews are always a learning opportunity. Both the candidate and the interviewer learn about themselves and their organization in this process. Therefore, this section is applicable both for people seeking ministry positions and people hiring for those positions.

Let's talk about the interview process goal: to determine whether a candidate is the right fit for the organization. Employers do not hire ministry professionals exclusively for their education, expertise, or skill set. They look for certain qualities—the abilities that come with mature personalities. Some of the most important characteristics for a ministry applicant to show are creativity, flexibility, teamwork, depth, and adaptability. I would hire a family ministry professional with no experience, but a high level of maturity and proven desire to learn and grow, over a seminary grad or a ministry veteran who appears stuck in their ways. Education and expertise are valuable and sought after, but at the end of the day, they don't matter if the person who wields them is a bad fit for the team.

With this in mind, a note to folks with graduate or seminary degrees: enter the interview space humbly. Seminary prepares people for ministry in wonderful ways, but there are many ministry skills that can't be learned in a classroom. Recognize your potential to learn on the job through the relationships you'll form through the ministry itself. After all, we ministry types are in the people business. Anyone who wants to succeed in ministry should pray for greater flexibility, a teamwork mindset, and grace for themselves and others.

The interview process is simply a search for authenticity. Those asking the questions are hoping to get a glimpse of the real person behind the best-foot-forward veneer of the business suit and manicure. This is the reason companies with high-level openings conduct long, stressful, repeat-visit interviews. If you find the interview process with an organization to be grueling, take heart—they are trying to get a look at the real you. It is impossible to know fully how a person will operate within an organization until that person is actually in the position for some time. That's why the interview is designed to give as accurate a picture of that person's character, personality, and abilities as possible. Do yourself a favor and be your real self in an interview. Promote your strengths, of course! Tell the organization why you believe you are right for the position, if indeed you do believe that. But do not hold back your concerns either. If a ministry position is going to drain the life from either you or the organization, better to discover that in the interview than years down the road.

Interviewer Tips

For those conducting interviews, there a few questions that can help give a clearer picture of candidates. Ask candidates to describe for you who has been their best supervisor in the past, and what made them so great.

Their answers will clue you in to how capable they are of operating autonomously and how they have responded to feedback in the past. Ask candidates to define their buzzwords. If someone says they dislike being "micromanaged," ask them what that means to them. If someone describes themselves as a go-getter, give them a chance to share an example of what that has looked like. Finally, ask candidates how you can pray for them, and look for an honest, meaningful response. Then close interviews with prayers of blessing over the candidate. Demonstrate the kind of spiritual and relational environment you want to offer.

There are a few red flags to note in an interview for a ministry position. If a candidate dumps on a previous employer, pay attention. Most people give some thought to how they will explain their employment history in an interview, so it is appropriate to expect a clear, rational explanation of why someone would leave their current situation to work for you. Someone who is still bitter over circumstances at a previous position may quite easily transfer that bitterness to a new workplace.

Another warning sign to watch for is if a ministry candidate comes in with no questions for you. Quality applicants will scour the church or organization's website before coming to an interview, and they will compile a list of questions that would not otherwise come up. Anyone who has performed well in a ministry position previously will bring experience with budgets, expectations, supervision, or event planning that will lead to meaningful questions. If a candidate does not have questions about the job or the organization, it is fair to wonder how important this opportunity is to them. Once a ministry professional is hired, then the real work begins! This next section will detail best practices for supervising ministry staff.

Being a Good Supervisor

If you are fortunate enough to supervise ministry leaders, count your blessings. You are in the business of developing people.[2] Supervisors are not responsible for doing all the work of ministry; a significant portion of their role in the organization is devoted to making strong, trustworthy leaders out of those they supervise. If the thought of this does not bring

---

2   Ibid., 28–29.

you joy, then consider finding other work. It should not come as a shock to hear that the best supervisors are those who love helping others develop.

Believing in People

I have benefitted from many stellar supervisors during my career, from pastors to business professionals, and I know that their investments in me are what have made me the leader I am today. There is, however, one supervisor in my past whose greatest contribution to my development was in teaching me how not to lead others.

Right after graduating from college, I took a job assisting an investment broker. To be honest, I was a truly lousy administrative assistant. I am so not into details, and I regularly forgot or simply ignored the minute tasks that were required of me. Still, my heart was in the right place—I wanted to be helpful to my boss, and I thought I was doing the best that I could. I don't blame my supervisor there one bit for being frustrated with me, but he committed the cardinal sin of leadership: he assumed the worst about me. Where I showed incompetence, he saw sabotage. With direction and kindness, I believe my attention to detail would have improved. Instead, he accused me of doing a poor job on purpose and insulted my intelligence. He insisted I document my every action, including any questions or messages I had for him. I was not allowed to talk to him in person, but rather had to write every question or comment on a note and put it in his inbox. He believed I was a failure, and that belief did not help me to succeed.

Assuming the best of others' intentions is critical. Giving people the benefit of the doubt can feel gullible and naive, but people cannot thrive in an environment where others believe they will fail, especially if those others are their supervisors. Extend to those you supervise the grace of believing in them. Supervision is about support—it is a matter of empowering people to do and be the best they can. This often means requiring people to do very hard things, not as a punishment, but as accountability, an investment in their growth. All ministry professionals must have hard conversations on a regular, sometimes daily basis. A good supervisor will walk their subordinates through those difficult conversations. The ability to communicate clearly in conflict with another person is one of the biggest challenges of ministry. It is an absolutely crucial quality in anyone who wants to become more like Jesus or lead others deeper into relationship with God. Supervisors cannot do the hard work for their people, but they can provide the listening, encouragement, and honest perspective to empower people to do the hard work themselves.

Setting Appropriate Expectations

Supervisors are often responsible for creating and helping to maintain job descriptions for those they lead. Unfortunately, in the church we tend to expect ministry staff to achieve full-time+ job responsibilities on a part-time salary and schedule. A travesty is committed by burning out so many pastors and staff, and the fault lies both with the workers and with the people who supervise them. Part of supervision in the church is providing pastoral care and promoting work-life balance for church leaders and staff. I wish more pastors and supervisors knew how to create a manageable job description. Pastors will sometimes send me the job descriptions for open positions in children's or youth ministry, asking me to refer candidates to them. Those job descriptions often look something like this:

- Lead Sunday school and worship every Sunday
- Recruit volunteers for all ministry areas
- Lead vacation Bible school each summer and special events throughout the year
- Provide childcare and programming for a mid-week program
- Maintain supplies and stick to a small budget
- Attend biweekly staff meetings
- Expected hours are 10-15/week
- Salary is $10/hour

Friends, this is ridiculous. If you are seeking or find yourself in a job with a description like this, it is time to make serious changes. It is no wonder church staffs are exhausted; we are asking them to do the impossible.

According to Ministry Architects, a consultancy that provides direction and training to churches, one full-time employee can sustain a ministry for about 75 children or 50 youth.[3] They warn that if your church's

---

3 "Staffing Your Ministry Strategically," Ministry Architects, August 27, 2018, https://ministryarchitects.com/staffing-your-ministry-strategically/.

participation numbers exceed this staffing, it is not a matter of "if," but "when" your staff will become overwhelmed and cease to be effective in their work, or even leave their positions. To extrapolate these numbers to smaller churches, a staff person that is expected to work only 15 hours a week can reasonably sustain a ministry of not more than 28 children or 19 youth. If this seems expensive to us, we may need to reconsider how realistic our expectations are for ministry staff. A church should seek to be a place of healing, growth, and empowerment for all its people, including its staff.

Being a Good Ministry Employee

You have been hired to a ministry position—congratulations! You are what we refer to in Christian-speak as the hands and feet of Jesus. Church staff and volunteers get to be in hands-on ministry, directly speaking life and truth into people's lives. It is an honor and a great responsibility.

But unless your name is at the very top of the organizational chart, you are beholden to a leader or supervisor. To at least some degree, your job is to implement that person's vision. Your creativity and personal mission may determine *how* you live out that vision, but your job begins by supporting someone else's leadership and ministry. Because this calling to live out someone else's vision for ministry can be tricky, this section is devoted to giving advice for working well under supervision.

Laying the Groundwork

As early as possible in your working relationship with your supervisor, there is a question you should ask. If you have already been working together for a length of time, it is still OK to have this conversation, but the sooner it happens in the working relationship, the better. The question is this: In the future, when there is conflict in our relationship, how would you like me to approach you with it?

This question presumes that there will be conflict at some point, because that is just a given. Two imperfect people working together will inevitably experience differences. By asking this question, you acknowledge the inevitability of that conflict while also indicating your desire to respect your boss' authority and wishes while working out the conflict.

Asking this question in the absence of conflict provides a road map when frustrations or disagreements in the relationship later emerge.

A supervisor may give many different answers to this question. The specifics here don't matter, as long as you are able to obtain permission to speak honestly behind closed doors. Even when a subordinate strongly disagrees with a supervisor's decisions or actions, it is not OK to express that conflict to anyone but the supervisor first. What you want to do is make a plan for how to do that as respectfully as possible. Participating in honest, loving conflict is hard enough, no matter what. The best thing you can do is to lay the groundwork for a helpful, meaningful, non-threatening conversation about it when the time comes.

Knowing how to express your honest beliefs and feelings to your supervisor is crucial. If it turns out that your supervisor is unable to hold space for a difficult conversation with you, it may be time to consider seeking other opportunities. While supervisors and subordinates do not need to be friends by any means, they do need to find a way to navigate conflict with one another honestly. If that is not possible, then productive ministry may not be possible either. You cannot stay in a toxic work environment just because the work you are doing is meaningful. There are needs to be met and callings to be fulfilled in many different places, and your time is valuable enough to be spent judiciously. Do not surrender yourself, your family, or your most productive years to a setting that will never free you up to do the work you were truly created for.

Boundaries in Ministry

Achieving a healthy working relationship with your supervisor is just the first step. Next, you want to figure out how to balance ministry with the rest of your life. It is far too easy to devote so much of ourselves to our ministries that we are no good either to our church or to anyone else. The pressure to perform in the church is every bit as suffocating as it can be in the business world. I remember as clear as crystal the feeling of resentment I used to entertain toward some of my colleagues as I walked to pick up my children from preschool. I was forced to consider work-life boundaries, unlike some of my coworkers who remained unmarried or childless, and could sit at their desks as late as they wanted, getting caught up and even working ahead! Shame on me for being jealous of that, but I was.

This desire to work insane hours in an effort to prove oneself and excel in one's work is what a former supervisor calls "over-functioning." It is unhealthy in a number of ways. First of all, it reveals a lack of trust, both in ourselves and in God to show up in our work. Over-functioning also communicates to everyone around us that they are unnecessary to the fulfillment of God's plan for the ministry. When we try to do everything ourselves, spinning into a frenzy of long work hours and postponed self-care, others learn to leave us to it, understanding that there is really no place for them in our strategy. Last and possibly worst, when we over-function, we almost always cross the borders of our own work arena into others'.

Disregarding proper work-life boundaries reveals deep insecurity. People who have found peace in their work and learned to find their worth in the right places do not need to attend every event, oversee every detail, and know everything about their work. They have forgotten that everyone is replaceable. Sometimes not showing up, not taking control, and not doing the work ourselves is the best gift we can give to a church. Because when we let go, others get to step in and learn to lead.

This is especially hard for people who are new to their positions. Culturally, men can sometimes rely on spouses to carry on with the household and family duties in their absence, so their work hours can be especially ridiculous. And it is so easy to excuse overwork when it is ministry! To be an emotionally and physically healthy ministry worker seems almost selfish. That is how twisted we can become.

Following are signs that you need to take a big, huge, step back from your work commitments and reevaluate:

- You catch yourself complaining about your long hours at work.
- Your friends, spouse, and/or kids begin to make resentful comments toward church and how much of your time it requires.
- Reading Scripture and praying no longer hold your interest or require your time.
- You feel a sense of pride over how few vacation/sick days you have taken in the past year. You can't remember your last real vacation.
- You answer every call, e-mail and text, no matter when they come.

- You are the first to arrive and the last to leave every church event.
- You are out of touch with your own sense of well-being.
- You have worked more hours than your church expects of you for several weeks in a row.

Rest assured, if you are overworking, you are hurting both yourself and others. Working in a helping profession requires that you stay connected to your own needs (physical, mental, and spiritual) and connected to your support systems.

Remember your call, but not as a to-do list or the beginning and end of your identity. We are all called to more than one thing—meaningful ministry, intimate relationships, pleasure in God's creation, fullness of life. No church job is so important that it should deprive us of those other places of fullness and joy.

Making Changes

Young ministry me had a lot of stellar ideas, which I introduced enthusiastically at staff meetings and which crumpled immediately under the weight of questions from supervisors and colleagues. I'd like to share some strategies I learned the hard way in the hope that others can glean them the easy way, just by reading.

The first rule of change management is to *be patient*. Give yourself time and give the church time. If you are in your first year of ministry at a church, dedicate yourself to learning everything you can about the people, the history, and the institution. Be extremely judicious about initiating change during that first year—change happens slowly in institutions. The improvements you'd like to make will likely happen just as quickly and much less painfully if you wait long enough to get your bearings before making them happen.

Use the time you have to build relationships before launching into fixing problems. Visit the families of your church, go to lunch with coworkers, stand in the hallways and talk to folks between services. Get to know your people and let them know you. People are much more likely to roll with changes proposed by a friend than by a stranger. I learned from experience: never propose change without first doing your homework.

Making a Proposal for Change

The church is never done changing. There will always be new people coming through the doors, new needs, new technologies, new ventures to attempt. However, change can be painful. Ironically, the people with the shortest tenure are often the ones with the best vantage point to identify areas of weakness and bring fresh ideas to the table. But having the idea is only the first 1 percent of the change process. Springing change on a church without sufficient preparation and thought will do more harm than good.

Thesis Statement

Step One in making a change proposal is to state your goal. This thesis statement should be short and clear, and it should both identify the problem you see and summarize the solution you propose. For example, let's suppose a first-year family ministry professional wants to change the Sunday morning schedule for elementary-aged kids. Whereas they have been dropped off in a separate worship room at the start of the service, our family minister wants to have them attend the first 15 minutes of the sanctuary worship service with their parents, then exit to a kids' worship time. A goal statement for making this change could be:

"To increase intergenerational worship opportunities and to empower parents and other adults to model worship for a younger generation, I propose that we include elementary-aged children in the first 15 minutes of sanctuary worship each week."

This statement delineates the problem (insufficient intergenerational worship experiences, families missing worshiping together) and states a simple, clear solution with just enough detail.

Name Those Affected

Before getting too far into the proposal process, name every single person and ministry area that will be affected by this change. You will thank me later. My unscientific prediction is that about 80 percent of frustration with ministry coworkers results from people implementing wonderful, quality changes without considering their effects on others and communicating about them. Don't be that person.

This is what you need to do—list every single ministry department, committee, family, age group, and ministry team in your church that could be affected. In our example, this list would include:

- Children's ministry staff
- Worship planning team
- Pastors
- Ushers and greeters
- Any family with an elementary-aged child
- Hospitality team

Before presenting your proposal to the whole staff or whole church body, make a point to have conversations with any staff or lay leaders who supervise the ministry areas you have named. Talk with the pastors, the worship planners, the head usher, and the head of hospitality separately. Ask them how this would affect them, what problems they see, and whether they would support the change. Solve those problems before they come up in the wider leadership group. Covering your bases in these separate conversations will prevent uncomfortable questions later on in front of the whole group. Listen for the language that folks use when reacting to your change and discussing the ways they will be affected, because that is the language you want to use in your eventual pitch.[4]

Pay attention to one important reaction: silence. People rarely keep silent when they are excited about a change, and silence has nothing to do with consent in any case. Take note of silent listeners, and give them a safe, private opportunity to share honestly with you. Interpret silence as a warning sign and assume that the person keeping silent does not feel speaking would be safe. Find a way to invite that person to speak safely. You may well receive your most helpful feedback from someone who was initially silent.

Write It Down

Take your thesis statement, along with the problems/solutions you have developed through individual conversations, and craft them into a one-page document. Anyone who isn't present to hear you talk about your proposed change can read about it later and get the gist, and visual learners

---

4   Diana R. Garland, *Family Ministry: A Comprehensive Guide*, 2nd edition (Downers Grove, IL: IVP Academic, 2012), 540–41.

will appreciate having the information in writing rather than just listening to your pitch. At this point, you have put the "pro" in "professional" and should feel like a total champion. Well done!

Making the Pitch

When you finally give your presentation to decision-makers, keep it simple and meaningful. State the initial problem you are trying to solve, then your thesis statement. Always, and I mean always, refer to your solution as an experiment.[5] Make it clear that your idea may or may not work, and there is an out if things go downhill. Name the primary challenges to implementation and your solutions for them. It is important to acknowledge the costs, whether financial, emotional, or logistical. You can bet that the people who will pay those costs are thinking about them! Give them the dignity of acknowledging the difficulty your proposal could cause.[6] Give folks your ideal timeline for moving forward. Leave out extraneous details and back story in the initial pitch—the time for anecdotes and history comes when folks begin asking questions. Take notes of any questions people ask, especially if they bring up problems you hadn't considered before. Thank the group for listening, and don't leave the conversation without naming a next step or receiving blessing to move forward.

Last, plan ahead of time what your evaluation strategy will be, and follow through on it. Design a survey, or set aside time to make phone calls, or set a focus group discussion on the calendar for after implementation.[7] It is too easy to forget or forgo evaluation if we don't plan for it ahead of time.

Important Conversations

Working in the church consists mostly of having one important conversation after another. Some are invigorating, many are exhausting. Nothing in ministry is more important than the way we talk to others, our ability to really listen, and the judgment we use to decide what we will and will not talk about.

---

5   Garland.
6   Ibid.
7   Ibid.

Listening

I don't care what your Myers-Briggs says or what Enneagram number you lean toward, in ministry we have all got to be good listeners. Maybe this comes naturally to you and maybe it doesn't, but knowing how to listen, when to set boundaries and when to be approachable is a fine art to which we all aspire. There are several situations when good listening skills are required.

Receiving Feedback

Listening while someone informs you of the ways you have disappointed is horrible, but also often quite necessary. Regardless of our educational attainment, our innate wisdom, and our ministry finesse, there will be times when we miss the mark and others let us know about it. Often, we will not agree with others' assessments of our performance, but we must listen to their feedback anyway. Remember, there is an outside chance they could be right and you could be wrong.

When someone gives constructive criticism, choke down your defenses and excuses, and listen. As always, assume the best of people—there is every chance that they are really on your side and that you both want your ministry to be as healthy and successful as possible. Even if they have insufficient information, their perspective is valid and valuable to you. Anyone who is willing to enter into confrontation with you is giving you a gift—a painful, awful gift. They have insight to which you would otherwise be blind. Listen to understand them. When someone approaches you with words that are difficult to hear, look for the truth in them. Realize that for most people, coming to you with negative feedback or honesty about their hurt feels difficult to them as well as to you, but they were willing to do it anyway. That's true love. Thank people for their honesty.

Occasionally, it is possible that someone will criticize you out of their own hurt rather than from a place of love. When this happens, pray for the maturity to listen well but not to allow their words to define you. Even when people hurl rude, thoughtless, or intentionally hurtful feedback at you, search for what they are really communicating underneath those words. A church member told me once that I had singlehandedly taken

Jesus out of Christmas for their family. That statement winded me completely, and I reeled from it for a good while. After considering, I realized that by changing the events our church offered during Advent without fully communicating my reasons for those changes, I had truly hurt her and probably many others. I had instigated a new way of celebrating Christmas, a way that made much more sense to me, but that had deprived her of Christmas experiences she had always counted on for her children. There was truth underneath her actual words.

Receiving Venting

Sometimes, those in leadership positions will just need to vent. This means that when a family in the church or a staff member that you supervise comes to your office and closes the door, you need to put aside the tasks at hand and make yourself available to listen. Remember that often, airing complaints in a safe place is all that a person needs. Just saying the words and getting them out of their system may be enough. Once someone has finished, ask, "OK, I have heard you. What do you need from me?" Perhaps they just needed a compassionate listener, and your job is done. However, it is also quite possible that the person in front of you needs to take action in order to resolve their own complaint. We do not fix other people's problems, nor do we speak on behalf of those they are complaining about. If someone gripes to you about a problem they're having with someone else, listen, then help them figure out how to bring up their problem with the offending person directly. Support people in conducting their own conflict resolution.

I once went to my executive director to complain about inappropriate comments I heard a colleague make to a group of church members. He had complained to them about the difficulty of his job requirements, and I felt frustrated about it. Instead of going to him to ask why he did that, I tattled on him. And the tattling felt good! Until my director, after listening without comment, told me I had to go talk to him about it, *and* tell him that I had already told on him. That was not a fun conversation, but it was the right thing to do at that point. You will not be shocked to hear that my colleague wasn't thrilled to know I had already gone over his head to share his comments with his own supervisor. But once we had that painful, short conversation, we were back on an even playing field with no dishonesty between us.

Gossip

There is a tiny, almost imperceptible line between venting and gossip, and sadly, churches are often gossip mills. Churches can break apart on gossip alone. If maintaining integrity between yourself and your supervisors is important at all, then you must have a no-gossip policy. For people-pleasers like myself, it is helpful to repeat gossip shut-down phrases such as, "I can't go there. Let's talk about something else," or "You should talk to your supervisor about this." Even remaining silent amid gossip, although one step up from contributing to it, can be interpreted as agreement and participation. Gossip has no place in a healthy church family.

Talking

Now that we have listening down, let's do some talking, a discipline that is just as hard to perfect. We are on the same page about receiving feedback and venting—so what about giving feedback and venting appropriately ourselves?

Giving Feedback

The first rule of entering into conflict is to not do it in writing! Speak difficult words in person whenever possible, or over the phone otherwise. There are so many problems with putting potentially hurtful words in writing. First, sending conflict through an e-mail or text means we have no idea what state the recipient is in when they read them. If they are already having a bad day, or if they are too busy to give our words their proper attention, it will be so much harder for them to hear our communication in the way we meant it. Second, written words can be obsessed over, reread, and shared with others out of context. They can become weapons that wound, then wound again. Third, written words cannot take into account the questions, reactions, facial expressions, and body language of our listeners. Compared to in-person communication, written words are harsh and unfeeling, a monologue that leaves no space for someone else to contribute to the conversation.

Having said this, I will admit that there have been times in my ministry when I have not had the emotional wherewithal to confront in person. When a powerful lay leader in my church wrote me a threatening e-mail, my supervisor looked me square in the eye and asked if I could call him back to respond. I remember feeling the blood drain out of my brain at the thought and shook my head "No," petrified just contemplating that. She helped me to craft a short e-mail response. I would handle that matter differently now, with almost ten years experience in the art of uncomfortable conversations since then. But there was grace at the time for me to do the best I could right then, and I'm grateful.

When others do communicate criticism or blame in writing, that does not excuse us to respond in kind. Whenever possible, and as long as it is safe, respond to criticism face-to-face. Consider it an excuse to take them to your favorite coffee place or restaurant, and remember that most of us are much more humane and gracious in person than in writing.

When giving feedback, assume the best of the person you are addressing. Find the things you can agree on, which almost always includes your shared goal for ministry. Name that shared goal, and admit that the disagreement most likely lies in methodology rather than theology or theory. Talk about how you feel and express your own perspective, but acknowledge that you could have incomplete information. Approach conflict with curiosity—your goal is to get on the same page with the person you don't understand, so recruit them to be your partner in reaching this goal. Share information and ask for their perspective.

Direct Communication

There may be times in church work when you learn about someone's hurt or hurtful comments second- or third-hand. This can be especially scary if you find that a supervisor or someone above you on the organizational chart has a problem with you. Before sinking into despair, adopt a healthy mistrust of data that has passed through others to get to you. Go to the source! If you have heard that someone else has a problem with you or your ministry, then that person is the only one who can tell you the truth. Go directly to the person who has been quoted to you and ask them for their version. Again, approach with curiosity, not blame.

Asking Forgiveness

Chances are that in the midst of all this wonderful conflict management, you will have an opportunity to ask forgiveness. Hurt does not have to be intentional to be real. Whether or not you meant to cause harm, once you know that you have, your only recourse is to apologize.

My husband is the best apologizer I have ever met. He is always the first one to bring resolution to an argument by saying he is sorry, admitting he is wrong, and plainly asking for forgiveness. I feel privileged to be married to someone with the humility and unselfish love to take responsibility for his actions and to ask for restoration.

Dr. Jennifer Thomas, who along with Gary Chapman wrote *When Sorry Isn't Enough*, writes on her blog about the five different aspects of good apologies. Just as everyone has a primary love language, everyone also appreciates different aspects of apology. As church leaders who try to model discipleship for others, we need to learn to cover each of these aspects of apology, not knowing which one will be most meaningful to the person receiving our apology.

1. Expressing Regret—This means telling the person we've wronged that we are truly sorry, being explicit about the fact that we feel sad and wish we had not caused the hurt.

2. Accepting Responsibility—We name exactly what we did or said that was wrong, without making excuses or shying away from the perspective of the person we hurt.

3. Making Restitution—Moving beyond words, in this stage we ask the person what we can do to restore the relationship, or we offer ways we have already thought of for making things right.

4. Genuinely Repenting—We tell the person we have wronged that we will change our behavior, offer some assurance that we will not continue to subject them to this hurt. We do not just apologize with our words, but with our actions.

5. Requesting Forgiveness—For me, this is the most painful part of apology. But an apology is incomplete until we have given the other person an opportunity to respond.[8]

Final Thoughts

The organizational chart is not designed to restrict or burden us. It is meant as a communication tool, a map to lead us to the people who can help us to succeed in ministry as well as those whom we can make successful. Understanding how to work within the power structures in the church is just smart leadership. The boundaries are set before we ever accept a position in the church; we do well when we honor them.

Working in the church is a lot like living with family. There are hierarchies to observe and rules to follow, and most of the time it feels super messy, because it is made up of relationships among imperfect humans. I hope in this chapter you have seen glimpses of how beautiful and impactful the church can be when we give others the benefit of the doubt and build relationships before insisting on our own way.

---

8   Jennifer Thomas, "What to Say When Sorry Isn't Enough," April 18, 2018, https://www.drjenniferthomas.com/2018/04/18/say-sorry-isnt-enough/.

RESOURCES

American Academy of Child & Adolescent Psychiatry. "Children with Lesbian, Gay, Bisexual and Transgender Parents." *Facts for Families,* August 2013.

American Academy of Pediatrics. "Child Abuse and Neglect." Healthy-Children.org, 2018. *http://www.healthychildren.org/English/safety-prevention/at-home/Pages/What-to-Know-about-Child-Abuse.aspx.*

American Psychiatric Association, "What Is Mental Illness?" accessed August 14, 2019, *https://www.psychiatry.org/patients-families/what-is-mental-illness.*

Anda, Robert F., Alexander Butchart, Vincent J Felitti, and David W. Brown. "Building a Framework for Global Surveillance of the Public Health Implications of Adverse Childhood Experiences." *American Journal of Preventive Medicine* 39, no. 1 (July 2010): 93–98. *https://doi.org/10.1016/j.amepre.2010.03.015.*

Anderson, Monica. "A Majority of Teens Have Experienced Some Form of Cyberbullying." Pew Research Center, September 27, 2018. *https://www.pewinternet.org/2018/09/27/a-majority-of-teens-have-experienced-some-form-of-cyberbullying/.*

Anderson, Monica, and Jingjing Jiang. "Teens, Social Media & Technology 2018." Pew Research Center, May 31, 2018. *https://www.pewinternet.org/2018/05/31/teens-social-media-technology-2018.*

-----. "Teens' Social Media Habits and Experiences," Pew Research Center, November 28, 2018. *https://www.pewinternet.org/2018/11/28/teens-social-media-habits-and-experiences/.*

Avis, Heather. *Scoot Over and Make Some Room.* Grand Rapids, MI: Zondervan, 2019.

Baker, Jessica H., M. K. Higgins Neyland, Laura M. Thornton, Cristin D. Runfola, Henrik Larsson, Paul Lichtenstein, and Cynthia Bulik. "Body Dissatisfaction in Adolescent Boys." *Developmental Psychology* 55, no. 7 (n.d.): 1566–78.

Baum, A. "Stress, Instrusive Imagery, and Chronic Distress." *Health Psychology: Official Journal of the Division of Health Psychology, American Psychological Association* 9, no. 6 (1990): 653–75.

Bell, Joanna H., and Rachel D. Bromnick. "The Social Reality of the Imaginary Audience: A Grounded Theory Approach." *Adolescence* 38, no. 150 (2003): 205–19.

Boer, Roland. "By Clans and Households: On the Malleability of the Kinship-Household in the Ancient Near East." *Memoria Ethnologica* 13, no. 48/49 (2013): 6–21.

Bogart, Kathleen R., Nicole M. Rosa, and Michael L. Slepian. "Born That Way or Became That Way: Stigma Toward Congenital versus Acquired Disability." *Group Processes & Intergroup Relations* 22, no. 4 (June 1, 2019): 594–612. *https://doi.org/10.1177/1368430218757897.*

Bohn, Annette, "Generational Differences in Cultural Life Scripts and Life Story Memories of Younger and Older Adults." *Applied Cognitive Psychology 24*, no. 9 (2010): 1324–45. *https://doi.org/10.1002/acp.1641.*

Boonstra, Heather D. "Matter of Faith: Support for Comprehensive Sex Education Among Faith-Based Organizations." Guttmacher Institute, March 5, 2008. *https://www.guttmacher.org/gpr/2008/02/matter-faith-support-comprehensive-sex-education-among-faith-based-organizations.*

Boylan, Anne M. *Sunday School: The Formation of an American Institution, 1790-1880.* Revised. New Haven: Yale University Press, 1990.

Braestrip, Kate, "The House of Mourning," The Moth Radio Hour (podcast), July 21, 2015, accessed November 11, 2019, *https://themoth.org/stories/the-house-of-mourning.*

Buckingham, David, Rebekah Willett, Sara Bragg, and Rachel Russell. "Sexualised Goods Aimed at Children: A Report to the Scottish Parliament Equal Opportunities Committee." January 1, 2010.

Cavalletti, Sofia. *The Religious Potential of the Child: Experiencing Scripture and Liturgy With Young Children.* Translated by Patricia M. Coulter and Julie M. Coulter. 2nd edition. Chicago: Liturgy Training Publications, 1992.

Cavelletti, Sofia, Patricia Coulter, Gianna Gobbi, and Silvana Q Montanaro. *The Good Shepherd and the Child: A Joyful Journey.* 1st edition. Chicago: Liturgy Training Publications, 1994.

Centers for Disease Control and Prevention. "About Adverse Childhood Experiences," April 15, 2019. *https://www.cdc.gov/violenceprevention/childabuseandneglect/acestudy/aboutace.html.*

Child Welfare Information Gateway. "Clergy as Mandatory Reporters of Child Abuse and Neglect." U.S. Department of Health & Human Services, Administration for Children and Families, Administration on Children, Youth, and Families, Childrens' Bureau, 2019. *https://www.childwelfare.gov/topics/systemwide/laws-policies/statutes/clergymandated/.*

-----. "What Is Child Abuse and Neglect? Recognizing the Signs and Symptoms." U.S. Department of Health & Human Services, Administration for Children and Families, Administration on Children, Youth, and Families, Childrens' Bureau, 2019. *https://www.childwelfare.gov/pubs/factsheets/whatiscan/.*

Corliss, Heather L., Susan D. Cochran, Vickie M. Mays, Sander Greenland, and Teresa E. Seeman. "Age of Minority Sexual Orientation Development and Risk of Childhood Maltreatment and Suicide Attempts in Women." *The American Journal of Orthopsychiatry 79*, no. 4 (October 2009): 511–21. *https://doi.org/10.1037/a0017163.*

Crone, Eveline A., and Ronald E. Dahl. "Understanding Adolescence as a Period of Social-Affective Engagement and Goal Flexibility." *Nature Reviews. Neuroscience* 13, no. 9 (2012): 636–50. *https://doi.org/10.1038/nrn3313.*

Denney, Andrew S., Kent R. Kerley, and Nikolas G. Gross. "Child Sexual Abuse in Protestant Christian Congregations: A Descriptive Analysis of Offense and Offender Characteristics." *Religions* 9, no. 1 (January 2018): 27. *https://doi.org/10.3390/rel9010027.*

Duckworth, Vicky, Karen Flanagan, Karen McCormack, and Jonathan Tummons. *Understanding Behaviour 14+*. Maidenhead: Open University Press, 2012.

Dulmas, Catherine N., and Carolyn Hilarski. "When Stress Constitutes Trauma and Trauma Constitutes Crisis: The Stress-Trauma-Crisis Continuum." *Brief Treatment and Crisis Intervention* 3, no. 1 (March 1, 2003): 27–36. *https://doi.org/10.1093/brief-treatment/mhg008*.

Dyregrove, Atle. *Grief in Children: A Handbook for Adults*. 2nd ed. London, England: Jessica Kingsley Publishers, 2008.

Dykstra, Robert C. "Ministry with Adolescents: Tending Boundaries, Telling Truths." *Pastoral Psychology* 62, no. 5 (October 1, 2013): 639–47. *https://doi.org/10.1007/s11089-013-0509-9*.

Eberhardt, Jo. "My Parenting Post Went Viral." *The Happy Logophile* (blog), January 7, 2019. *https//joeberhardt.com/2019/01/07/my-parenting-post-went-viral/*.

Edgar-Bailey, Meredith, and Victoria E. Kress. "Resolving Child and Adolescent Traumatic Grief: Creative Techniques and Interventions." Journal of Creativity in Mental Health 5 no. 2 (2010): 158–76.

Elliott, J. H. "Temple versus Household in Luke-Acts: A Contrast in Social Institutions," *HTS Teologiese Studies / Theological Studies* 47, no. 1 (January 9, 1991): 88–120. *https://doi.org/10.4102/hts.v47i1.2356*.

Felitti, V. J., R. F. Anda, D. Nordenberg, D. F. Williamson, A. M. Spitz, V. Edwards, M. P. Koss, and J. S. Marks. "Relationship of Childhood Abuse and Household Dysfunction to Many of the Leading Causes of Death in Adults. The Adverse Childhood Experiences (ACE) Study." *American Journal of Preventive Medicine* 14, no. 4 (May 1998): 245–58.

Finer, Lawrence B., and Mia R. Zolna. "Unintended Pregnancy in the United States: Incidence and Disparities, 2006." *Contraception* 84, no. 5 (November 2011): 478–85. *https://doi.org/10.1016/j.contraception.2011.07.013*.

Fowler, James W. *Faithful Change: The Personal and Pubic Challenges of Postmodern Life*. Nashville: Abingdon Press, 2000.

-----. *Stages of Faith: The Psychology of Human Development and the Quest for Meaning*. San Francisco: Harper & Row, 1981.

Freedman-Doan, Carol R., Leanna Fortunato, Erin J. Henshaw, and Jacqueline M. Titus. "Faith-Based Sex Education Programs: What They Look Like and Who Uses Them." *Journal of Religion and Health* 52, no. 1 (March 2013): 247–62. *https://doi.org/10.1007/s10943-011-9463-y*.

Friedman, Matthew J., and Anica Mikus-Kos, eds. *Promoting the Psychosocial Well Being of Children Following War and Terrorism*. Vol. 4. NATO Security through Science Series. Amsterdam: IOS Press, 2005.

Garceau, Camille, and Scott T. Ronis. "The Interface Between Young Adults' Religious Values and Their Sexual Experiences Before Age 16." *The Canadian Journal of Human Sexuality,* July 31, 2017. *https://doi.org/10.3138/cjhs.262-a6*.

Garland, Diana R. *Family Ministry: A Comprehensive Guide*. 2nd edition. Downers Grove, IL: IVP Academic, 2012.

Gates, Gary. "LGBT Parenting in the United States." The Williams Institute, February 26, 2013. *https://williamsinstitute.law.ucla.edu/research/census-lgbt-demographics-studies/lgbt-parenting-in-the-united-states/Gates.*

Gillis, John R. *A World of Their Own Making: Myth, Ritual, and the Quest for Family Values.* Cambridge, MA: Harvard Univerity Press, 1997.

Gilmore, Karen, and Pamela Meersand. *The Little Book of Child and Adolescent Development.* 1st edition. Oxford: Oxford University Press. 2014.

Glass, Valerie Q., and April L. Few-Demo. "Complexities of Informal Social Support Arrangements for Black Lesbian Couples." *Family Relations* 62, no. 5 (2013): 714–26. *https://doi.org/10.1111/fare.12036.*

Goldsmith, Connie. *Understanding Suicide: A National Epidemic.* Minneapolis: Twenty-First Century Books, 2016.

Gould, Elise, and Cooke Tanyell. "High Quality Child Care Is Out of Reach for Working Families." Economic Policy Institute (blog), October 6, 2015. *https://www.epi.org/publication/child-care-affordability/.*

Guttmacher Institute. "Adolescent Sexual and Reproductive Health in the United States." Guttmacher Institute, September 2017. *https://www.guttmacher.org/fact-sheet-/american-teens-sexual-and-reproductive-health.*

Hach, Alexa, and Susan Roberts-Dobie. "Give Us the Words: Protestant Faith Leaders and Sexuality Education in Their Churches." *Sex Education* 16, no. 6 (November 1, 2016): 619–33. *https://doi.org/10.1080/14681811.2016.1151778.*

Hagar, Mark A., and Jeffrey L. Brudney. "Volunteer Management Practices and Retention of Volunteers." Technical Volunteer Management Capacity Study Series. Washington, D.C.: The Urban Institute, June 2004.

Hansen, Berit Hjelde, Beate Oerbeck, Benedicte Skirbekk, and Hanne Kristensen. "Non-Obsessive-Compulsive Anxiety Disorders in Child and Adolescent Mental Health Services–Are They Underdiagnosed, and How Accurate Is Referral Information?" *Nordic Journal of Psychiatry* 70, no. 2 (2016): 133–39. *https://doi.org/10.3109/08039488.2015.1061053.*

Hay, David, and Rebecca Nye. *The Spirit of the Child.* Revised. London: Jessica Kingsley Publishers, 2006.

Henry, Lynette M., Julia Bryan, and Carlos P. Zalaquett. "The Effects of a Counselor-Led, Faith-Based, School-Family-Community Partnership on Student Achievement in a High-Poverty Urban Elementary School." *Journal of Multicultural Counseling and Development* 45, no. 3 (2017): 162–82. *https://doi.org/10.1002/jmcd.12072.*

Herdt, Gilbert, and Martha McClintock. "The Magical Age of 10." *Archives of Sexual Behavior* 29, no. 6 (December 1, 2000): 587–606. *https://doi.org/10.1023/A:1002006521067.*

Hindman, David. "An Order for Blessing New Drivers." Discipleship Ministries, 2013. *https://www.umcdiscipleship.org/resources/an-order-for-blessing-new-drivers.*

Hinshaw, Stephen P. "The Stigmatization of Mental Illness in Children and Parents: Developmental Issues, Family Concerns, and Research Needs." *Journal of Child Psychology and Psychiatry* 46, no. 7 (2005): 714–34. *https://doi.org/10.1111/j.1469-7610.2005.01456.x.*

Hoffman, Jennifer, and Edward Miller. "Engaging with Volunteers." *NonProfit Times* 32, no. 9 (September 2018): 14.

Hughes, Michelle, and Whitney Tucker. "Poverty as an Adverse Childhood Experience." *North Carolina Medical Journal* 79, no. 2 (March 1, 2018): 124–26. *https://doi.org/10.18043/ncm.79.2.124.*

Huisman, Martijn. "King Saul, Work-Related Stress and Depression." *Journal of Epidemology and Community Health* 61, no. 10 (October 2007): 890. *https://doi.org/10.1136/jech.2007.066522.*

Johnstone, Lucy, and Mary Boyle. "The Power Threat Meaning Framework: An Alternative Nondiagnostic Conceptual System." *Journal of Humanistic Psychology,* August 5, 2018. *https://doi.org/10.1177/0022167818793289.*

Kezelman, Cathy, and Pam Stravrospoulos. "'The Last Frontier'--Practice Guidelines for Treatment of Complex Trauma and Trauma Informed Care and Service Delivery." Blue Knot Foundation (Formerly Adults Surviving Child Abuse). 2012.

Konieczny, Mary Ellen. "Individualized Marriage and Family Disruption Ministries in Congregations: How Culture Matters." *Sociology of Religion* 77, no. 2 (June 2016): 144–70. *https://doi.org/10.1093/socrel/srw010.*

Kost, Kathryn, Isaac Maddow-Zimet, and Alex Arpaia. "Pregnancies, Births and Abortions Among Adolescents and Young Women in the United States, 2013: National and State Trends by Age, Race and Ethnicity." Guttmacher Institute, August 16, 2017. *https://www.guttmacher.org/report/us-adolescent-pregnancy-trends-2013.*

Kropf, Nancy P., and Barbara L. Jones. "When Public Tragedies Happen: Community Practice Approaches in Grief, Loss, and Recovery." *Journal of Community Practice* 22, no. 3 (July 3, 2014): 281–98. *https://doi.org/10.1080/10705422.2014.929539.*

Kulikoff, Allan. *From British Peasants to Colonial American Farmers.* Chapel Hill, NC: The University of North Carolina Press, 2000.

Larsen, Debra, and Beth Hudnall Stamm. "Professional Quality of Life and Trauma Therapist." In *Trauma, Recovery, and Growth: Positive Psychological Perspectives on Posttraumatic Stress,* 275–93. Hoboken, NJ, US: John Wiley & Sons Inc. 2008.

Law, Bridget Murray. "Biting Questions," *Monitor on Psychology,* February 2011.

Lazarus, Richard S. "Puzzles in the Study of Daily Hassles." *Journal of Behaviorial Medicine* 7, no. 4 (December 1984): 375–89. *https://doi.org/10.1007/BF00845271.*

Legg, Pamela Mitchell. "The Work of Christian Education in the Seminary and the Church: Then (1812) and Now (2012)," *Interpretation* 66, no. 4 (October 1, 2012): 425, *https://doi.org/10.1177/0020964312451420.*

Leproult, Rachel, and Eve Van Cauter. "Role of Sleep and Sleep Loss in Hormonal Release and Metabolism." *Endocrine Development* 17 (2010): 11–21. *https://doi.org/10.1159/000262524.*

Li, Gu, Karson T. F. Kung, and Melissa Hines. "Childhood Gender-Typed Behavior and Adolescent Sexual Orientation: A Longitudinal Population-Based Study." *Developmental Psychology* 53, no. 4 (2017): 764–77. *https://doi.org/10.1037/dev0000281.*

Liazos, Alex. *Families: Joys, Conflicts, and Changes.* New York: Routledge. 2015.

Lipari, Rachel N., and Struther L. Van Horn. "Children Living with Parents Who Have a Substance Use Disorder." Substance Abuse and Mental Health Services Administration, 2017. *https://www.samhsa.gov/data/report/children-living-parents-who-have-substance-use-disorder.*

Lock, Robin H., and Kelly Prestia. "Incorporate Sensory Activities and Choices Into the Classroom." *Intevention in School and Clinic* 39, no 3 (January 1, 2004): 172–75. *https://doi.org/10.1177/10534512040390030701.*

Macduff, Nancy L. "Managing Older Volunteers: Implications for Faith-Based Organizations." *Journal of Religious Gerontology* 16, no. 1–2 (January 3, 2004): 107–22. *https://doi.org/10.1300/J078v16n01_07.*

MacKay, Tommy. "False Allegations of Child Abuse in Contested Family Law Cases: The Implications for Psychological Practice." *Educational and Child Psychology* 31 (September 1, 2014): 85–96.

Manlove, Jennifer, Cassandra Logan, Kristin A. Moore, and Erum Ikramullah. "Pathways from Family Religiosity to Adolescent Sexual Activity and Contraceptive Use." *Perspectives on Sexual and Reproductive Health* 40, no. 2(June 2008): 105–17. *https://doi.org/10.1363/4010508.*

Manning, Wendy D., Marshal Neal Fettro, and Esther Lamidi. "Child Well-Being in Same-Sex Parent Families: Review of Research Prepared for American Sociological Association Amicus Brief." *Population Reserach and Policy Review* 33, no. 4 (August 1, 2014): 485–502. *https://doi.org/10.1007/s11113-014-9329-6.*

Marsiglio, William. "Stepfathers With Minor Children Living at Home: Parenting Perceptions and Relationship Quality." *Journal of Family Issues* 13, no. 2 (June 1, 1992): 195–214. *https://doi.org/10.1177/019251392013002005.*

Mathew, Stephen K., and Jeyaraj D. Pandian. "Newer Insights to the Neurological Diseases Among Biblical Characters of Old Testament." *Annals of Indian Academy of Neurology* 13, no. 3 (July 2010): 164–66. *https://doi.org/10.4103/0972-2327.70873.*

Mayo Clinic. "Alcohol Use Disorder - Symptoms and Causes." Accessed September 20, 2019. *https://www.mayoclinic.org/diseases-conditions/alcohol-use-disorder/symptoms-causes/syc-20369243.*

McBride, Neal F. *How to Lead Small Groups.* Colorado Springs, CO: NavPress, 1990.

McGoldrick, Monica, Nydia A. Garcia Preto, and Betty A. Carter. *The Expanding Family Life Cycle: Individual, Family, and Social Perspectives.* 5th edition. Boston: Pearson, 2015.

Meindl, James N. and Jonathan W. Ivy. "Mass Shootings: the Roles of the Media in Promoting Generalized Imitation." *American Journal of Public Health* 107, no. 3 (March 2017): 368–70. *https://doi.org/10.2105/AJPH.2016.303611.*

MennoMedia. "Faith Markers: Marking Each Child's Faith Journey." MennoMedia. Accessed July 23, 2019. https://www.faithandliferesources.org/Curriculum/FaithMarkers/pdf/FaithMarkersMin.pdf.

Metzler, Marilyn, Melissa T. Merrick, Joanne Klevens, Katie A. Ports, and Derek C. Ford. "Adverse Childhood Experiences and Life Opportunities: Shifting the Narrative." *Children and Youth Services Review,* Economic Causes and Consequences of Child Maltreatment, 72 (January 1, 2017): 141–49. *https://doi.org/10.1016/j.childyouth.2016.10.021.*

Ministry Architects. "Staffing Your Ministry Strategically," August 27, 2018. *https://ministryarchitects.com/staffing-your-ministry-strategically/.*

Morris, Amanda Sheffield, Lindsay M. Squeglia, Joanna Jacobus, and Jennifer S. Silk. "Adolescent Brain Development: Implications for Understanding Risk and Resilience Processes Through Neuroimaging Research." *Journal of Research on Adolescence* 28, no. 1 (2018): 4–9. *https://doi.org/10.1111/jora.12379.*

Moss, Candida. "Biblical Families: Families Have Never Been Just a Mom, Dad, and 2.5 Children." *U.S. Catholic* 83, no. 4 (April 2018): 17–19

Moxnes, Halvor, ed. *Constructing Early Christian Families: Family as Social Reality and Metaphor.* 1st ed. London: Routledge, 1997.

Musu-Gillette, L., A. Zang, K. Wang, J. Zhang, J. Kemp, M. Diliberti, and B. A. Oudekerk. "Indicators of School Crime and Safety: 2017." National Center for Education Statistics, March 2018. *https://nces.ed.gov/pubs2018/2018036.pdf.*

National Alliance on Mental Illness. *https://www.nami.org/Learn-More/Mental-Health-By-the-Numbers.*

-----. "Closing the Gap for Children's Mental Health," May 8, 2012. *https://www.nami.org/Blogs/NAMI-Blog/May-2012/Closing-the-Gap-for-Children-s-Mental-Health.*

-----. "Know the Warning Signs." Accessed September 30, 2019. *https://www.nami.org/Learn-More/Know-the-Warning-Signs.*

"Principles of Adolescent Substance Use Disorder Treatment: A Research-Based Guide." National Institute on Drug Abuse, 2014. *https://www.drugabuse.gov/publications/principles-adolescent-substance-use-disorder-treatment-research-based-guide/frequently-asked-questions/what-are-signs-drug-use-in-adolescents-what-role-can-parents-play-in-getting-treatment.*

Nelson, J. Ron, Gregory J. Benner, Kathleen Lynne Lane, and Benjamin W. Smith. "Academic Achievement of K-12 Students With Emotional and Behavioral Disorders." *Exceptional Children* 71, no. 1 (2004): 59–73.

Nesbit, Rebecca, Robert K. Christensen, and Jeffrey L. Brudney. "The Limits and Possibilities of Volunteering: A Framework for Explaining the Scope of Volunteer Involvement in Pubilc and Non-profit Organizations." *Public Administration Review* 78, no. 4 (July 2018): 502–13. *https://doi.org/10.1111/puar.12894.*

Newport, Frank. "In U.S., Estimate of LGBT Population Rises to 4.5%." Gallup.com, May 22, 2018. *https://news.gallup.com/poll/234863/estimate-lgbt-population-rises.aspx.*

Okoro, Catherin A., NaTasha D. Hollis, Alissa C. Cyrus, and Shannon Griffin-Blake. "Prevalence of Disabilities and Health Care Access by Disability Status and Type Among Adults–United States, 2016." *Morbidity and Mortality Weekly Report* 67, no. 32 (2018): 882–87. *https://doi.org/10.15585/mmwr.mm6732a3.*

Osiak, Carolyn, and David L. Balch. *Families in the New Testament World: Households and House Churches.* Louisville, KY: Westminster John Knox Press, 1997.

Ott, Kate. *Sex + Faith: Talking with Your Child from Birth to Adolescence.* Louisville, KY: Westminster John Knox Press, 2013.

-----. "Using Sex + Faith as a Parent and Teen Sunday School Curriculum." *</Kate>* (blog), September 19, 2014. *http://kateott.org/using-sex-faith-as-a-parent-and-teen-sunday-school-curriculum/.*

Peoples, Sandra. "Reflections on the #disabilityinchurch Discussion." *Key Ministry* (blog). Accessed October 28, 2019. *https://www.keyministry.org/church4everychild/2017/4/27/disability-in-church.*

Perdue, Leo G., Joseph Blenkinsopp, John J. Collins, and Carol Meyers. *Families in Ancient Israel.* Louisville, KY: Westminster John Knox Press 1997.

Perrin-Wallqvist, Renée, and Josephine Lindblom. "Coming Out as Gay: A Phenomenological Study About Adolescents Disclosing Their Homosexuality to Their Parents." *Social Behavior and Personality* 43, no. 3 (January 22, 2015): 467–480. *https://doi.org/10.2224/sbp.2015.43.3.467.*

Porfeli, Erik, and Bora Lee. *Career Development During Childhood and Adolescence.* Vol. 2012, 2012. *https://doi.org/10.1002/yd.20011.*

Porter, Susan Eva. *Relating to Adolescents: Educators in a Teenage World.* Lanham, MD: Rowman & Littlefield Education, 2009.

Powell, Kara E., and Chap Clark, *Sticky Faith: Everyday Ideas to Build Lasting Faith in Your Kids.* Grand Rapids, MI: Zondervan, 2011.

Provance, Brett Scott. *Pocket Dictionary of Liturgy & Worship.* Downers Grove, IL: InterVarsity Press, 2009.

The reThinkGroup, host, "How Transparency Can Save Marriages in Your Church." the Think Orange Podcast (podcast), February 5, 2019, accessed November 11, 2019, http://orangeblogs.org/thinkorangepodcast/081-how-transparency-can-save-marriages-in-your-church/.

Roberts, Stephen B., Kevin J. Flannelly, Andrew J. Weaver, and Charles R. Rigley. "Compassion Fatigue Among Chaplains, Clergy, and Other Respondents After September 11th." *Journal of Nervous and Mental Disease* 191, no. 11 (2003): 756–58. *https://doi.org/10.1097/01.nmd.0000095129.50042.30.*

Root, Andrew, and Kenda Creasy Dean. *The Theological Turn in Youth Ministry.* Downers Grove, IL: InterVarsity Press, 2011.

Rozendaal, Esther, Moniek Euijzen, and Patti Valkenburg. "Children's Understanding of Advertiser's Persuasive Tactics." *International Journal of Advertising*, 2011, 30(2), pp. 329–350.

Rumney, Philip. "False Allegations of Rape." *The Cambridge Law Journal* 65 (March 12, 2006). *https://doi.org/10.1017/S0008197306007069.*

Rutter, Michael. "Psychopathological Development Across Adolescence." *Journal of Youth and Adolescence* 36, no. 1 (January 1, 2007): 101–10. *https://doi.org/10.1007/s10964-006-9125-7.*

Saffron, L. "Raising Children in an Age of Diversity-Advantages of Having a Lesbian Mother." *Journal of Lesbian Studies* 2, no. 4 (1998): 35–47, *https://doi.org/10.1300/J155v02n04_04.*

Sanders, Cody J. *A Brief Guide to Ministry with LGBTQIA Youth.* Louisville, KY: Westminster John Knox Press, 2017.

Sasnett, Sherri. "Are the Kids All Right? A Qualitative Study of Adults with Gay and Lesbian Parents." *Journal of Contemporary Ethnography* 44, no. 2 (April 1, 2015): 196–222. *https://doi.org/10.1177/0891241614540212.*

Schofield, Thomas J., M. Brent Donnellan, Melissa T. Merrick, Katie A. Ports, Joanne Klevens, and Rebecca Leeb. "Intergenerational Continuity in Adverse Childhood Experiences and Rural Comunity Environments." *American Journal of Public Health* 108, no. 9 (September 2018): 1148–52. *https://doi.org/10.2105/AJPH.2018.304598.*

Schofield, Thomas J., Rosalyn D. Lee, and Melissa T. Merrick. ."Safe, Stable, Nurturing Relationships as a Moderator of Intergenerational Continuity of Child Maltreatment: A Meta-Analysis." *The Journal of Adolescent Health* 53, no. 4 (October 2013): S32–38. *https://doi.org/10.1016/j.jadohealth.2013.05.004.*

Scott, Donald M., and Bernard W Wishy, eds. *America's Families: A Documentary History.* New York: Harper & Row Publishers, 1982

Senter III, Mark H. "A History of Youth Ministry Education in the USA." Journal of Adult Theological Education 11, no. 1 (2014): 46–60.

Shell, Marc. "Moses' Tongue." *Common Knowledge* 12, no. 1 (January 4, 2006): 150–76.

Silcoff, Mireille. "A Mother's Journey Through the Unnerving Universe of 'Unboxing' Videos." *The New York Times,* January 19, 2018. *https://wwwnytimes.com/2014/08/17/magazine/a-mothers-journey-through-the-unnerving-universe-of-unboxing-videos.html.*

Smith, Christian, and Melina Lundquist Denton. *Soul Searching: The Religious and Spiritual Lives of American Teenagers.* Oxford: Oxford University Press, 2009.

Sodeke-Gregson, Ekundayo A., Sue Holttum, and Jo Billings. "Compassion Satisfaction, Burnout, and Secondary Traumatic Stress in UK Therapists Who Work with Adult Trauma Clients." *European Journal of Psychotraumatology* 4 (December 30, 2013). *https://doi.org/10.3402/ejpt.v4i0.21869.*

Solansky, Stephanie T., Dennis Duchon, Donde Ashmos Plowman, and Patricia G. Martinez. "On the Same Page: The Value of Paid and Volunteer Leaders Sharing Mental Models in Churches." *Nonprofit Management and Leadership* 19, no. 2 (September 2008): 203–19. *https://doi.org/10.1002/nml.215.*

Sorenson, Jacob. "The Summer Camp Experience and Faith Formation of Emerging Adults." *Journal of Youth Ministry* 13, no. 1 (Fall 2014): 17–40.

Stonehouse, Catherine. *Joining Children on the Spiritual Journey: Nurturing a Life of Faith.* Grand Rapids, MI: Baker Academic, 1998.

Straka, Silvia M., and Lyse Montminy, "Family Violence: Through the Lens of Power and Control." *Journal of Emotional Abuse* 8, no. 3 (August 26, 2008): 255–79. *https://doi.org/10.1080/10926790802262499.*

Strother, Eric, Raymond Lemberg, Stevie Chariese Stanford, and Dayton Turberville. "Eating Disorders in Men: Underdiagnosed, Undertreated, and Misunderstood." *Eating Disorders* 20, no. 5 (2012): 346–55. *https://doi.org/10.1080/10640266.2012.715512.*

Takishima-Lacasa, Julie Y., Charmaine K. Higa-McMillan, Chad Ebesutani, Rita L. Smith, and Bruce F. Chorpita. "Self-Consciousness and Social Anxiety in Youth: The Revised Self-Consciousness Scales for Children." *Psychological Assessment* 26, no. 4 (December 2014): 1292–1306. *https://doi.org/10.1037/a0037386.*

Thomas, Jennifer. "What to Say When Sorry Isn't Enough," April 18, 2018. *https://www.drjenniferthomas.com/2018/04/18/say-sorry-isnt-enough/.*

The United Methodist Church. *The Book of Discipline of the United Methodist Church.* Nashville, TN: The United Methodist Publishing House, 2016.

UN General Assembly. "Universal Declaration of Human Rights," 1948. *https://www.un.org/en/universal-declaration-human-rights/index.html.*

US Department of Health and Human Services. "Child Maltreatment 2017," 2019, 261.

United States Department of Justice Civil Rights Division. "Americans with Disabilities Act of 1990, AS AMENDED with ADA Amendments Act of 2008." Accessed August 14, 2019. *https://www.ada.gov/pubs/adastatute08.htm#12102.*

Watson, Kevin M. *Pursuing Social Holiness: The Band Meeting in Wesley's Thought and Popular Methodist Practice.* 1st Edition. Oxford: Oxford University Press, 2014.

Watts, Fraser N., Rebecca Nye, and Sara B. Savage. *Psychology for Christian Ministry.* London: Routledge, 2002.

Welch, Robert H. *Church Administration: Creating Efficiency for Effective Ministry.* Nashville: B & H Pub. Group, 2011.

Wilcox, Brian L., Dale Kunkel, Joanne Cantor, Peter Dowrick, Susan Linn, and Edward Palmer. "Report of the APA Task Force on Advertising and Children." American Psychological Association, 2004. *https://www.apa.org/pi/families/resources/advertising-children.pdf.*

Wilson, John P. "PTSD and Complex PTSD: Symptoms, Syndromes and Diagnoses." In *Assessing Psychological Trauma and PTSD,* edited by John P. Wilson and Terence M. Keane, 2nd Edition, 7–44. New York, NY: Guilford Publications, 2004.

Wooden, Cherie L., and Frances R. Anderson. "Engaging Parents in Reproductive Health Education: Lessons Learned Implementing a Parent Designed, Peer-Led Educational Model for Parents of Preteens." *American Journal of Sexuality Education* 7, no. 4 (October 1, 2012): 461–73. *https://doi.org/10.1080/15546128.2012.740963.*

Wymer, Walter W. "Strategic Marketing of Church Volunteers." *Journal of Ministry Marketing & Management* 4, no. 1 (April 8, 1998): 1–11. *https://doi.org/10.1300/J093v04n01_01.*

Wymer, Walter W., and Becky J. Starnes. "Conceptual Foundations and Practical Guidelines for Recruiting Volunteers to Serve in Local Nonprofit Organizations: Part I." *Journal of Nonprofit & Public Sector Markeing* 9, no. 1–2 (January 10, 2001): 63–96. *https://doi.org/10.1300/J054v09n01_05.*

Yong, Amos. "Zacchaeus: Short and Un-Seen." *Christian Reflection: A Series in Faith and Ethics–Disability,* 2012, 11–17.

Zappia, Ron & Jody. *The Marriage Knot: 7 Choices that Keep Couples Together,* Moody Publishers: Chicago, IL, 2019, 27–46.